Constitutional Consciousness

Dia-Logos

Schriften zu Philosophie und Sozialwissenschaften
Studies in Philosophy and Social Sciences

Edited by
Piotr W. Juchacz

Volume 31

Skirgailė Žalimienė / Bartosz Wojciechowski (eds.)

Constitutional Consciousness

In Search of a Remedy for the Crisis of Discourse and Democracy Deficit in the European Union

PETER LANG

Lausanne - Berlin - Bruxelles - Chennai – New York – Oxford

Bibliographic Information published by the Deutsche Nationalbiblio-Bibliographic
The Deutsche Nationalbibliothek lists this publication in the Deutsche Nationalbibliografie; detailed bibliographic data is available in the internet at http://dnb.d-nb.de.

Library of Congress Cataloging-in-Publication Data
A CIP catalog record for this book has been applied for at the Library of Congress.

The book has been prepared within the framework of the research project no. 2017/27/L/HS5/03245, financed by the National Science Center of Poland (dec. no. DEC-2017/27/L/HS5/03245) and of Lietuvos mokslo taryba (contract no. S-LL-19-4 / LSS-220000-1395).

ISSN 1619-005X
ISBN 978-3-631-89556-6 (Print)
ISBN 978-3-631-90521-0 (E-PDF)
ISBN 978-3-631-90522-7 (E-PUB)
DOI 10.3726/b21009

Published by Peter Lang GmbH, Berlin, Deutschland

info@peterlang.com - www.peterlang.com

This publication has been peer reviewed.

Table of Contents

Karolina M. Cern[1]

Introduction: A Typically European Approach…?

Perhaps, there is nothing more European than a crisis. It is crisis that animates the Socrates-Gadfly to bite and thus launches practical philosophical reflection. Perhaps crisis might be deemed the driver of Europeanism and also be marketed as a European best-seller. The story of the struggle against the many faces of crisis and the way Europeans responded to them, is the history of our development – but are we aware of the cost we are paying for this development? The papers collected in the volume oscillate reflexively between the identification of the various types of crises currently affecting the European Union, Europe and even the entire world, and the awareness of the ways of formulating legal remedies for them. In particular, constitutional consciousness is considered as a remedy for the crisis in discourse and the democracy deficit in the European Union.

We can perhaps say the same thing about the common European legal culture and union law lawyers as Chris Ballinger said about the Lords and English constitutional law: "The Lords themselves are still in doubt about their origin."[2] And so are we still in doubt about the true origins of our common European legal culture, firstly as a background and a condition for discourse – legal and institutional as well as political and to

1 Karolina M. Cern – philosopher of law specialising in processes of Europeanisation, constitutionalisation and public law. Author of several articles in law and ethics, author and co-author of three books (*Conception of Time by Early Heidegger*, 2004; *The Counterfactual Yardstick: Normativity, Self-Constitutionalisation and the Public Sphere*; 2014; with Ewa Nowak *Ethos in Public Life*, 2011); editor and co-editor of a dozen of collected volumes. Cern is currently working on a deliberative philosophy of law, particularly administrative law and the relationship between the ideas, concepts and conceptions of the *Rule of Law* and *Rechtsstaat*. She is a professor at the Faculty of Philosophy, Adam Mickiewicz University in Poznań, Poland.

2 Ch. Ballinger, *The House of Lords 1911–2011. A Century of Non-Reform*, Hart Publishing, 2012, p. 4.

some extent cultural or economic, but above all also a transnational civic discourse articulated in the name of common values, mutually recognised rights and shared interests. Indeed, for many, perhaps even most of us, discourse seems to be the most typical way for Europeans – post-Socratic beings – to deal with problems of all kinds, including crises.

However, as much as we consider the discourse and the common European legal culture that makes it possible, we probably also harbour some doubts. Should we trace the common European legal culture to "ancient" times, to the days of yore, to protect it from any (legal) questioning? Or should we stick to the turbulence of recent times for discursively setting the common rules right now, and let them be (politically) challenged at any time by any of us? Or should we boldly look forward to where none has looked before to present a big picture of what we might one day (economically) benefit from together?

In other words, when we refer to and look for the common European legal culture as a common European legal resource for discourse, in what terms should we do so? And exactly what kind of resource is it in the first instance? These are important questions that seem to enable us to define the reasonable expectations regarding this concept. So, is it to be a resource for overcoming crisis and reaching an agreement on how we, Europeans, should develop? Actually, agreement is also needed in the face of the physical threat of war that Russia has sparked right now, next door, in Europe. For it is extremely difficult (or perhaps impossible) to conduct a discourse without establishing a common ground; thus common European legal culture would provide a massive context (as a resource) for potential agreement-reaching.

So, let us first consider whether the common European legal culture is in some way related to our identity – European and/or national, our inherited and therefore constitutive values, as well as our respect for the past. Would that work? Well, following John H. Langbein, Renée Lettow Lerner, and Bruce P. Smith:

> "The reception [of Roman law] produced a common European legal culture, called the *ius commune* (common law). Thus, both England and Europe experienced what was called a common law. The English common law was national law, rooted in the authority of the king and his courts. The European *ius*

commune was transnational law, rooted in a university-centred intellectual tradition of studying and teaching the medieval Roman law."[3]

As we can see, *ius commune*, from the very outset, might be understood in at least two ways: as a result of the creative and intellectual (elite-driven) reception of something mainly external and, therefore, as a result, as international law; or as a product of the internal (close to the individual) everyday practice, i.e. as a law that is a common national achievement. As one can clearly see, the most *sui generis* constitutive element of the *ius commune* is *tension*. This is the in-built tension between the ruler and subjects; the state power(s); the different power-holders; the authorities and the capital (e.g. of the kings, popes, nobles and the resourceful bourgeoisie, as well as those *sin-nobles*); interests or values vs. emancipatory movements and rights... And what is intriguing is that the significance of the abovementioned elements, as tension triggers, depends on the time/historical moment and the (non)common consciousness of Europeans as reflexively shaping the resource for discourse. Crucially, all these terms suggest that specific *reflexive flexibility* is the next core feature (besides the tension) of the common European legal culture.

Coming back to the common European legal culture as the common resource for discourse produced in the medium of law. Perhaps yet another factor is at play here, namely a European achievement of the post-metaphysical morality for which the key question is not what is good for me or for us, but what is the right and just thing to do?[4] Especially when dealing with diverse tensions, revealed in different times/historical moments, and the flexibly reflexive mode. Thus, the pressing puzzle to solve would be the following: which moral-democratic principles should be discursively established on a rolling basis and, therefore, constantly modified? More specifically: which *or* whose principles and how much

3 J.H. Langbein, R. Lettow Lerner, B.P. Smith, *History of the Common Law. The Development of Anglo-American Legal Institutions*, Aspen Publishers, Wolters Kluwer, Law & Business, 2009, p. 137.

4 J. Habermas, *Lawrence Kohlberg and Neo-Aristotelianism*, [in:] *Justification and Application. Remarks on Discourse Ethics* (trans. C.P. Cronin), The MIT Press, third edition, 2001, pp. 117–118.

could they be challenged? This is the question, because the problem – as already rooted in the one indicated above – is that:

> "According to Thompson, and contrary to popular myth, the Peace of Westphalia (1648) 'did not result in external state sovereignty against all other states'. Rather, it 'legitimized the sovereignty of powerful modern states and the right of those states to impose limits on the statehood of defeated and aspiring states. It defined an external world in which sovereignty depended on power and in which distinctions were made between strong and weak states' (pp. 25–6). Seen in this light, the policies of contemporary institutions such as the World Bank and the IMF, where tough conditions are imposed on states in the developing world, conditions that increasingly speak to constitutional values such as 'good governance', 'accountability' and 'transparency', are not so much a break from the Westphalia model as its continuation by new means: 'An international economy in which indebted states find that richer states succeed in controlling their economic decision-making and the parameters of their internal politics is repeating past history' (p. 36)."[5]

The above-outlined problem, in which our common European legal culture seems to have been immersed for centuries, is related to the tension between the powers of states and other international institutions and authorities defining *who is to be a participant in the discourse*, on what basis, and how much they are to be allowed to influence this common (inter)national discourse. Thus: who will be part of the subject reflecting on and at the same time deciding on actions? This discourse, for which our common European legal culture seems to be a resource and, as such, also a condition for the possibility of reaching an agreement, is then translated into already rigid legal regulations dictating the rules of the game played by the European Union and its citizens. Of course, one can think, after Jürgen Habermas, Karl-Otto Appel and Robert Alexy, of a discourse almost doing justice to the ideal conditions of communication – but whether all participants in the discourse want such a discourse is not that obvious. As Jeoffrey T. Checkel highlights, "the new member states have had a different relationship to Europe; they have unique historical memories that

5 C. Turpin, A. Tomkins, *British Government and the Constitution. Texts and Materials*, sixth edition, CUP, 2007, p. 20.

will not be Europeanized away."[6] This in-built tension – who is European actually – has always fuelled the various crises swirling through Europe too. And it is particularly important to bear this in mind and not deny it, as *the concepts of difference, diversity, as well as inequality, are also products of internal European tensions and the reflexive dealing with them.*

Thus, tensions, since the modern era arising predominantly around the category of the state, power and economy, are then translated into rigid rules of the game in discourse, existential aspirations, and the quality of life of ordinary people. They are the foundations of the shared European legal culture, which is a resource and a condition for participating in discourse and reaching a potential and negotiable agreement.

Or is there something else, something more promising, a benefit from having a common resource that will be fully revealed to us in the future one day? But who will decide on this? *Who are the gatekeepers of our beneficial future?* When a common resource was generated through Roman law and the universities, academics were the gatekeepers; for generating *ius commune* as a national achievement, the royal centralisation of the common law courts played the paramount role; but who is playing and who will soon play a central role *on the stage* of the common European legal culture?

Let us listen to Turpin and Tomkins again, to their book issued years before Brexit was "called on" and came into force.

> "Ours has traditionally been a political constitution, in which change is directed and conflicts are largely resolved through the political process (see Griffith, *The Political Constitution*, 1979, MLR, vol. 42, no. 1). When a written constitution is in place, arguments about its effect are conducted in legal terms, as an exercise in interpretation, and are displaced from the political forum into the courts. As Ian Holliday remarks (in G. Parry and M. Moran (eds.), *Democracy and Democratization*, 1994, p. 253), 'juridification of politics is one of the major problems created by a written constitution': much power, and much trust, are given to judges. The role which they may assume is exemplified by the history of the United States Supreme Court."[7]

6 J.T. Checkel, *Identity, Europe, and the world beyond public spheres*, [in:] T. Risse (ed.) *European Public Spheres. Politics Is Back*, CUP, St. Ives, 2015, pp. 236–237.

7 C. Turpin, A. Tomkins, *British Government and the Constitution. Texts and Materials*, sixth edition, CUP, 2007, p. 31.

Actually, this comment on the constitution poses a question: who would we like to be? How would we like to communicate with one another? In other words, why would the man on the Clapham omnibus, that is, an ordinary and reasonable person, want to be ruled by legal elites, rather than by a political process? By legal elites without very compelling democratic legitimisation (bearing in mind that this is precisely what the EU judiciary lacks)? Brexit showed that the man on Clapham omnibus did not want them. Why should other ordinary and reasonable persons, from other Member States, want these elites to make decisions apart from them? In other words, the time has come for citizens to be taken seriously, for them to be shown respect and paid heed; time for citizens across the EU to engage in respectful discourse – instead of them being subject to paternalization and written about by the formidable elites who know best how to Europeanise the Continent by means of law, and for economic reasons.

Now, the pivotal question is, therefore: what and how is the discourse to be conducted in the face of the plethora of crises battering the European Union? Whose resource is the discourse of the common European legal culture? Exactly what kind of resource is it? What kind of discourse should it be: Academic? Legal? Political? Or perhaps civic (but again: civic-national or civic-pan-European)? *Should each of these discourses play the same or a similar role in the debate on the current crises and how to overcome them, or is any one of them distinguished, for example, from the perspective of the legitimisation of democratic law?* This is, in fact, one of the main questions posed by Dimitry V. Kochenov and Graham Butler,[8] although unfortunately it is not asked anywhere there… The question of the difference between legality and legitimisation, which Kochenov and Butler do not pose when discussing, with remarkable vigour, the issue of the termination of the mandate of the UK Advocate General as a "sitting member of the Court of Justice."[9]

8 D. Kochenov, G. Butler, *Independence of the Court of Justice of the European Union: Unchecked Member States power after the Sharpston Affair*, "European Law Journal" vol. 27, no. 1–3, pp. 262–296.

9 *Ibidem*, p. 263.

Here, the fundamental point is to rethink how the EU can be made a union of citizens for citizens, not of distant elites, one that is capable of responding to the concerns of ordinary citizens. How to strengthen the transnational channels of communication between different groups of citizens speaking different languages but perhaps facing and struggling with quite similar problems, how to involve these citizens in various initiatives of participation and deliberation about themselves in their EU, whose future is theirs.

Thus, the most important thing that emerges from the above is that the three options identified provide differing definitions of the participants in the discourse, and of the tasks they can and should perform. Again, who are the gatekeepers of our future? If this role is no longer to be played by academics, then is it to be taken up by judges and Justices or politicians? Is there any place assigned to citizens? And finally, how do we understand democracy, with what terms do we conceptualise it?[10] Let us look a little bit more closely at this point, namely, by looking at some of the issues vividly pointed out in the *ELJ* article cited above.

Well, paradoxically, the tension inherent in the concept of a common European legal culture is also created by the notions underlying the principle of the *Rule of Law* and *Rechtsstaat*. Currently "A globally accessible mode of communication – a kind of *lingua franca* – has emerged in international development cooperation under the banner of the rule of law to describe the 'correct' way to structure societies and governance."[11] The *Rule of Law*, this legal yardstick – a kind of legal "lingua franca" on an international level – grew out of the English political and ethical philosophy, culture, history and tradition (naturally, it has also been developed in many other countries that remain under the British influence). As we can recall, Brexit came into life on 31 January 2020. The rival concept to

10 P.W. Juchacz, *Deliberative Law-Making: A Case Study of the Process of Enacting of a 'Constitution of the Third Sector'in the Polish Sejm*, "International Journal for the Semiotics of Law" 2020, vol. 33, p. 81.

11 D. Dedov, *The Rule of Law and Legal State Doctrines as a Methodology of the Philosophy of Law*, [in:] J.R. Silkenat, J.E. Hickey Jr., P.D. Barenboim (eds.), *The Legal Doctrines of the Rule of Law and the Legal State (Rechtsstaat)*, Springer, Berlin, 2014, p. 78.

the *Rule of Law*, coined in the 19th century, was *Rechtsstaat*, which grew out of the Continental political and ethical philosophy, culture, history and tradition.[12] (Here "Continental" can mean German and/or French and/or Italian and so on – depending on how detailed the discussion is). The problem is that comparatively little has been written on this profound issue, namely the philosophical provenance and the basic net of philosophical concepts operating behind the *Rule of Law* and *Rechtsstaat*. The well-known exception is, of course, the philosophical reflection on the *concept* of the government/sovereign.[13] This diagnosis applies to both the historical and contemporary perspectives.

This is actually surprising, because the philosophical concepts people are taught at schools, or just become socialised to, deeply structure their minds,[14] in the sense of creating their capabilities, resources and competencies for creating, building and maintaining relations with others, as well as those relations that are institutionally mediated. Further, the assumptions, images and design of public institutions are based upon a fundamental philosophical understanding of elementary ethical, social and political issues,[15] such as, for example, reason and emotions/ affects/ sentiments, individual freedom and liberties, the role of political authority, the function of law (and its sources), or the idea of justice in relationship to the previously listed ideas.

Additionally, the different philosophical backgrounds of the citizenry may give rise to different expectations with regard to public institutions and, on the other hand, a different functioning of public institutions may be perceived and regarded as trustworthy by citizens. Paul Tiedemann, for

---

12 D. Zolo, *The Rule of La: A Critical Reappraisal*, [in:] P. Costa, D. Zolo (eds.), *The Rule of Law. History, Theory, Criticism*, Springer, Dordrecht, 2007.

13 M. Loughlin, *Foundations of Public Law*, OUP, 2010; G. Palombella, *The rule of law beyond the state: Failures, promises, and theory*, "*I*CON*", vol. 7, no. 3, 2009; P. Costa, *The Rule of Law: A Historical Introduction*, [in:] P. Costa, D. Zolo (eds.), *The Rule of Law. History, Theory, Criticism*, Springer, Dordrecht, 2007.

14 E. Nowak, *Experimental Ethics. A multidisciplinary approach*, LIT, Münster–Berlin, 2013.

15 F.J. Goodnow, *Comparative administrative law. An analysis of the administrative systems national and local, of the United States, England, France and Germany*, G.P. PUTNAM's SPNS, New York, London, 1893, vol. I & II, p. 5.

example, argues that respect for the formal principle of *Rechtsstaat* can be sustained and maintained only "where an appropriate culture of legality is firmly established."[16] Neil MacCormick, agreeing on the role of *habits* for the effective sustaining of law, stresses, however, the role of affective human nature: "the critical rational discussion depends on an understanding of real people as they have really acted in the past and go on acting now. [...] Without empathy there is no understanding of (other) people as people. Without understanding of other people, there is no self-understanding."[17] Thus, how shall we understand the addressees of *Rechtsstaat* and the *Rule of Law*? Are they the same addressees, or are the addressees very similar?

In other words, the way people – meaning ordinary citizens, office holders, lawyers, including judges and Justices, and also politicians – understand the *Rule of Law* and *Rechtssaat*, and whether they do so in similar or different ways, depends, to a certain extent, on the philosophical assumptions and conceptual nets operating behind the two concepts. And the question is: which – and precisely what – concept is used by prominent legal experts in widely read legal journals, when they write (to whom?) about the *Rule of Law*? And how is this concept democratically legitimised?

What is particularly significant in this collected volume is the genuine interest in European citizens, their communities and nationalities, as well as the values they adhere to and simultaneously contest (Paulius Gricīūnas, *National Identity: Constitutional Patriotism or Dialogue on Values*; Anna Kalisz, *The Margin of Appreciation – a Safety Anchor for Constitutional Identity in Semiotic and Legal Contexts*; Martin Škop, *The Indifference of Law to Literature*) – versus the common European consciousness, rights and identity, in short, common European legal culture (Milena Korycka-Zirk, *The Political versus Proportionality – Methods of Justifying Conflicts of Constitutional Values*). Although the questions about citizens and their concerns are posed from the perspective of both national and European

16 P. Tiedemann, *The Rechtsstaat-Principle in Germany: The Development from the Beginning Until Now*, [in:] J.R. Silkenat, J.E. Hickey Jr., P.D. Barenboim (eds.), *The Legal Doctrines of the Rule of Law and the Legal State (Rechtsstaat)*, Springer, Berlin, 2014, p. 177.

17 N. MacCormick, *Practical Reason in Law and Morality*, OUP, Oxford, 2008, p. 9.

institutions, most of all by Justices and/or professors in law, they genuinely express interest in and concern for citizens, the democratic principles that enable them to exercise democratic power (Bartosz Wojciechowski, Skirgailė Žalimienė, *The Role of Democratic Thinking in the Shaping of Legal Awareness and Legal Recognition*), their rights as individuals also vis-à-vis the state (Marcin Górski, *"Tempering Steel" – on Shaping the Standard of Interpretation of the Convention as Exemplified by the Legal Recognition of Same-Sex Relationships*). This volume is, therefore, unique in that it deals with how to enable citizens to participate in discussions and decisions on issues as urgent and important as the participatory budget and the citizen (Jarosław Sułkowski, *Participatory Budgeting as a Tool for Increasing Constitutional Awareness*), environmental sustainability (Rasa Ragulskytė-Markovienė, Jurgita Paužaitė-Kulvinskienė, *The Right of Access to Justice in Environmental Matters as One of the Forms of Public Participation in Governance and an Instrument for Upholding the Values of the European Union*), and their national, constitutional and European identity (Anna Chmielarz-Grochal, *The Limits to Constitutional Amendments and the Question of Constitutional Identity and Citizens' Consciousness (the Polish case)*; Vygantė Milašiūtė, *Freedom of the Rule of Law-Promoting Expression of Prosecutors under European Law*).

Bibliography

Ballinger, Ch., *The House of Lords 1911–2011. A Century of Non-Reform*, Hart Publishing, Oxford, 2012.

Checkel, J.T., *Identity, Europe, and the World Beyond Public Spheres*, [in:] T. Risse (ed.) *European Public Spheres. Politics Is Back*, CUP, St. Ives, 2015.

Costa, P., *The Rule of Law: A Historical Introduction*, [in:] P. Costa, D. Zolo (eds.), *The Rule of Law. History, Theory, Criticism*, Springer, Dordrecht, 2007.

Dedov, D., *The Rule of Law and Legal State Doctrines as a Methodology of the Philosophy of Law*, [in:] J.R. Silkenat, J.E. Hickey Jr., P.D. Barenboim (eds.), *The Legal Doctrines of the Rule of Law and the Legal State (Rechtsstaat)*, Springer, Berlin, 2014, pp. 71–89.

Goodnow, F.J., *Comparative Administrative Law. An Analysis of the Administrative Systems National and Local, of the United States, England, France and Germany*, G.P. PUTNAM's SPNS, New York–London, 1893, vol. I & II.

Habermas, J., *Lawrence Kohlberg and Neo-Aristotelianism*, [in:] *Justification and Application. Remarks on Discourse Ethics* (trans. C.P. Cronin), The MIT Press, third edition, 2001, pp. 117–118.

Juchacz, P.W., *Deliberative Law-Making: A Case Study of the Process of Enacting of a 'Constitution of the Third Sector' in the Polish Sejm*, "International Journal for the Semiotics of Law" 2020, vol. 33, pp. 77–100.

Kochenov, D., Butler, G., *Independence of the Court of Justice of the European Union: Unchecked Member States power after the Sharpston Affair*, "European Law Journal" vol. 27, no. 1–3.

Langbein, J.H., Lettow Lerner, R., Smith, B.P., *History of the Common Law. The Development of Anglo-American Legal Institutions*, Aspen Publishers, Wolters Kluwer, Law & Business, Austin, New York, NY, 2009.

Loughlin, M., *Foundations of Public Law*, OUP, Oxford, 2010.

MacCormick, N., *Practical Reason in Law and Morality*, OUP, Oxford, 2008.

Nowak, E., *Experimental Ethics. A Multidisciplinary Approach*, LIT, Münster–Berlin, 2013.

Palombella, G., *The Rule of Law Beyond the State: Failures, Promises, and Theory*, "*I*CON*", vol. 7, no. 3, 2009, pp. 442–467.

Rawls, J., *Political Liberalism. With a new introduction and the "Reply to Habermas"*, Columbia University Press, New York, 1996.

Tiedemann, P., *The Rechtsstaat-Principle in Germany: The Development from the Beginning Until Now*, [in:] J.R. Silkenat, J.E. Hickey Jr., P.D. Barenboim (eds.), *The Legal Doctrines of the Rule of Law and the Legal State (Rechtsstaat)*, Springer, Berlin, 2014, pp. 171–192.

Turpin, C., Tomkins, A., *British Government and the Constitution. Texts and Materials*, sixth edition, CUP, 2007.

Zolo, D., *The Rule of La: A Critical Reappraisal*, [in:] P. Costa, D. Zolo (eds.), *The Rule of Law. History, Theory, Criticism*, Springer, Dordrecht, 2007.

Part I

Bartosz Wojciechowski,[2] Skirgailė Žalimienė[3]

The Role of Democratic Thinking in the Shaping of Legal Awareness and Legal Recognition[1]

Abstract

The article conceptualises democracy as an institution anchored in a cooperative social consciousness, and thus as an ideal of free and open cooperative association between individuals who are afforded rights of equal consideration and respect. This is based on the assumption that by publicly affirming basic freedoms, citizens in a well-governed society express mutual respect towards each other, as reasonable and trustworthy individuals, and recognise the value that all citizens place on their own way of life. The institution capable of fostering such affirmation and recognition is discursively agreed law, based on the consensus of all co-operating citizens and guided by Habermas' "constitutional patriotism", which expresses the solidarity of

---

1 The article was prepared under the grant of the National Science Center no DEC-2017/27/L/HS5/03245 and of Lietuvos mokslo taryba, contract no. S-LL-19-4 / LSS-220000-1395

2 Bartosz Wojciechowski is a professor at the University of Lodz (Poland), the director of the Center for Theory and Philosophy of Human Rights, a member of the Editorial Board of the journals: *The Intellectum. A Journal of Generating Understanding* (Greece), *Przegląd Sejmowy* (the journal of the Sejm of the Republic of Poland), *Folia Iuridica. Acta Universitatis Lodziensis*. An international expert in the EU-funded project "Pravo-Justice" (European Justice for Ukraine). He is a judge in the Supreme Administrative Court. He has published and co-edited several books on legal philosophy, the interpretation of law, and legal responsibility.

3 Skirgaile Žalimiene, professor of EU Law at the Faculty of Law, Vilnius University, since 2008 Judge of the Supreme Administrative Court of Lithuania, since 2022 the president of the Lithuanian Supreme Administrative Court. She is the author or co-author of numerous publications on international and EU law. Constitutional law of the European Union, EU legal remedies, and regulation of the EU internal market are among her scientific interests. Since 2012 she has been a member of the Lithuanian European Law Association and member of the Lithuanian Association of Judges.

citizens. Although "constitutional patriotism" underpins the validity of liberal democracy, it must also promote maximum goodwill towards difference, thus ensuring the most tolerant and flexible political system possible. "Constitutional patriotism" therefore requires a certain common minimum, to unite exclusive groups and communities guided by different lifestyles, while ensuring the protection of the rights of minorities and groups subject to discrimination.

Keywords: community identity, pluralistic societies, deliberative democracy, legal recognition, constitutional patriotism

1. Introduction

Democracy allows crucial values to be realised in social life, and this system has an advantage over other regimes when it comes to guaranteeing the freedom and equality of all people. A democratic society is one in which those in power are obliged to treat the governed "with concern, that is, as human beings who are capable of suffering and frustration, and with respect, that is, as human beings who are capable of forming and acting on intelligent conceptions of how their lives should be lived."[4]

Nowadays community identity is defined less by common territory, shared language, or adherence to tradition, and more by active membership (citizenship) based on mutual respect. A community has thus come to be defined as a group of people who are loyal to one another, who are brought together by an affiliation arising from the conscious adoption and acceptance of the specific values that unite them, by shared responsibility for their fate, and by a certain affinity in the way they view the world. Democracy functions successfully in a wide range of societies: those that are culturally homogeneous, those that are culturally heterogeneous, and those that are geographically and culturally distant from the places of its birth. A democratic system does not pursue axiological goals that were set in advance; instead, it grants equal rights to everyone pursuing the axiological goals that have been agreed upon, and when it comes to deciding on common goals, this is done within the framework of democratic institutions and procedures. In other words, democracy is not specific to any particular culture; on the contrary, the proponents of democracy and

4 R. Dworkin, *Taking Rights Seriously*, Duckworth, London, 1977, pp. 272–273.

democracy itself are found in very diverse cultural circles.[5] As a result, every culture seeks to make democracy one of its component parts. In multicultural and pluralistic societies, democracy is particularly necessary because it is through democratic procedures that diversity comes to the fore, thereby enriching social thought and enlivening the state. It can be said that the essence of democracy lies in the clash of different views, values and interests.

2. Deliberative democracy as a requirement for responsive legal policy

An issue of particular interest today is how contemporary democratic theory can explain why every citizen should be willing to participate actively in the social and political processes of collective thought and will-formation, including negotiated law-making. The active role of normal citizens in political processes is understood today, especially in the theories of deliberative democracy, as a normative condition for the legitimate exercise of state power. Nowadays, different citizens express their preference for different value hierarchies, and democratic participation is the plane in which pre-political consensus is manifested.[6] A way out of the malaise of democratic participation is now chiefly offered by the theories of deliberative democracy: John Dewey's re-popularised theory of democracy as a reflexive form of cooperation, and Ronald Dworkin's partnership view of democracy.[7]

In general terms, according to the representatives of deliberative currents, politics (democracy) can be understood as the transformation of citizens' preferences through rational discussion, and thus takes the form of open and public activity aimed at formulating the idea of the

5 A. Gutmann, *Identity in Democracy*, Princeton University Press, Princeton, 2004, p. 80.

6 Ch.F. Zurn, *Anerkennung, Umverteilung und Demokratie. Dilemmata in Honneths Kritischer Theorie der Gesellschaft*, "Deutsche Zeitschrift für Philosophie" 2005, vol. 53, no. 3, p. 439.

7 On the partnership view of democracy, see R. Dworkin, *Is Democracy Possible Here?: Principles for a New Political Debate*, Princeton University Press, Princeton, 2006, p. 131 ff.

common good.[8] The figure most representative of this theory is Jürgen Habermas,[9] but it also includes advocates of participatory democracy such as John Stuart Mill and Carole Paterman.[10] James Bohman notes that the various conceptions of deliberative democracy are united in their strong emphasis on the interconnectedness of normative, descriptive and practical issues. The theory of deliberative democracy must be adequate at all three levels if it is to guide political practice and reform.[11] In Bohman's view, normativity is concerned with resisting the reduction of politics and decision-making processes to instrumental and strategic rationality. In deliberative processes, therefore, the arrival at a particular political decision is preceded by deliberation, involving the presentation of all the relevant arguments in a public forum. In principle, this allows unlimited freedom of

---

8 It is worth noting that various terms are used interchangeably in the literature: deliberative democracy, discursive democracy, communicative democracy and dialogical democracy, which, as one can easily see, are embedded in different philosophical concepts and do not necessarily mean exactly the same thing. A representative distinction between liberal and constitutional deliberative democracy, on the one hand, and discursive democracy on the other has been made by John Dryzek, who states that the deliberative democracy model is characterized by the narrowing of public debate to the content contained in the political culture of liberal democratic states, while the discursive model, in contrast, focuses on an inclusive, multicultural and pluralistic public sphere open to all participants – including new and foreign ones – in the formation of public opinion and will, and especially the views they formulate, J. Dryzek, *Deliberative Democracy and Beyond: Liberals, Critics, Contestations*, Oxford, 2002.

9 Habermas's views on democratic proceduralism will be discussed in the next chapter. At this point, it is only worth hinting that, according to this German philosopher (and Hannah Arendt, a representative of republicanism also believes the same), the idea of democratic will and opinion formation can only take place in the public sphere of linguistic agreement and only in this way can individuals realise a fundamentally communicative freedom. Cf. J. Habermas, *Between Facts and Norms. Contributions to a Discourse Theory of Law and Democracy*, The MIT Press, Cambridge, MA, 1998, Chapter 3 and *Popular Sovereignty*, pp. 463–490.

10 For more on this topic, see J. Elster, *The Market and the Forum*, [in:] J. Bohman, W. Rehg (eds.), *Deliberative Democracy. Essays on Reason and Politics*, The MIT Press, Cambridge, 1997, pp. 3–33.

11 J. Bohman, *Public Deliberation. Pluralism, Complexity, and Democracy*, The MIT Press, Cambridge, MA, 1996, p. 4.

argumentation, but more importantly it obliges the participating citizens to consider common interests or arguments that could be accepted by all the participants in the decision-making process.[12] However, deliberative democracy only accepts the claims put forward by individual citizens that treat other citizens as equals.

The answer to the question posed above concerning the reason for (or source of) each citizen's willingness to participate in the process of democratic public decision-making can be found in the conception of Joshua Cohen, for whom deliberative democracy means a relationship in which citizens are obliged to coordinate their activities, using appropriate institutions that make deliberation possible and drawing on norms that have been agreed upon during collective deliberation.[13] Consequently, it can be argued that it is the free debate of equal citizens, i.e. equal members of the established union, that constitutes the basis for the legitimacy of public and state institutions. Deliberative democracy promotes reasoned discussion and consensus, thereby contributing to the elimination of intolerance, inequality and violence from public life. This view of democracy assumes that public decisions are the result of free and reasoned deliberation between actors who are treated as morally and politically equal.[14] Deliberation attains its great significance because a central characteristic of democratic states is the fact there is a plurality of conflicting reasonable

---

12 *Ibidem*, p. 5.

13 J. Cohen, *Deliberation and Democratic Legitimacy*, [in:] A. Hamlin, Ph. Pettit (eds.), *The Good Polity. Normative Analysis of the State*, Basil Blackwell, Oxford, 1989, p. 21: "The notion of a deliberative democracy is rooted in the intuitive ideal of a democratic association in which the justification of the terms and conditions of association proceeds through public argument and reasoning among equal citizens".

14 S. Benhabib, *Toward a Deliberative Model of Democratic Legitimacy*, [in:] S. Benhabib (ed.), *Democracy and Difference: Contesting the Boundaries of the Political*, Princeton University Press, Princeton 1996, p. 68 ff. In this regard, Thomas McCarthy writes that all participants in the discourse of global modernity function at essentially the same discursive level, and this discursive symmetry makes all epistemic and evaluative assumptions essentially debatable (contestable). T. McCarthy, *Dialogical Freedom and Democratic Deliberation*, [in:] O.A.P. Shabani (ed.), *Multiculturalism and law: a critical debate*, Cardiff, 2007, p. 51.

religious, philosophical and moral doctrines. Rawls notes that "the ultimate idea of deliberative democracy is deliberation", which implies that citizens exchange views among themselves in political debate, and that their opinions are not immutable – they can be revised in the course of discussion.[15] In other words, democracy requires the contractual establishment, as a result of deliberation, of procedural rules of agonistic confrontation and competition, in which free human subjects can freely participate on an equal footing, being endowed with a dignity that no political competition – and therefore no failure of such – is able to deprive them of.

In contemporary scholarship, a great deal of attention is being devoted to updating Dewey's model of democracy,[16] according to which social cooperation is possible only when individual problems, as socially shared, are taken into consideration. Only then will citizens, as cooperating actors, engage in deliberative processes in which they evaluate the competing means to achieve the postulated goals, allocate special tasks according to abilities and interests, and reflexively justify these processes in the light of experience.[17] The medium for such cooperation is, of course, law. In particular, this refers to intersubjectively shared human rights, especially individual freedom, the right to political participation and so-called social rights.[18] John Dewey understood democracy as a reflexive form of communal cooperation. He maintained that democracy represents the political form of organisation in which human intelligence reaches its most complete development, because it is only where the methods of publicly debating individual convictions have taken institutional form that a rational

---

15 J. Rawls, *The Law of Peoples*, Harvard University Press, Cambridge 1999, p. 135.

16 I present this theory in order to indicate its validity and relevance, especially for my key Honnethian conception of recognition, but only in outline so as not to lose the essential thread of this study. Furthermore, I would like to take this opportunity to refer to the alternative justification of human rights presented within American pragmatism.

17 Ch.F. Zurn, *Anerkennung, Umverteilung und Demokratie...*, p. 440.

18 A. Honneth, *Das Andere der Gerechtigkeit. Aufsätze zur praktischen Philosophie*, Suhrkamp, Frankfurt am Main 2000, p. 271.

solution of a communicative nature can emerge from within the framework of social life.[19]

The terrain on which the solution of common problems takes place is the state, which encompasses the public as a discursive medium for cooperative problem-solving in accordance with democratic conditions. In this situation, social action manifests itself in the various forms of interaction taking place, the consequences of which – in the ideal, simplest case – affect only the direct participants of the interaction,[20] but which, after a certain time, also affect non-participants. This is why the necessity of joint public control and resolution of social problems arises. "The public" is that sphere of social action with regard to which a particular social group can demonstrate that its consequences require universal regulation, including administrative control, because they affect the whole community. Of course, this involves making an essentialist distinction between the "private" and the "public", which, as we know, is no straightforward matter.[21]

Assistance in the resolution of social problems is to be provided by the state, understood as a "secondary form of association." The state also formalises the resolution of these social problems by creating the conditions, underpinned by legal norms, from within which citizens can articulate and agree on their interests and claims. In this context, Dewey writes that state officials are supposed to create the conditions in which members of society are able "to count with reasonable certainty upon what others will do…", while creating "respect for others and for one's self."[22] Honneth astutely observes that, for Dewey, the political sphere is the cognitive medium through which society attempts to examine its problems, within the framework of the coordination of social action, and then to elaborate and solve them. Consequently, it is indisputable that society's political self-governance must be democratically organised, and that the more actively the public responds to social problems, the more

19 J. Dewey, *Die Öffentlichkeit und ihre Probleme*, Bodenheim, 1996, p. 175.

20 A. Honneth, *Das Andere der Gerechtigkeit…*, p. 300. In discussing Dewey's views, I draw on the critical view that Honneth presented in this text.

21 J. Dewey, *Die Öffentlichkeit und…*, p. 29.

22 *Ibidem*, p. 72.

rational will be the process through which the state can develop solutions to social problems that deserve popular approval.[23] Honneth notes that social cooperation makes it possible to arrive at more intelligent solutions to emerging problems, because in the process participants exchange information in an unforced and equally legitimate way, then propose different solutions to be discussed later. In this way, each individual learns, both on an individual and collective level, about the optimal conditions for social cooperation.[24] The experience of collective problem-solving and conflict resolution creates contexts in which individuals – *as individuals* – can find recognition for their own particular contribution and action. In other words, such contexts create the basis for the formation of the individual's proper self-appraisal and self-evaluation. A positive evaluation will encourage such an individual to continue their participation in the socio-political problem-solving process, gaining social esteem and personal benefit in the process.[25]

Here democracy is anchored in the consciousness of social cooperation; it is the ideal of free and open cooperative association between individuals in a well-organised society, but it is not an ideal in the sense of a prescribed political course of action aimed at finding a solution to a social problem within the formal state apparatus. Dewey identifies the premise of the revitalisation of the democratic public as being embedded in the pre-political scope of the social division of labour, which must be organised in such a just and equitable way that each member of society can see themselves as an active participant in a cooperative enterprise, because without this awareness, responsibility and cooperation will not be shared by individuals and,

---

23 A. Honneth, *Demokratie als reflexive Kooperation. John Dewey und die Demokratie-theorie der Gegenwart*, [in:] H. Brunkhorst, P. Niesen (eds.), *Das Recht der Republik*, Suhrkamp, Frankfurt am Main, 1999, p. 302.

24 Dewey discusses in detail the relationship between the democratic form of community life, the division of labour and the educational value of cooperative action in a work published under the title *Democracy and Education. An Introduction to the Philosophy of Education*, Free Press, New York, 1966, particularly in chapter VII: *The Democratic Conception in Education*.

25 Ch.F. Zurn, *Anerkennung, Umverteilung und Demokratie…*, p. 440.

as a result, they will not perceive the democratic conduct of will-making as a means for arriving at common solutions to social problems.[26]

The role of social cooperation is also emphasised by Rawls, in whose conception this entails acting for mutual benefit. In other words, "fair terms of social cooperation" are those which individuals "think others as equal citizens with them might reasonably accept."[27] Consequently, fair terms of social cooperation express the idea of reciprocity and mutuality. We can only cooperate as equals, and on the basis of mutual respect. In this sense, Rawls' "partial consensus" requires the kind of agreement that enables society to exist as a fair system of cooperation between rational and reasonable citizens, who are also free and equal persons. This is particularly important in view of the fact that people differ not only in their opinions and preferences, but also in their skills and abilities. Social cooperation provides a platform for the externalisation of one's own expectations, thereby fostering a plurality of values and socially diverse views, but it also provides an opportunity for all individuals – being equally valuable – to contribute to the common good through full participation in a particular social relationship. Thus it can be argued that Dewey's paradigm of social cooperation and a fair social division of labour provides both a sound epistemic justification for the democratic procedure of resolving social conflicts and a convincing explanation of the motivational sources of democratic participation.[28]

Dewey's theory of radical democracy becomes particularly attractive and topical given the ever-increasing pluralisation, heterogeneity and diversity of contemporary lifestyles. Paradoxically, the plurality of diverse lifestyles, and thus divisions of labour, does not necessarily have a destructive effect on society, but can instead make it possible to effectively

26 A. Honneth, *Demokratie als reflexive Kooperation...*, pp. 304–305. In other words, the fair and equitable division of labour is justified on the one hand by the motivational assumptions of political democracy, and on the other by the intersubjective assumptions of undistorted identity formation. Such a division of labour enables the positive self-validation of the individual, which in effect makes the individual realise the meaningfulness of social cooperation.

27 J. Rawls, *Political Liberalism*, Columbia University Press, New York, 1996, p. 300.

28 Ch.F. Zurn, *Anerkennung, Umverteilung und Demokratie...*, p. 441.

realise social goals by necessitating social consensus, for example in the form of specific laws. The formation of certain patterns of behaviour operating within the institutionalised forms of social life, and the formation of certain ethical systems, does not take place as an isolated process in the consciousness of the human individual, but occurs precisely within the commonly accepted category of the consciousness of the political community. In this sense, Herbert L.A. Hart treats the political community as a cooperative community, i.e. one in which the voluntary cooperation of the members of the community creates moral obligations and laws for the realisation of a common goal.[29]

The attractiveness of democracy is primarily due to the fact that its basic premise of equality implies equal participation in humanity. It is therefore a political and legal affirmation of the need to respect the right to be treated as equal to others, in the form of the right to equal care and respect. Democratic humanity is *one*, and shared belonging to this unity is the basis for both democratic equality and democratic bonding: the other is equal to me as a human being, and as a human being is my neighbour and brother. Therefore, the democratic bond intrinsically transcends all empirical barriers, divisions and differences: the other is like me, he is my alter ego – not because of a common culture, social background, education, wealth, or any other empirical fact, but simply as a human being. The task of democracy is to create a platform for the diverse and thus beautiful ability of human beings to choose between and enjoy a wealth of diverse lifestyles, and also to ensure the peaceful coexistence of people living in different ways, preferring different values. The existence and guarantee of the possibility for citizens to freely pursue their happiness is, together with freedom and equality, a key feature of democracy, and one which at the same time gives it an ethical dimension.[30]

---

29 H.L.A. Hart, *Social Solidarity and the Enforcement of Morality*, [in:] *Essays in Jurisprudence and Philosophy of Law*, Oxford University Press, Oxford, 2001, pp. 252–253; *idem*, *'Are There Any Natural Rights?'*, [in:] J. Waldron (ed.), *Theories of Rights*, Oxford University Press, Oxford, 1984, p. 77 ff.

30 A. Gutmann, *Identity in…*, p. 26 ff.

3. Legal recognition as a component of civil society

At this point, the cognitive-formal relationship of recognition in law (or rather in civil society) comes to the fore. Legal recognition means that we are the bearers of certain rights and, as such, we can demand their fulfilment, but only on condition that we are aware of the normative obligations that we must honour towards other subjects.[31] In this sense, recognition has a double reference – firstly, the norm, the legal order in force; secondly, other human beings – which compels everyone to identify other subjects as free individuals equal to all others. Legal recognition thus combines the universal validity of the norm and the uniqueness of each person.

Self-respect makes us feel that we are fully valued, cooperative members of society, capable of being guided throughout our lives by the principles of a particular conception of the good that is worth striving for and realising. Through the public affirmation of fundamental freedoms, citizens in a well-ordered society express mutual respect for each other as reasonable and trustworthy, and recognize the value that all citizens attach to their own way of life.[32] It is therefore important that a person should be able to live in such a way as to safeguard the inherent value of his or her own dignity, determined by a certain minimum resulting from the fact of being human.[33] The measure of this value is the respect we have for ourselves, our respect for others, and the respect that others show towards us. Hence it is accurate to say that if we do not respect ourselves, it is difficult to demand such respect from others, or to hold others in high esteem. It

---

31 A. Honneth, *Kampf um Anerkennung. Zur moralischen Grammatik sozialer Konflikte*, Suhrkamp Verlag, Frankfurt am Main, 1994, p. 174.

32 J. Rawls, *Political Liberalism...*, p. 15 ff.

33 This is why Honneth devotes so much space in his later works to the problem of redistribution, which is supposed to guarantee recognition. See the discussion between Axel Honneth and Nancy Fraser on this topic: N. Fraser, A. Honneth, *Umverteilung oder Anerkennung? Eine politisch-philosophische Kontroverse*, Suhrkamp, Frankfurt am Main 2003; also S. Thompson, *Is Redistribution a Form of Recognition? Comments on the Fraser – Honneth Debate*, "Critical Review of International Social and Political Philosophy" 2005, vol. 8, no. 1, pp. 85–102.

is therefore important to be aware of and cultivate one's own personal dignity. This is sometimes very difficult, if not impossible, due to the economic, social or political situation. Thus the protection of one's own dignity requires that we expect it to be recognised by other people, and reflection on our own sense of dignity should be accompanied by awareness of the need to respect the dignity of others.

From a positivist legal perspective, we can conclude that legal recognition consists in mutual recognition as a person, since such an obligation arises from the legal norms in force. Such recognition is rational rather than emotional. It consists in the realisation of one's own worth, which is confirmed by the norms of the democratic legal order. Recognition makes it possible for individuals to participate in the interactions taking place between equal subjects equipped with individual rights, without the possession of which it is not possible to develop self-respect.[34] In other words, the result of recognition – in this second distinguished sphere – is self-respect from the perspective of public law relations, which is dependent on one's sense of dignity being ensured. Habermas's observation that rights are not properties that individuals possess by nature, but rather relations based on mutual recognition, which is at the same time a form of social cooperation, is thus very astute and fitting.[35]

In the sense presented above, legal recognition implies "the connection between the enlarging of the sphere of rights recognized as belonging to persons and the enriching of the capacities that these subjects recognize in themselves."[36] Honneth and Ricoeur aptly note that the enlargement

34 A. Honneth, *Kampf um Anerkennung...*, p. 194.

35 A similar position is articulated by J. Habermas in *Between Facts and Norms...*, pp. 88–89. The German philosopher writes here: "At a conceptual level, rights do not immediately refer to atomistic and estranged individuals who are possessively set against one another. On the contrary, as elements of the legal order they presuppose collaboration among subjects who recognize one another, in their reciprocally related rights and duties, as free and equal citizens. This mutual recognition is constitutive for a legal order from which actionable rights are derived. In this sense 'subjective' rights emerge co-originally with 'objective' law, to use the terminology of German jurisprudence".

36 P. Ricoeur, *The Course of Recognition*, Harvard University Press, Cambridge, 2005, p. 198.

of the normative sphere of rights corresponds to the enlargement of the capacities granted to legal subjects, and thus on the one hand entails the presentation (enumeration) of a catalogue of such subjective rights (privileges) and on the other hand the allocation of these rights to new categories of individuals or groups.[37] In other words, legal recognition implies the protection of the individual's sphere of freedom and legally assured participation in the public will-making process, which, after all, is not possible without ensuring a certain level of living standards. If they are equipped with individual rights, subjects can make socially acceptable claims and thus carry out legitimate social activity, with the conviction that all other members of society must relate to them with respect. Rights thus serve to develop self-respect, since they provide individuals with a symbolic means of expression that allows them to engage in social activities outwardly and leads to their widespread recognition (also morally) as complete and capable people.[38]

Honneth's conception of recognition is grounded in the belief that the subject should be treated in the field of legal and state recognition as a subject who shares with all other members of their community the qualities that allow participation in the discursive production of public will-formation.[39] This makes it possible to create a political community understood as the totality of democratic institutions that formulate the purpose to be served by a given legal order in the state, and what distinguishes it from other

37 A. Honneth, *Kampf um Anerkennung…*, p. 186. In presenting the catalogue and justification of such individual rights, both authors refer to Robert Alexy's concept of fundamental rights presented in his well-known work *Theorie der Grundrechte* (Baden-Baden, 1986). Thus, Honneth classifies them as follows: "The first category refers to negative rights that protect a person's life, liberty, and property from unauthorized state interference; the second category refers to the positive rights guaranteeing a person the opportunity to participate in processes of public will-formation; and the third category, finally, refers to the similarly positive rights that ensure a person's fair share in the distribution of basic goods" (*ibidem*, p. 186).

38 A. Honneth, *Kampf um Anerkennung…*, p. 194.

39 *Ibidem*, p. 195.

social groups is precisely the possibility of shaping through its activity the vision of the individual's place in society.[40]

In this context, James Tully's suggestion that we are now in the third phase of anti-authoritarian politics seems correct: the first was the struggle for democratic citizenship, the second was the fight against global imperialism, while the third is the "politics of cultural recognition." He distinguishes two areas of the struggle for recognition: the first being the struggle for the legal and political recognition of various types of difference and equality – endogenous, ethnic, national, transnational, religious, cultural, civilisational and linguistic; the second being the practical response to the former – in the form of multiple law-making practices.[41] Tully therefore believes that modern constitutions should take cultural diversity into account and thus be based on intercultural dialogue.[42] Only this will guarantee that everyone's voice is given due consideration. In his view, intercultural dialogue constituted in this way, based on cooperative, deliberative democracy and popular discourse, would ensure fair cultural recognition while also rejecting unjust claims.

The issue is approached somewhat differently by Habermas in his discourse theory, since he does not appeal to moral recognition in order to justify the recognition of equality and the equality of citizens. He treats the equality of all people-citizens as a basic requirement of the discursive situation. For this reason, he treats the integration of members of different cultural, religious and world-view communities, including ethnic or sexual minorities, as a basic condition for the social integration of a multicultural and pluralistic democratic society. Members of such groups must gain the status of equal and free members of a cooperative society (the

40 John Finnis notes that community (or rather, togetherness and association) should be conceptualised as an evolving states of affairs, living together, acting together and having a community of interests, grouping together and connecting with each other. In other words, community is a relationship that unites human beings, not a social group or association. J. Finnis, *Natural Law and Natural Rights*, Clarendon Press, Oxford, 1992, pp. 136, 154–156.

41 J. Tully, *The Practice of Law-Making and the Problem of Difference: An Introduction to the Field*, [in:] O.A.P. Shabani (ed.), *Multiculturalism…*, p. 19.

42 *Ibidem*, p. 27 ff.

state) in order to participate fully in discursive democracy. From this point of view, the right to be different must be treated as basic. Difference cannot be a source of restriction or discrimination. On the contrary, discursively grounded procedures, discursively reconstructed law and deliberative politics ought to guarantee the respect of the "rights of others" and the recognition of their equality in their difference. The structure of the "system of rights" presented by Habermas thus encompasses the individual forms of the "struggle for recognition"; in other words, it already contains and recognises the achievements of the individual forms of this struggle. The state, through the medium of law, ought to enable the cultural reproduction of life-worlds, but should not guarantee the survival (persistence) of a particular culture.[43] From a theoretical-legal point of view, the plurality of values and worldviews imposes the requirement of ethical neutrality on the legal order and the political sphere.[44] In this context, the primary task of a state based on discursive democracy is to enable citizens to freely choose their lifestyles, values or culture and, furthermore, to ensure equal access to the political system for all citizens regardless of the form of life they ultimately choose. At the same time, the moral self-realisation of the political community is to be expressed through enabling the principle of democracy to be respected, that is, through allowing the authentic will of the general public to be heard in the public sphere. It also follows that the private autonomy of the equal citizen can only be ensured if their state-citizen autonomy is activated. The defect of the "liberal" variant of the system of rights lies precisely in the fact that it ignores this relationship, which means the universalism of fundamental rights cannot be conceived

---

43 J. Habermas, *Kampf um Anerkennung...*, p. 259.

44 *Ibidem*, p. 252. By 'ethical', Habermas means "all questions that relate to conceptions of the good life, or a life that is not misspent. Ethical questions cannot be evaluated from the 'moral point of view' of whether something is 'equally good for everyone'; rather, impartial judgment of such questions is based on strong evaluations and determined by the self-understanding and perspectival life-projects of particular groups, that is, by what is from their point of view 'good for us,' all things considered. The first-person reference, and hence the relationship to the identity of a group (or an individual) is grammatically inscribed in ethical questions."

of as an abstract equalisation of differences.[45] In other words, it makes it difficult to pursue a correct politics of recognition. Meanwhile, the contemporary democratic framing of the rights system also includes collective goals that are articulated in struggles for recognition.

4. The idea of constitutional patriotism as an expression of citizen solidarity

The institutional impregnat here is to be discursively agreed law based on the consensus of all cooperating citizens, guided by Habermas's "constitutional patriotism", which is an expression of citizen solidarity.[46] The constitution must obviously guarantee the equal coexistence of different ethnic groups and their cultural forms of life. It must safeguard the structures of communication that reflect the fact that the identity of each individual is intertwined with collective identities and can only be embedded in a cultural network.[47] Despite the fact that "constitutional patriotism" supports

45 *Ibidem*, p. 245.

46 Similarly, Neil MacCormick: "We need not overstress the requirements of culture or common ethnicity or language as essentially constitutive of a *demos* in the sense required for the concept of democratic government. I should like to suggest the possibility of our conceiving such a thing as a 'civic' *demos*, that is, one identified by the relationship of individuals to common institutions of civic rather than an ethnic or ethnic-cultural kind. People can have a civic identity constituted perhaps by what Habermas has dubbed 'constitutional patriotism', *Verfassungspatriotismus*. This is a common loyalty to a common constitutional order, regardless of differences of language, ethnic background, and the rest. People are sometimes willing to sink differences of culture, of language, of heritage, of history for the sake of their common participation in a lawfully constituted polity of commonwealth." N. MacCormick, *Questioning Sovereignty*, Oxford University Press, Oxford, 2001, p. 144.

47 In this context, Habermas considers the issue of "reverse discrimination". Indeed, he points out that some endangered cultures of some previously unfavored groups have a moral right to be supported. However, this does not mean that every culture is of "equal value" in the sense that its contribution to the creation of world civilization is equal, or that it has something important to impart to all people. *Ibidem*, p. 258 ff. Susan Wolf also made similar statements, *Comment*, [in:] A. Gutman (ed.) *Multiculturalism. Examining the Politics of Recognition*, Princeton University Press, Princeton, 1994, p. 84. Therefore, the state is only obliged to enable the cultural reproduction of life-worlds by means of the

the validity of liberal democracy, it must promote maximal consideration of difference and provide the most tolerant and flexible political system possible. "Constitutional patriotism" thus represents a common minimum that unites organic groups and communities guided by different lifestyles, while ensuring that the rights of minorities and discriminated groups are protected. In other words, discourse theory assumes that the consensus it aims for will be achieved by ensuring correct democratic procedures and through the communicative network of political public spheres. Habermas states that the content of such an agreement is human rights, which are discursively woven into the code of law that institutionalises them in the form of positive law. In turn, the system of rights and the principles of the democratic rule of law find their source in the rational practice which led to the acceptance of the legal community in the first act of self-constitution.[48] This situates Habermas's conception somewhere between legal positivism and natural law theories.

A deliberated agreement leading to mutual respect is not possible if the representatives of different cultures, religions, worldviews and moral attitudes refuse to refrain from asserting their professed truths through violence (by military, state or terrorist means).[49] They must recognise

law. In other words, in multicultural societies, the equal coexistence of diverse lifestyles provides the opportunity for each person, each member of a given organic community, to be able to continue the traditions maintained by it, but it also makes it possible to abandon them self-critically. Hence there is no room here for fundamentalist positions prohibiting a break with one's own culture or for unreflective adherence to certain traditional dogmas. Habermas points out that such positions lack awareness of the fallibility of their claims and fail to respect the "burdens of reason" of which Rawls writes. Fundamentalism does not allow for the reflexive consideration of foreign ways of life with which, after all, it shares the same universe of discourse. Hence, fundamentalism should not be confused with dogmatism and orthodoxy.

48 J. Habermas, *Zur Legitimation durch Menschenrechte*, [in:] H. Brunkhorst, P. Niesen (eds.), *Das Recht der Republik*, Suhrkamp, Frankfurt am Main, 1999, pp. 386–403; *idem*, *Faktyczność i obowiązywanie. Teoria dyskursu wobec zagadnień prawa i demokratycznego państwa prawnego* (trans. A. Romaniuk, R. Marszałek), Wydawnictwo Naukowe Scholar, Warszawa, 2005, p. 579.

49 J. Habermas, *Od wrażenia zmysłowego do symbolicznego wyrazu*, Oficyna Naukowa, Warszawa, 2004, p. 48.

each other as equal partners and participants in discourse, regardless of their mutual respect for the values of each other's traditions and preferred lifestyles. Habermas points out here that it is necessary to overcome the "fundamentalist self-understanding" that constitutes a distortion of communication, and this involves a reflexive analysis of dogmatic claims to truth. In a multicultural society, the constitution can only tolerate lifestyles that are not based on fundamentalist premises, because the equal coexistence of different ways of life requires the mutual recognition of different cultural life-worlds.[50] It is therefore necessary to create a political community of a constructivist nature, the basic condition of which is that its members should reciprocally recognise each other's freedom and provide opportunities for changing perspectives, guaranteeing equality and mutual recognition. Only such a community can be sensitive to the necessity of institutionalising certain conditions of communication in order to to guarantee human rights.[51]

In this regard, Jürgen Habermas aptly observes that "In multicultural societies basic rights and the principles of the constitutional state form the points of crystallization for a political culture which unites all citizens. This in turn is the basis for the coexistence of different groups and subcultures, each with its own origin and identity."[52] In other words, the integration of citizens should foster loyalty to a common political culture rooted in a shared interpretation of constitutional principles. The primary objective for the members of such a community is not to maximise their own interests but rather to discover the public (common) interest. Such common interests include security and institutional protection from violence. Hence the role of ethically integrated organic communities in such a constructivist community must not be diminished – instead the differential

50 J. Habermas, *Kampf um Anerkennung...*, p. 262.

51 J. Habermas, *The Liberating Power of Symbols*, The MIT Press, Cambridge, MA, 2001, p. 87.

52 *Ibidem*, p. 87. He goes on to state that "The *uncoupling of these two levels of integration* is needed to prevent the majority culture from exercising a power of definition over the whole political culture. Indeed, the majority culture must subordinate itself to the political culture, and enter into a non-coercive exchange with the minority cultures."

multiplicity and integrity of different coexisting lifestyles in a multicultural society must be reinforced. It is worth emphasising once again that the binding element of such a political community of a constructivist nature, which respects and incorporates the multiplicity of diverse lifestyles, will be the discursive procedure of law-making and the exercise of power (deliberative politics or discursively grounded democracy), as well as the mutual recognition of the members of a community. In other words, the universality and acceptability of legal rules is manifested in a procedural consensus that must be proposed in the form of constitutional patriotism in the context of each historically determined political culture.[53] An inclusive community, that is, one embracing pluralism of values, worldview, ethnicity and culture, functions through the fundamental premise of co-operation and, moreover, through the ability and willingness to transcend the divisions resulting from the multiplicity of lifestyles, while grounded in the idea of human dignity and discursive democracy. In this context, we can say that society is not defined by a quasi-contractual definition of the scope of individual freedom, but by the mutual recognition of others as members of this community and respect for these others as human beings. R. Antony Duff aptly observes that in a society (community) constructed in this way, the law is not merely the command of the sovereign, but the language of its members expressing their own – by definition – shared political values.[54] Consequently, the requirements of law are normative expressions of the values to which every member of the community or society should be committed. Hence, it should be emphasised once again that inclusion in the community entails being recognised and treated as a full member of the community in question. This encompasses the right to participate both in the political sphere of the community through involvement in the creation of law and the exercise of power, as well as participation in the goods produced by that community (the state). Furthermore, such an inclusive community is supposed to provide – by means of the law and the state structure thus shaped – protection guaranteeing that I am treated as

53 J. Habermas, *Kampf um Anerkennung…*, p. 264.

54 R.A. Duff, *Punishment, Communication and Community*, Oxford University Press, Oxford, 2001.

a fellow citizen worthy of respect and esteem, which encompasses protection from violence.

The greatest threat to such a community is violence, which Habermas describes as communicative pathology. He asserts that: "The spiral of violence begins as a spiral of distorted communication that leads through the spiral of uncontrolled reciprocal mistrust, to the breakdown of communication."[55] It is therefore necessary to consider how to protect our political community from attacks of violence and what to do with the perpetrators. In doing so, it is important to make a distinction between, on the one hand, the violence typical of Western liberal democracy, which is expressed either through social inequality, discrimination and marginalisation, or through the perpetration of crimes, and, on the other hand, intercultural violence, which consists in the fact that "those who first become alienated from each other through systematically distorted communication" do not subsequently recognise themselves as participating members of the community.[56] The remedy for the violence of unequal distribution is, as I noted earlier with reference to the views of Nancy Fraser and Axel Honneth, to restore recognition by improving the material situation of the oppressed group and, furthermore, by ensuring their social respectability and participation in the public formation of will and opinion. Ronald Dworkin's words are significant here: "Government must treat those whom it governs with concern, that is, as human beings who are capable of suffering and frustration, and with respect, that is, as human beings who are capable of forming and acting on intelligent conceptions of how their lives should be lived."[57] This implies the realisation of a contemporary *civic humanism* in political life, which at the same time plays an enormous emancipatory and empowering role for ordinary citizens as active co-creators of the socio-political reality in which they live. Such a citizen becomes a "critical

---

55 J. Habermas, [in:] G. Borradori, *Philosophy in a Time of Terror: Dialogues with Jurgen Habermas and Jacques Derrida*, University of Chicago Press, Chicago, 2003, p. 35.

56 *Ibidem*, p. 35.

57 R. Dworkin, *Taking Rights Seriously*, Duckworth, London, 1977, pp. 272–273.

citizen" and thus a subject of the democratic processes taking place in their political-legal community.[58]

58 See P. Norris, *Critical Citizens. Global Support for Democratic Government*, Oxford University Press, Oxford 1999, pp. 1–27.

Bibliography

Alexy, R., *Theorie der Grundrechte*, Baden-Baden, 1986.

Benhabib, S., *Toward a Deliberative Model of Democratic Legitimacy*, [in:] S. Benhabib (ed.), *Democracy and Difference: Contesting the Boundaries of the Political*, Princeton University Press, Princeton, 1996.

Bohman, J., *Public Deliberation. Pluralism, Complexity, and Democracy*, The MIT Press, Cambridge, MA, 1996.

Cohen, J., *Deliberation and Democratic Legitimacy*, [in:] A. Hamlin, Ph. Pettit (eds.), *The Good Polity. Normative Analysis of the State*, Basil Blackwell, Oxford, 1989.

Dewey, J., *Democracy and Education. An Introduction to the Philosophy of Education*, Free Press, New York, 1966.

Dewey, J., *Die Öffentlichkeit und ihre Probleme*, Bodenheim, 1996.

Dryzek, J., *Deliberative Democracy and Beyond: Liberals, Critics, Contestations*, Oxford University Press, Oxford, 2002.

Duff, R.A., *Punishment, Communication and Community*, Oxford University Press, Oxford, 2001.

Dworkin, R., *Is Democracy Possible Here?: Principles for a New Political Debate*, Princeton University Press, Princeton, 2006.

Dworkin, R., *Taking Rights Seriously*, Duckworth, London, 1977.

Elster, J., *The Market and the Forum*, [in:] J. Bohman, W. Rehg (eds.), *Deliberative Democracy. Essays on Reason and Politics*, The MIT Press, Cambridge, 1997.

Finnis, J., *Natural Law and Natural Rights*, Clarendon Press, Oxford, 1992.

Fraser, N., Honneth A., *Umverteilung oder Anerkennung? Eine politisch-philosophische Kontroverse*, Suhrkamp, Frankfurt am Main, 2003.

Gutmann, A., *Identity in Democracy*, Princeton University Press, Princeton, 2004.

Habermas, J., [in:] G. Borradori, *Philosophy in a Time of Terror: Dialogues with Jurgen Habermas and Jacques Derrida*, University of Chicago Press, Chicago, 2003.

Habermas, J., *Between Facts and Norms. Contributions to a Discourse Theory of Law and Democracy*, The MIT Press, Cambridge, MA, 1998, Chapter 3 and *Popular Sovereignty*.

Habermas, J., *Faktyczność i obowiązywanie. Teoria dyskursu wobec zagadnień prawa i demokratycznego państwa prawnego* (trans. A. Romaniuk, R. Marszałek), Wydawnictwo Naukowe Scholar, Warszawa, 2005.

Habermas, J., *Kampf um Anerkennung im demokratischen Rechtstaat*, [in:] *idem*, *Die Einbeziehung des Anderen. Studien zur politischen Theorie*, Suhrkamp, Frankfurt am Main, 1999.

Habermas, J., *Od wrażenia zmysłowego do symbolicznego wyrazu*, Oficyna Naukowa, Warszawa, 2004.

Habermas, J., *The Liberating Power of Symbols*, The MIT Press, Cambridge, MA, 2001.

Habermas, J., *Zur Legitimation durch Menschenrechte*, [in:] H. Brunkhorst, P. Niesen (eds.), *Das Recht der Republik*, Suhrkamp, Frankfurt am Main, 1999.

Hart, H.L.A., *'Are There Any Natural Rights?'*, [in:] J. Waldron (ed.) *Theories of Rights*, Oxford University Press, Oxford, 1984.

Hart, H.L.A., *Social Solidarity and the Enforcement of Morality*, [in:] *Essays in Jurisprudence and Philosophy of Law*, Oxford University Press, Oxford, 2001.

Honneth, A., *Das Andere der Gerechtigkeit. Aufsätze zur praktischen Philosophie*, Suhrkamp, Frankfurt am Main, 2000.

Honneth, A., *Demokratie als reflexive Kooperation. John Dewey und die Demokratie-theorie der Gegenwart*, [in:] H. Brunkhorst, P. Niesen (eds.), *Das Recht der Republik*, Suhrkamp, Frankfurt am Main, 1999.

Honneth, A., *Kampf um Anerkennung. Zur moralischen Grammatik sozialer Konflikte*, Suhrkamp Verlag, Frankfurt am Main, 1994.

MacCormick, N., *Questioning Sovereignty*, Oxford University Press, Oxford, 2001.

McCarthy, T., *Dialogical Freedom and Democratic Deliberation*, [in:] O.A.P. Shabani (ed.), *Multiculturalism and Law: A Critical Debate*, University of Wales Press, Cardiff, 2007.

Norris, P., *Critical Citizens. Global Support for Democratic Government*, Oxford University Press, Oxford, 1999.

Rawls, J., *Political Liberalism*, Columbia University Press, New York, 1996.

Rawls, J., *The Law of Peoples*, Harvard University Press, Cambridge, 1999.

Ricoeur, P., *The Course of Recognition*, Harvard University Press, Cambridge, 2005.

Thompson, S., *Is Redistribution a Form of Recognition? Comments on the Fraser – Honneth Debate*, "Critical Review of International Social and Political Philosophy" 2005, vol. 8, no. 1.

Tully, J., *The Practice of Law-Making and the Problem of Difference: An Introduction to the Field*, [in:] O.A.P. Shabani (ed.), *Multiculturalism and Law: A Critical Debate*, University of Wales Press, Cardiff, 2007.

Wolf, S., *Comment*, [in:] A. Gutman (ed.) *Multiculturalism. Examining the Politics of Recognition*, Princeton University Press, Princeton, 1994.

Zurn, Ch.F., *Anerkennung, Umverteilung und Demokratie. Dilemmata in Honneths Kritischer Theorie der Gesellschaft*, "Deutsche Zeitschrift für Philosophie" 2005, vol. 53, no. 3.

Paulius Griciūnas[2]

National Identity: Constitutional Patriotism or Dialogue on Values[1]

Abstract
The national identity clause, established in Article 4(2) TEU gave an incentive for broad academic discussions on the scope, purpose and overall position of this clause in EU law. This article explores the concept of national identity by providing an analysis of academic works and the jurisprudence of the ECJ. It also addresses the existing challenges to the judicial application of the national identity clause. However, in the environment of constitutional pluralism, the lack of inclusion of the national constitutional courts in the direct judicial dialogue on national identity might be an additional reason for maintaining the *controlimiti* doctrine. This doctrine is not addressed in the article, but attention is paid to the notion of constitutional identity, which is often equated with the notion of national identity. In the context of the national identity concept, probably the most important and well-known decision is *Vardyn* – a case which is related to Lithuania. Accordingly, the final part of the article addresses the concept of national identity in the Lithuanian legal system.

Keywords: constitutional pluralism, national identity, judicial dialogue, EU law primacy constitutional identity.

---

1 The research was conducted within the scope of the project "Constitutional Consciousness as a Remedy for the Crisis of Discourse and Democracy Deficit in the European Union", Lietuvos mokslo taryba. Narodowe Centrum Nauki. DAINA – Polish-Lithuanian Funding Initiative, contract no. S-LL-19-4 / LSS-220000-1395, 10 August 2018

2 Paulius Griciūnas is a graduate of the University of Vilnius Faculty of Law and of the Faculty of Economics. He is a PhD candidate at the University of Vilnius, with his areas of academic interest being EU law, national constitutional law, and human rights. Since 2018 he has been the Secretary-General of the Lithuanian Bar. He served as the Vice-minister of Justice for the last five years. Moreover, for five years he was a Chairman of the Scientific Council of the Lithuanian Law Institute.

1. Introduction

European constitutional pluralism assumes that the interaction of autonomous legal systems based on heterarchical judicial dialogue (Toader, Safta, 2016, p. 110) does not itself resolve conflict, but instead "helps to rationalise the outcome of legal disputes" (Popelier, 2012, p. 77). This dialogue presupposes an exchange of arguments between two apex courts of different legal systems – the ECJ and the national Constitutional Courts,[3] neither having authority over the other, but rather competing over the "final say."[4] Constitutional Courts hold a privileged position in national legal systems, allowing them to "forge closer ties between different but interacting legal regimes" (Pollicino, 2010, pp. 66–67). However, despite being spokespeople of national legal systems, it is questionable whether national Constitutional Courts are being properly taken into consideration by the ECJ.

The interaction between the highest judicial authorities would not, in principle, pose any (major) challenge at the level of ordinary law. For instance, if the cooperation were to take place in the framework of EU law and were based on the unconditional primacy of EU law.

However, the situation changes significantly when it concerns national constitutional law.[5] Therefore, in order to accommodate the peculiarities of national constitutional law within the framework of EU law, the notion of national identity was introduced in EU primary law. Article 4(2) TEU

---

3 Specialised constitutional courts have been established in 18 EU Member States: Austria, Belgium, Bulgaria, Croatia, Czechia, Germany, Hungary, Italy, Latvia, Lithuania, Luxemburg, Malta, Poland, Portugal, Romania, Slovakia, Slovenia, and Spain. France is also included in this group. In Ireland, Denmark, Cyprus, and Estonia, the supreme courts are also institutions of constitutional review. In the Netherlands, Sweden, Finland, and Greece, there is no specialised constitutional review institution (Mayer, 2009, pp. 400–401; Dicosola *et al.*, 2015, p. 1318).

4 A complicated picture can be noticed in the relationship between the ECJ and the Constitutional Courts (Martinico, 2013, p. 107) as in multilevel cooperation, each constitutional court "is competent for safeguarding 'its' Constitution" (Voßkuhle, 2013, pp. 83, 85).

5 C. Van de Heyning defines such situations such as "having constitutional content" (Van de Heyning, 2012, p. 182).

established the national identity clause in the Lisbon Treaty, paving the way for its transformation from a mere declaratory intention in the Maastricht Treaty, to a justiciable autonomous ground.

This clause has a significant potential to ensure that the ECJ addresses concerns over the constitutional traditions of Member States. However, national identity cannot be straightforwardly equated with Article 4(2) TEU, as this Article encompasses three important principles: the national identity clause, the equality of Member States, and the respect for the essential State functions (Bogdandy, Schill, 2011, p. 1425). These principles represent the former pillars structure (Dobbs, 2014, pp. 325–326).

However, although Article 4(2) TEU is mentioned, the present article exclusively analyses the national identity clause from both viewpoints: theoretical background and practical application. Until now, the national identity clause has received more scholarly attention than practical application, as references to the national identity clause are extremely rare in the jurisprudence track record of the ECJ.

The national identity clause could be regarded as a midpoint between two extremes: the "orthodox" primacy of EU law and the protection of the constitutional core outside the bounds of EU law.[6] This midpoint creates an opportunity to have an open dialogue on values, at least temporarily setting aside the constitutional patriotism of its legal system, be it on the scale of the EU or on a national level, and in all likelihood currently remains the only sustainable solution.

This article provides an overview of academic writings and jurisprudence on the notion of national identity in EU law. It starts by explaining the notion and elements of national identity, supplemented by an analysis of challenges to the application of the identity clause, and followed by

6 It is worthwhile mentioning that the views of Constitutional Courts on the relationship between national constitutional law and EU law are "controversial and inconsistent" (Grabenwarter, 2009, pp. 84–85). The Constitutional Courts "have never accepted the primacy of EU law without conditions" (Tuori, 2015, p. 326), or have accepted it "only relatively" (Auby, 2018, p. 9). National Constitutional Courts "challenge the preference of EU law over the constitution or set limits" (Pérez, 2012, p. 121) and behave like "constitutional guards against incompatible EU legislation" (Van de Heyning, 2012, p. 189).

an analysis of relevant jurisprudence. One such example is the *Vardyn* case, which has also been viewed from the point of view of Lithuanian constitutional law.

2. Explaining the concept of the national identity clause

2.1. Historical developments establish a legal framework for national identity

The national identity clause,[7] established in Article 4(2) TEU of the Lisbon Treaty, did not appear *ex nihilo* (Preshova, 2012, p. 269). Its history begins with the Maastricht Treaty, which was a leap in integration (Cloots, 2015, p. 123), and created a new political system (Chalmers et al., 2014, p. 25). Article F of the Maastricht Treaty did not maintain a previously inherent "constitutional blindness" towards the Member States (Claes, 2012, pp. 214–215), and became a turning point in the narrative of European integration, aiming to restrict the ECJ and protecting the constitutional identity of the Member States (Martinico, 2013, p. 100). The national identity clause remained in the Amsterdam Treaty Article 6(3), recognising that the EU is based on national participation and respect, and not on the overcoming of national identities (Besselink, 2010, pp. 40–41). This provision remains unchanged in the Nice Treaty.

The development of the national identity clause sped up in the preparation of the Treaty establishing a Constitution for Europe (the Constitutional Treaty). Working Group V, led by H. Christophersen, was given the goal of delineating complementary competences. H. Christophersen proposed a clause to define the limits of EU competence.[8] This proposal, later to be known as a "Christophersen clause", suggested wording the clause rather than listing the exclusive competences of the Member States (Guastaferro, 2012, p. 271). Furthermore, it was a proposal made to

7 The national identity clause, established in Article 4(2) provides: "the Union shall respect [...] Member States [...] national identities, inherent in their fundamental structures, political and constitutional, inclusive of regional and local self-government."

8 Working Group V, Working document 5, Option paper by H. Christophersen, 11 July 2002.

ensure the EU's respect for certain competences of the Member States, but they were not listed because of the fear that a "competence creep" would be possible in other areas. The condition of national identity was therefore formulated (Bogdandy, Schill, 2011, p. 1426), which was more a limitation rather than a delineation of EU competences (Guastaferro, 2012, p. 279).

However, two important points were highlighted by Working Group V: first, that the national identity clause "was not a derogation clause", and second, that the ECJ should be "the ultimate interpreter of the provision."[9] Thus, the national identity clause was significantly extended in comparison to previous Treaties and was established in Article I-5 of the Constitutional Treaty.

However, the failure to ratify the Constitutional Treaty resulted in a "period of reflection",[10] and after "two years of uncertainty over the Union's treaty reform process",[11] it was proceeded with the preparation of a new Treaty, in which, as an outcome, the national identity clause from the Constitutional Treaty was transposed to Article 4(2) TEU of the Lisbon Treaty (Preshova, 2012, p. 270).

Moreover, one may consider that Article 4(2) TEU is of the most significant in the whole Lisbon Treaty due to its reference to national constitutional law (Martinico, 2018, p. 83). It became clear that the national identity clause did not have a historical, linguistic, or sociological reference, but, on the contrary, has a legal meaning, or rather a constitutional one (Faraguna, 2016, p. 498; Faraguna, 2017, p. 1628; Bogdandy, Schill, 2011, p. 1427; Murphy, 2017, pp. 98–99). This is a reason this clause has attracted the attention of legal scholars (Konstadinides, 2011, pp. 196, 198; van der Schyff, 2016a, p. 230; Pérez, 2013b, p. 141). The wording of Article 4(2) TEU shows that the position of the Member States was strengthened (Pernice, 2011a, p. 86) even compared to the Constitutional

9 Final report of Working Group V, November 2002 (CONV 375/1/02 REV 1), p. 11.

10 Declaration by the Heads of State or Government on the ratification of the Treaty establishing a Constitution for Europe, 18 June 2005 (SN 117/05), p. 2.

11 Presidency Conclusions of the Brussels European Council 21/22 June 2007 (11177/1/07REV 1), p. 2.

Treaty (Dobbs, 2014, pp. 310–312), and requires respect for constitutional and political structures (Chalmers et al., 2014, p. 235).

The notion of national identity before the Lisbon Treaty was more moderate and less manifestly constitutional (Besselink, 2012, p. 678). Nevertheless, the importance of Article 4(2) TEU when compared to the Amsterdam Treaty, is not exclusively related to the extension of wording. This is due to the fact that in the Lisbon Treaty, for the first time, national identity fell within the jurisdiction of the ECJ (Guastaferro, 2012, p. 264). Therefore, it became available for judicial proceedings before the ECJ (Grewe, 2013, p. 37). Consequently, this provision gained an autonomous legal force (Dobbs, 2014, p. 316), and was now enforceable by judicial procedure (van der Schyff, 2016a, p. 230).

2.2. The content of the concept of the national identity clause

Article 4(2) TEU references multilevel constitutionalism (Murphy, 2017, p. 98), including the possibility of different constitutional structures (Priban, 2015, p. 330), as well as constitutional reservations. All the elements mentioned are above all essential for the relations between the EU and Member States (Dobbs, 2014, p. 334). And although the Lisbon Treaty has strengthened the national identity clause as a legal instrument, the content of this instrument itself remains ambiguous (Faraguna, 2015, p. 24). This is a widely accepted perception, confirmed by many researchers.[12]

It is likely that the most encompassing description was provided by A. Arnaiz and C. Llivina, who stated that this clause had the potential "to be anything from the cornerstone of a pluralistic European polity to the single most disintegrative clause" (Arnaiz, Llivina, 2013, p. 10). However, this provision would hardly be regarded as a means to reverse or to stall European integration (Gisbert, 2013, pp. 88–89).

Every element of the national identity clause could be analysed in detail, however, some of the most important elements should be discussed first.

12 For example, A. von Bogdandy and S. Schill (Bogdandy, Schill, 2011, p. 1422), J.H. Reestman (Reestman, 2009, p. 380), E. Cloots (Cloots, 2016, p. 86), M. Wendel (Wendel, 2013, p. 999), G. Rugge (Rugge, 2017, p. 24), and others.

First, it is necessary to mention that the element "Union" encompasses not just the EU as an entity, but also all EU institutions, including the ECJ itself (Kröll, 2012, pp. 113–114; Konstadinides, 2013, p. 2; Cloots, 2015, p. 80), therefore, the ECJ should respect this clause (Tatham, 2013, p. 293).

Second, the requirement of "respect"[13] is another element worthy of mention. Notably, it requires that national identity and democracy be respected (Mayer, 2009, p. 424). By extension, any kind exemption from this rule should be impermissible (Chalmers et al., 2014, pp. 235–236).

This element of respect is not used exclusively for interpretation – it provides an independent ground for the ECJ to assess the legality of an EU act (Bogdandy, Schill, 2011, p. 1443). Moreover, as this respect is addressed to the national identity inherent in fundamental structures (Grewe, 2013, p. 38), it is closely related to the third element – constitutional structures. Thus, it is to be noted that the formula used in the national identity clause refers not to "constitutional values", but instead to "constitutional structures" (Preshova, 2012, p. 274). Such explicit reference to these aforementioned fundamental structures suggests the clause has constitutional significance (Kovács, 2017, p. 1704). However, the national identity clause should not be interpreted as an injunction created to protect every constitutional rule, otherwise, the autonomy of EU law would no longer be possible (Bogdandy, 2012, p. 771).

The term "constitutional structures" does not signify an ordinary relationship, but rather an exclusive one (Guastaferro, 2012, p. 313). Unlike, for example, the respect of, say, cultural expression (Cloots, 2015, p. 163). The EU, therefore, only has a general obligation to respect national identity inherent in respective "constitutional structures" (Kröll, 2012, p. 114). Therefore, what is to be "national identity" is not to be seen from an "external perspective", but rather by referring to national constitutional law and the notions it includes (Bogdandy, Schill, 2011, pp. 1428–1429).

---

13 See for example, the opinion of Advocate General M.P. Maduro delivered on 21 May 2008 in *Arcelor* case (C-127/07) points 15–16. See also the opinion of Advocate General M.P. Maduro delivered on 8 October 2008 in *Michaniki* case (C-213/07) points 31–32.

Simply because a national constitution expresses national identity (Cloots, 2015, pp. 163–164).

The national identity clause allows for the preservation of individual characteristics despite legal, political, and economic integration (Murphy, 2017, pp. 96, 115). In a way, it is a safeguard clause, created to ensure that EU institutions respect the interests of Member States, and to avoid any resistance arising from them (Klamert, 2014, p. 20). Therefore, respect for national identity has a unique value for such a multinational entity as the EU (Cloots, 2015, p. 81).

It could be considered that the notion of "respect for national identity" covers fundamental constitutional rights (Pérez, 2013a, p. 62), fundamental constitutional values (Preshova, 2012, p. 274) and fundamental constitutional norms (Konstadinides, 2013, p. 3). Especially if we consider that, according to researchers, national identity comprises features of the national community: history, language, values and traditions (Cloots, 2016, pp. 90–91), as well as religion, culture, and customs (Wójtowicz, 2014, p. 146). Therefore, the changes in national identity might impact changes in the identity of the national community itself (Martí, 2013, p. 21). Consequently, the national identity clause is related only to those fundamental principles which are not common to all Member States (Claes, Reestman, 2015, p. 934).

2.3. The place of the national identity clause in the EU legal system

First of all, it is necessary to stress that the national identity clause should be interpreted on the basis of EU law, rather than on the constitutional law of respective countries (Tremps, 2013, p. 264; Rugge, 2017, p. 28). Due to its very nature, the national identity clause is conflictual, as it has to reconcile respect for national identity with the integratory nature of the EU (Cloots, 2015, p. 196).

Consequently, the notion of national identity could only be applied in "exceptional" cases (Konstadinides, 2011, p. 206; Bogdandy, Schill, 2011, p. 1431). Moreover, ideally, it would, be regarded as a measure of last resort (Faraguna, 2016, p. 500).

The national identity clause allows for a "special rule" – a provision derogative from EU law (Konstadinides, 2011, p. 200). Because of this clause, even primary EU law may be applied variously in different Member States (Cloots, 2015, pp. 176–177), but tolerable deviations in the long-term perspective of uniform application of EU law are more valuable than ensuring short-term absolute compliance (Flynn, 2019, p. 222).

Accordingly, the national identity clause is not a unilateral clause, which could outweigh[14] other EU law principles (Wendel, 2011, p. 104). Article 4(2) TEU should not be considered as a provision separate from the rest of EU law, because EU law protects not only national identity but also EU values, enshrined in Article 2 TEU (Tuori, 2015, p. 106). National identity as a legitimate argument can be accepted only if it complies with the values of Article 2 TEU (Faraguna, 2017, p. 1639; Koncewicz, 2015, p. 54). Even if the national identity clause could be regarded as establishing limits on the competence of the EU, these limits could not be contrary to EU values (Preshova, 2019, p. 171), or regarded as an exemption from the fundamental constitutional principles of EU law (Bogdandy, Schill, 2011, p. 1430). National identity itself is a part of EU values, therefore, it is protected only if it complies with other values (Rodin, 2011, pp. 14–15). A "reversed Solange" could be applied to explain the effect of national identity – it is respected as long as it does not affect the values of Article 2 TEU (Bogdandy et al., 2015, p. 237).

Some also assert that Article 3 TEU takes priority over Article 4(2) TEU, consequently establishing the EU's aims (Murphy, 2017, p. 103; Konstadinides, 2011, p. 199). However, this position is difficult to accept. First, the EU's goals do not have independent legal value (Kellerbauer et al., 2019, p. 32) and thus they do not create obligations.[15] Accordingly, as they do not create legal obligations, they could not be considered as EU law principles and weighted against the national identity clause.

On the other hand, it is apparent that the national identity clause is one of the EU's fundamental law principles (Cloots, 2015, pp. 134–135;

14 See the ECJ *Omega* decision (C-36/02) para 36. See also the following ECJ decisions: C-444/05, para 23; C-33/07, para 23; C-73/08, para 28.

15 See the ECJ *Caja de Ahorros* decision (C-484/08), para 46.

Faraguna, 2016, p. 500). It has autonomous legal power and could be used "in relation to the entirety of EU law" (Dobbs, 2014, p. 316). However, this has not yet been confirmed[16] by the ECJ.

Moving on, despite the national identity clause possessing autonomous legal power, it is not an autonomous concept (Rugge, 2017, pp. 24–25); it requires judicial interpretation, and the ECJ is assigned the role of reconciling any national constitutional differences (de Boer, 2013, p. 1097). As a result, the ECJ might confirm constitutional interests or institutional circumstances as grounds for derogation from EU law. Nevertheless, such a derogation will be based on EU law and supervised by the ECJ (Claes, 2015a, p. 205).

For instance, only the ECJ can justify deviations from uniform application of freedom of movement (Pérez, 2013b, p. 154), flexibly interpret existing derogations, or create new ones all together (Dobbs, 2014, p. 325).

In any case, derogations based on the national identity clause would have to preserve the unity and consistency of EU law (Maduro, 2003, pp. 99–100), and as a result, they would be based on EU law (Schnettger, 2020, p. 33). This would inevitably lead to the national identity clause being weighed against other EU law principles; for example, if a decision had to be made regarding whether a derogation ought to be applied in a particular situation in accordance with its unique circumstances.

A much more significant impact of the clause can be found *vis-à-vis* secondary EU law; it ensures the limits of a potential "competence creep", and functions as an effective measure in the prevention of conflicts (Guastaferro, 2012, p. 317). Moreover, scholars agree that secondary EU law which disregards the national identity clause is subject to annulment (Cloots, 2015, p. 324; de Boer, 2013, p. 1099), as it contradicts primary EU law.

The binding force of the national identity clause provides an opportunity for the revision of the legality of acts on independent grounds, in

16 So far the ECJ has accepted that the "preservation of the Member States' national identities is a legitimate aim respected by the [EU] legal order", see ECJ case C-473/93 (*Commission* v. *Luxembourg*), para 35. However, see *note 51*.

accordance with Article 263 TFEU. This potentially affects the development of EU law (Dobbs, 2014, p. 325; Konstadinides, 2013, p. 2).

All of this means that Article 4(2) TEU provides an autonomous ground for evaluating EU acts. Thanks to the wording of the quote "shall respect", we can see that it is not only the basis for interpretation. Thus the ECJ can examine the legality of an act, and analyse whether the provisions could be formulated and implemented in other ways (for example, in respecting national identity) (Bogdandy, Schill, 2011, p. 1443). However, using Article 4(2) TEU as a basis for challenging the legality of an EU act would be novel, as the ECJ has yet to find any EU act that violates the national identity clause (Cloots, 2015, p. 64).

There are examples of an even broader approach, implying that Article 4(2) TEU allows disapplying EU law on the basis of national constitutional law.[17] In general, there is a clear division of opinions.

On one hand, if we were to take a more cautious viewpoint, EU acts could potentially be challenged in the ECJ under Article 4(2) TEU. But a more revolutionary approach suggests that, based on Article 4(2) TEU, EU acts could be disapplied in Member States, on the basis of a disregard of national constitutional law.

The second option is only understandable provided national identity is treated as a synonym for the notion of constitutional identity, which is not the case. This will be elaborated on later in this article.

Based on Article 19(1) TEU, only the ECJ handles the interpretation and application of the Treaties, therefore, and Article 4(2) TEU. The ECJ also has an exclusive jurisdiction to review the legality of EU acts according to Article 263 TFEU. Accordingly, the presumption that an EU act could be declared inapplicable by the Constitutional Court on the basis of Article 4(2) TEU would be contradictory to the very purpose of the national identity clause.[18]

---

17 See as an example: Dobbs, 2014, p. 325; Pernice, 2011b, p. 388; Konstadinides, 2013, p. 2; Paris, 2018, p. 220.

18 As already mentioned, this was also confirmed by the Final report of Working Group V: "it seems possible to meet the main concerns expressed in the Working Group and elsewhere of safeguarding the role and importance of the Member States in the Treaty while at the same time allowing the necessary margin of flexibility. In the latter respect, it was noted that the provision was not a derogation

Meanwhile, one aspect requires clarification. National identity, as a general argument, could be used by any privileged applicant.[19] Though it is rather doubtful whether any privileged applicant, but the Member State, has *locus standi* to use Article 4(2) TEU as a basis for the legality necessary to review an EU act. We could safely assume this, as there is an inevitable need to interpret national constitutional law.

2.4. National identity and the principle of EU law primacy

Any analysis of the national identity clause would be incomplete without a mention of the debate about the impact of this clause on the EU's law primacy principle. Three major conditional directions of these principles could be highlighted, as they explain the interdependence between those two EU laws.

First, some suggest maintaining the "orthodox" primacy of EU law, on which the national identity clause has no impact at all. Because the primacy of EU law is absolute, the national identity clause has no effect on it (Claes, 2015a, p. 178) and could not be used to rebut it (Kellerbauer et al., 2019, p. 44). The clause could thus not be regarded as a possibility permitting derogation (de Boer, 2013, p. 1099), and it could therefore not be regarded as making any changes between EU and national law (Rosas, Armati, 2018, pp. 67–68). Neither could it be interpreted as a limitation of EU law, or as an integration of national values into EU law (Burgorgue-Larsen, 2013, pp. 293, 299).

According to the opinions of this direction, the national identity clause should be regarded as a horizontal clause which would create more favourable conditions for constitutional and cultural diversity (Guastaferro, 2012, pp. 316–317), but it would not automatically affect EU protected interests (Wendel, 2014, p. 286). The national identity clause should not be interpreted as a *carte blanche* with which one could deny EU law its

---

clause. The Member States will remain under a duty to respect the provisions of the Treaties" (p. 11).

19 See for example the ECJ *Gibraltar* decision (C-145/04), where the European Commission submits that "it is appropriate to take account of different approaches, such as that resulting from the constitutional tradition of the United Kingdom" (para 53).

primacy (Fabbrini, Sajó, 2019, p. 16). Nor should it be used to avoid the obligations to adopt national constitutional provisions existing under EU law (Kröll, 2012, p. 115).

As a result, national identity cannot change the relationship between national and EU law, only the arguments of the ECJ (Guastaferro, 2012, p. 264). Therefore, the Court does not take this clause seriously (Kosta, 2009, pp. 506–507), rather giving preference to the principles of primacy and uniform application of EU law (Safjan, 2015, p. 388). The principle of the primacy of EU law is unconditional according to the position of the ECJ, and it is hardly possible to imagine seeing any changes, especially considering some recent decisions.[20]

The second direction to be discussed could be summarised as being based on an understanding of unilateral exemptions from the principle of the primacy of EU law (Claes, 2013, p. 129), or a revocation of the primacy principle, based on national Constitutional Court decisions (Mayer, 2011, p. 781). This direction is not as coherent as the previously discussed direction, and it might be divided into two sub-directions. The first one is based on *jurisdictional criteria*, which allows national courts to disapply EU law without infringing on it (Kumm, Comella, 2003, p. 479; Kumm, 2012, p. 61).

Fundamental constitutional structures serve as *controlimiti* for European integration, and Member States retain the authority to review nonconformity in order to avoid negative consequences for the national legal system (Tremps, 2013, p. 266). Such a review should be carried out by national Constitutional Courts (Halmai, 2018, p. 477), which would be able to reject EU competence based on values established in their respective Constitutions (Konstadinides, 2011, p. 198). Therefore, Article 4(2) TEU should be understood as an implicit limit on the primacy of EU law (De Witte, 2011, p. 357) and an acknowledgement of the jurisprudence of Constitutional Courts overcoming absolute primacy and controlling the expansion of EU competence (Gamba, Lentzis, 2017, p. 1684).

20 See for example the following ECJ decisions: *Tanja Kreil* (C-285/98), *Connect Austria* (C- 462/99), *Winner Wetten* (C-409/06) *Angelidaki* (C-378/07 to C-380/07), *Michaniki* (C-213/07), *Filipiak* (C-314/08), *Elchinov* (C-173/09) and *Melloni* (C-399/11).

The second sub-direction is based on the *normative hierarchy* of the national identity clause with regard to the EU law primacy principle, creating a conflict-solving criteria based on which constitutional nucleus has hierarchical supremacy over EU norms (Bofill, 2013, p. 239). Article 4(2) TEU could be interpreted as a principle contradictory to and overcoming the primacy principle (Klamert, 2014, pp. 20, 39). Or as a superiority clause of constitutional elements against primacy, prohibiting the application of EU law (Dobbs, 2014, pp. 301, 325; Wendel, 2014, p. 287), based on "constitutional structures" (Sarmiento, 2013, p. 177). Therefore, Article 4(2) TEU is attractive for Constitutional Courts, providing at least a theoretical opportunity to disapply EU law or establish an exemption from the application of EU law (Murphy, 2017, p. 102). Using Article 4(2) TEU, Constitutional Courts are able to establish the infringement of national identity (Paris, 2018, p. 220).

First of all, both sub-categories could be summarised by the approach of M. Dobbs – she claims that Article 4(2) TEU could be used as a unilateral derogation (Dobbs, 2014, p. 317), while F. Mayer claims that national identity outweighs any other loyalty to the EU (Mayer, 2017, p. 282). It is debatable whether such an understanding of Article 4(2) TEU is consistent, because, as N. Murphy underlines, in such a case the national identity clause could be used against almost any EU act (Murphy, 2017, pp. 111–112). Second, following an interpretation of this direction, Member States would be free to extend the boundaries of national identity with no external control. Third, despite visible changes in the entrenchment of the primacy of EU law from the Constitutional Treaty to the Lisbon Treaty, there has been no radical change in the primacy principle, which could be regarded as a rejection of this principle. And finally, such an approach could not be based on the jurisprudence of either the ECJ or Constitutional Courts.

The third direction searches for a middle way and could be regarded as representing the position of most researchers,[21] as it is based on variable priority. That said, this approach is not based on the dominance

21 The search for a "middle path" can be found not only in legal works, but also in the Advocate General M.P. Maduro's opinion in case C-160/03, see point 35.

of the national identity clause.[22] According to this direction, the national identity clause could be understood as a "special rule", offering an exemption[23] from the principle of primacy in certain cases. Although it is doubtful whether such a "special rule" could be regarded as a "pure" exemption from the principle of primacy. It is more likely that a "special rule" could be regarded as an exemption from the uniform application of EU law, which is based on the primacy of EU law. However, it should be admitted that without the national identity clause, there would be no basis for the exemption. Thus, it could also be considered as an exemption from primacy.

As a result, despite the monistic approach of the ECJ in the *Simmenthal* and *Internationale Handelsgesellschaft* cases (Craig, de Búrca, 2011, p. 300), EU law undergoes "subtle changes", shifting from absolute autonomy to heteronomy (Koncewicz, 2015, pp. 64–66). Legal scientists agree that Article 4(2) TEU could create exemptions from uniform application of EU law, and the principle of primacy should not be automatically applied (Pérez, 2013b, pp. 147–148). It has become almost obvious that EU law has primacy over national law, with the theoretical exception of founding constitutional principles (Menéndez, 2011, p. 220). The national identity clause requires a more flexible approach to EU law primacy, and there are signs of the adoption of a more flexible, non-absolutist approach (Sadurski, 2012, p. 134). It is important to notice that neither the primacy principle nor the national identity clause are principles of normative hierarchy but principles of the application of EU law. Therefore, national constitutional law could not be the basis for derogation from EU law (Baquero Cruz, 2018, p. 50; Guastaferro, 2012, pp. 310–311).

Because of the national identity clause, the primacy of the EU should not be radical, otherwise it becomes very difficult to accommodate national identity (Kosta, 2009, p. 507). The national identity clause does not establish the primacy of national constitutional principles over EU

22 See the opinion of Advocate General M.P. Maduro in the *Arcelor* case (C-127/07), see point 16.

23 See the opinion of Advocate General N. Wahl in the *Torresi* case (joined cases C-58/13 and C-59/13), see point 100. Also see the opinion of Advocate General M.P. Maduro in the *Michaniki* case (C-213/07), see point 33.

law, but at the same time it does not allow intervention in national identity disproportionately. Because of that, the clause creates the possibility of overcoming the absolute primacy of EU law (Bogdandy, Schill, 2011, pp. 1419–1420, 1441) in order to accommodate constitutional differences instead of strict application of the primacy principle (de Boer, 2013, p. 1103). When the question of applying the national Constitution arises, the ECJ should not automatically refer to primacy (Pérez, 2013b, p. 157).[24]

Moving on, for a "special rule" to be created, several preconditions should be met. First, the national identity clause should not be seen as *carte blanche* in all situations (Konstadinides, 2011, p. 206). It has to be reconciled with the principle of primacy (Bogdandy, Schill, 2011, p. 1420; Pérez, 2014, p. 327). It seems that the revision of the EU law primacy principle is inevitable to avoid or mitigate conflicts, but it is unrealistic to expect that the national identity clause could serve as a unilateral derogation from EU law (Preshova, 2019, p. 199).

Second, the national identity clause has a limiting effect on primacy (Avbelj, 2011, p. 748), serves as a counterbalance to primacy (Konstadinides, 2011, p. 198), and overcomes the "blindness" of EU law regarding constitutional limits (Bogdandy, Schill, 2011, p. 1452). Therefore, the national identity clause stipulates a relationship between EU and constitutional law based on a "qualified" primacy and not an absolute one (Murphy, 2017, p. 97).

Third, not all national constitutional norms, but only the core ones, will satisfy the national identity clause (de Boer, 2013, p. 1098; Murphy, 2017, pp. 111–112, 119; Besselink, 2010, pp. 48–49). The opinions of the third direction show that despite the EU's "orthodox" primacy, as maintained by the ECJ, this principle could (should) change. However, there are also enough arguments to support the position that the national identity clause could be regarded as affecting the uniform application of EU law rather than the primacy itself. As the "special rule" to be established in a particular case, it is still applicable on the basis of the primacy principle.

Accordingly, the national identity clause has the potential to protect certain features, "but on the basis of EU law and the cooperation between

24 However, see *note 20*.

the ECJ and national Constitutional Courts" (Dobbs, 2014, p. 302). As a result, a national identity-based "special rule" from uniform application of EU law does not undermine EU primacy. However, this is not the same as claiming that EU law has unconditional primacy (Pérez, 2013b, p. 148). It is important that the national identity clause limits unconditional primacy, but it is no less important that application of this clause is based on cooperation and dialogue between Constitutional Courts and the ECJ (Preshova, 2019, pp. 197–198). As a result, deciding on the national identity clause "remains in accordance with the ECJ's jurisprudence on primacy" (Dobbs, 2014, p. 306) and "remains a question of EU law" (Wendel, 2011, p. 103). Therefore, national identity is a concept of EU law (Tremps, 2013, p. 264), and "should not be read" as allowing unilateral disapplication[25] of EU law (Claes, 2013, p. 122).

However, the principle of sincere cooperation entails that neither can the ECJ decide unilaterally (Murphy, 2017, p. 114) as the national identity clause is binding on the ECJ itself (Cloots, 2015, pp. 75–76).

2.5. National and/or constitutional identity

Perhaps because of the potential effect of national identity on EU law primacy, the notion of national identity in EU law was thought to correspond to the notion of constitutional identity derived from national constitutional law. The logic of the national identity clause is consistent with the approach of Constitutional Courts regarding constitutional identity (Murphy, 2017, p. 99). According to F.B. Callejon, the Lisbon Treaty has Europeanised the *controlimiti* doctrine (Callejon, 2012, p. 270). However,

25 See the opinion of Advocate General M.P. Maduro in cases C-53/04 and C-180/04, point 40: "Doubtless the national authorities, in particular the constitutional courts, should be given the responsibility to define the nature of the specific national features that could justify such a difference in treatment. Those authorities are best placed to define the constitutional identity of the Member States which the European Union has undertaken to respect. The fact remains, however, that it is the duty of the Court of Justice to ensure that that assessment is made in accordance with the fundamental rights and objectives with which it must ensure compliance within the Community context."

as mentioned already, the *travaux préparatoires* of the Lisbon Treaty do not imply such an assumption (Cloots, 2016, p. 84).

The majority of scholars construe the national identity clause as an instrument for protecting constitutional identity (Schnettger, 2020, p. 11), or even commonly identified with constitutional identity (Claes, 2013, p. 123). There is a strong tendency to equate the notion of national identity with that of constitutional identity (Cloots, 2016, p. 83). There are sufficient examples to support such a position, and several (conditional) techniques could be identified.

First, the "*merger*" technique is based on giving the same meaning to both notions: "national identity as constitutional identity" (Toniatti, 2013, p. 65), "constitutional or national identity" (Drinóczi, 2020, p. 106), or "national (constitutional) identity" (Wendel, 2013, p. 999).

The second technique is "*convergence*", equating or cohering both notions in Article 4(2) TEU. Some[26] examples of such a technique can be cited: national identity is "legally determined" by constitutional identity (Besselink, 2010, p. 47); constitutional identity is explicitly mentioned in Article 4(2) TEU (Konstadinides, 2011, p. 216); Article 4(2) TEU establishes a clear obligation for the EU to "respect the constitutional identity" of its Member States (Groussot, 2012, p. 331), and codifies "national constitutional identity" (Faraguna, 2016, p. 498); national identity is "constituted by constitutional identity" (Murphy, 2017, pp. 100–101) and "must be exclusively read as a constitutional identity clause" (Gamba, Lentzis, 2017, pp. 1700–1701).

The third technique is "*inclusion*", implying that the notion of national identity also includes a notion of constitutional identity. Here are some examples: "national identity includes constitutional identity" (Mayer, 2009, p. 424), "national identity concerned includes evidently the constitutional identity" (Groussot, 2012, p. 331). Or, the "concept of national identity [...] is the functional equivalent of constitutional identity" (Callies, van der Schyff, 2020, p. 330).

26 See also Priban, 2015, p. 330; Drinóczi, Mohay, 2017, pp. 192, 204; Arnull, 2012, p. 133; Tuori, 2017, p. 53; Panara, 2015, p. 58; Pérez, 2013b, pp. 147–148; Kumm, 2012, p. 61.

The fourth and final technique could be identified as "*conjunction*", underlining the bond between the two concepts. For example: the "connection between national and constitutional identity has gradually been taken as a self-evident truth" (Faraguna, 2016, p. 496); "There is a shift in emphasis from national identity as such to constitutional identity" (Besselink, 2010, p. 44); "Article 4(2) TEU [...] understands national identity mainly in terms of constitutional identity" (Bogdandy, Schill, 2011, p. 1435); "National identities is generally interpreted as protecting national constitutional identity" (van der Schyff, 2016b, p. 173).

To summarise, despite the nuanced differences in these techniques, there is a clear trend to equate notions of national identity and constitutional identity. There is also a second major group of opinions, which detach those two notions. They propose it would be "too hasty" to conclude that constitutional identity is protected under Article 4(2) TEU (Cloots, 2015, pp. 165–166).

First, the Lisbon Treaty wording refers to national identity, not to a constitutional identity (Wójtowicz, 2014, p. 145). The ECJ has never used the notion of constitutional identity (Konstadinides, 2011, p. 202), except when presenting the arguments of the parties. The ECJ "has not drawn an analogy" between national identity and constitutional identity, although such an approach is often used in the literature (Polzin, 2017, p. 1607). Therefore, the first argument to separate these two notions is that the ECJ has not used the concept of constitutional identity in its jurisprudence.

Second, if the concept of national identity coincides (overlaps) with the concept of constitutional identity, it would be incompatible with many tenets of EU law, from absolute primacy to the autonomous character of EU law (Guastaferro, 2012, p. 317). It would also result in the final decision being taken by the Constitutional Courts, not by the ECJ. However, if the ECJ were to be considered as the ultimate arbiter, in that case it would mean that the ECJ is also protecting constitutional identity, and therefore, Constitutional Courts remain irrelevant (Paris, 2018, p. 221). National identity establishes a European perspective, whereas constitutional identity – a national perspective founded on the national constitution, clearly does not fall within the ECJ's interpretation competence (Gérard, Verrijdt, 2017, p. 200). Therefore, the second argument is based on the separation of two different review mechanisms. National identity is to be reviewed by the ECJ, while constitutional identity is reviewed by the Constitutional Courts. The equation of those two notions removes the limits of those jurisdictions and, as a result, is incompatible with the rule of law.

Third, the concept of constitutional identity is to be linked with normative or formal elements, whereas the notion of national identity is related to particularity irrespective of formalisation (Tremps, 2013, p. 264). Constitutional identity may not comprise fundamental structures unrelated to the national Constitution, such as language (Cloots, 2015, p. 168). National identity is more neutral, based on Article 4(2) TEU.

In summary, national identity, might in certain cases encompass elements of constitutional identity, but it is important to establish limitations. Essentially, the concept of national identity should not be identified with the concept of constitutional identity.[27] At a minimum, because constitutional identity might preserve founding constitutional principles unaffected by EU law. And vice versa, the concept of national identity might enclose constitutional structures not covered by constitutional identity. Last, the national identity notion remains an EU law category, while the one of constitutional identity is a concept of national constitutional law. Therefore, to summarise, it is possible to consider the similarity or proximity of those two concepts, but not their equation.

3. Challenges to the judicial application of the national identity clause

3.1. Adjudication on national identity as a duality of competences

Following the overview of the concept of national identity, the possibilities of its judicial application can now be explored. Despite the concept

27 For a comparison, see the opinion of Advocate General Y. Bot in the *Melloni* case C-399/11, point 142: "national identity or, more specifically, the constitutional identity of a Member State", and alternatively, a request for a preliminary ruling by the German Constitutional Court in *OMT* case, para 29: "the identity review performed by the Federal Constitutional Court is fundamentally different from the review under Art 4 sec. 2 sentence 1 TEU by the Court of Justice of the European Union."

of national identity being present in the Treaties from 1993, it "has not yet found relevant use" by the ECJ (Rugge, 2017, pp. 23–24) and "has not yet played a prominent role" (Claes, Reestman, 2015, p. 934). In the pre-Lisbon period, "no reference [had] ever been made" to the national identity clause in ECJ case-law (Besselink, 2010, p. 41). The ECJ "has not really seriously embraced" national identity in its doctrine (Preshova, 2019, p. 199). This might be explained by the coherence of national and EU legal orders and the compatibility of constitutional principles, making the application of this clause extraordinary (Baquero Cruz, 2018, p. 50). However, it cannot be ruled out that the ECJ did not have any intention of making any concessions to the well-established principle of primacy.

Some emphasize the possibility for Member States to use national identity in order to avoid obligations under EU law (Mayer, 2011, p. 784; Mayer, 2017, p. 283; Pérez, 2013b, p. 155) and, as a result, the creation of discriminatory situations between Member States (Groussot, 2012, p. 333). Such approaches could be accepted in certain conditions only. First, if the national identity clause unconditionally overcomes the EU's law primacy principle, and second, if the ultimate arbiter on the national identity clause is national Constitutional Courts. That means equating the national identity clause with the notion of constitutional identity. But as discussed above, these two concepts should be understood as detached.

The functioning of the national identity clause is quite uncertain. First, we may begin by noticing that it has not yet been substantiated by the practice of the ECJ or/and Constitutional Courts. Therefore, even after almost 30 years since its creation, its functioning has mostly been explained in scholarly literature. Legal science brings invaluable and important insights into how the national identity clause works and raises several highly debatable issues, which will be briefly addressed in this article.

As N. Murphy observes, "the meaning, or the effect of the clause is anything but clear" (Murphy, 2017, p. 109). The bipolar position of competence and "interpretative competition" (Martinico, 2013, p. 97) leads to the question "who is in charge of defining what belongs to the idea of national identity?" and to the possibility of "interpretative anarchy" (Martinico, 2018, p. 84). The functioning of the national identity clause raises the questions of "who decides" and "who decides last" (Rodin, 2011, p. 34), and the question of the "competent authority in charge of interpretation" (Faraguna, 2016, p. 500). As L.F.M. Besselink points out, the question of the deciding body is "one of the most intriguing legal questions" (Besselink, 2010, p. 44). These opinions could be outlined briefly as "how to reconcile the possible overlap of competences [...] and what role the respective (EU and national) courts should play in the process" (Koncewicz, 2015, p. 66). Particularly when "both sides claim ultimate authority but avoid direct conflict" (Dobbs, 2014, p. 334).

Absolutist positions of both judicial sides would be difficult to maintain, as Article 4(3) TEU requires sincere cooperation (Bogdandy, Schill, 2011, p. 1447) and "may solve conflicts" (Bogdandy, 2009, p. 41).[28] In other words, the principle of sincere cooperation complements the national identity clause and "indicates the EU's duty to show consideration for the Member State's most fundamental constitutional norms" (Gragl, 2018, p. 226). Despite the national identity clause, the ECJ has not been "particularly keen on framing conflicts between EU law and national constitutional orders under the aegis" of this clause (Rugge, 2017, p. 24). This might be understandable, because the question of what makes up national identity and the interpretation of national identity is "open to reasonable disagreement" (de Boer, 2018, p. 214).

The national identity clause "provides the normative basis for a balancing between the fundamental structures of national Constitutions and essential principles of EU law" (Baquero Cruz, 2018, p. 50). However, because Article 4(2) TEU enables Member States to protect national identity by relying on EU law, the conflict "is no longer between national and EU law, but between aspects of EU law" (Dobbs, 2014, p. 325). A slightly different aspect is noted by A. von Bogdandy and S. Schill, who suggest that Article 4(2) TEU is subject to the interpretation and control of the ECJ, whose "authority extends to determining the conceptual framework of what a Member State can determine to form part of its national identity" (Bogdandy, Schill, 2011, p. 1448). Accordingly, the ECJ has no competence in determining the national identity of a particular Member State, as this surpasses the jurisdiction of the ECJ under Article 19(1) TEU.

---

28 However, the relationship between the ECJ and national Constitutional Courts cannot be founded on the principle of loyal cooperation (Klamert, 2014, p. 323).

Therefore, Article 4(2) TEU "incorporates two dimensions": first, the elements to be determined by Constitutional Courts along with normative relevance and, second, limits on the EU law to be determined by the ECJ (Preshova, 2012, p. 296). It is for Constitutional Courts to interpret the meaning of national identity and for the ECJ to consider this interpretation (Pérez, 2013b, p. 154).

Consequently, the national identity clause assumes there will be judicial dialogue between two judicial institutions – the ECJ and the Constitutional Court, two "complementary parts of European composite constitutional adjudication" (Bogdandy, Schill, 2011, p. 1447). However, the "stakes are so high" in this case that neither the ECJ nor the Constitutional Courts can be "entrusted with balancing or holding the scales" (Cloots, 2015, p. 219). This adjudication "is distributed between supranational and national levels": Constitutional Courts decide on the content of national identity; the ECJ decides "if and in how far the identity-claim prevails over (hypothetically) conflicting principles of EU law" (Wendel, 2011, p. 103). Constitutional Courts should define and explain national identity, but the ECJ takes the lead in interpreting this explanation in terms of EU law (Claes, 2013, p. 137; Halmai, 2018, p. 477; Konstadinides, 2011, p. 206).

To summarise, there is no "ultimate jurisdictional claim" because interpreting national identity requires the participation of both apex courts (Mayer, 2009, p. 431). There is no definitive answer to the question of who has the power to decide, "as there is no final arbiter" (Bogdandy, Schill, 2011, p. 1452). Features of constitutional pluralism, intrinsic in Article 4(2) TEU, predetermine non-hierarchical relations, permeated by ambiguities and ambivalences (Toniatti, 2013, p. 72).

3.2. Cooperation, balance of competence and proportionality test

Before the Lisbon Treaty, national identity "neither constituted the battleground, nor the meeting point" (Murphy, 2017, p. 99), but in the Lisbon Treaty, Article 4(2) TEU became "one of the central points in the relationship between legal orders" (Preshova, 2019, p. 107). There is no doubt that the fundamental importance of the (successful) application of the national identity clause will depend on the stances taken by the Constitutional

Courts, and especially the ECJ. It is unlikely that both counterparts will have a similar approach, as what the national identity clause "entails or means exactly remains unclear" (Dobbs, 2014, p. 326). M. Claes draws attention to the fact that agreement "on terms of negotiations" regarding the identity clause "is indispensable" (Claes, 2013, p. 124). The national identity clause itself cannot ensure that no judicial conflicts arise, but it is a "channel for discussion" (Tuori, 2017, p. 53), to manage "potential conflicts in the process of mutual accommodation" (Pérez, 2012, p. 128).

As already explained, there is no single court capable of adjudicating the national identity clause alone. In a situation of dual or composite adjudication, both the national Constitutional Court and the ECJ adjudicate within the limits of their competence (Tatham, 2013, p. 292). As was also explained, national identity does not refute the EU's law primacy principle. Such an approach fits constitutional pluralism, which seeks to find a variable balance. As K. Tuori states, every legal system defends its interpretive autonomy and avoids outright conflicts to maintain a pluralist equilibrium (Tuori, 2015, p. 104). Therefore, the national identity clause does not establish "absolute protection", but requires finding a "proportional balance" (Bogdandy, Schill, 2011, p. 1441). Accordingly, national identity could not be regarded as an "absolute obligation" but preferably as a "balance against other interests" (Claes, Reestman, 2015, p. 937). The notion of "balancing" of fundamental constitutional structures against the principles of EU law is also underlined by other legal scholars: J. Baquero Cruz (Baquero Cruz, 2018, p. 50), A.T. Pérez (Pérez, 2013b, p. 157) and M. Dobbs (Dobbs, 2014, p. 317). "Balancing" is a keyword in the understanding of a functioning national identity clause, otherwise Member States would be left with only the option of Article 50 TEU (Wilkinson, 2017, p. 223).

Under such circumstances, the "absolutist position is unattractive" as it "dismisses the goods and values instituted by other legal order" (Chalmers et al., 2014, p. 219). The national identity clause "fosters dialogue" (Groussot, 2012, p. 334). What is "attractive" under Article 4(2) TEU, that feasibility of "convergence between the national Constitutional Courts and the ECJ is far greater", even "permitting simultaneous derogations" (Dobbs, 2014, p. 333). Therefore, Article 4(2) TEU can work only in a "genuine spirit of cooperation" (Mayer, 2014, p. 133) and may be applied only "through constant dialogue between legal orders" (Tremps, 2013, p. 264). Direct and "true dialogue" between the ECJ and national Constitutional Courts is required, rather than a "rhetorical reference to conversations and dialogue" (Claes, 2012, p. 208; Preshova, 2019, pp. 197–198).

It may appear that Article 4(2) TEU foresees some special procedure for the ECJ to establish the matter of national identity. However, it is widely accepted by scholars that the national identity clause is adjudicated by applying a proportionality test (Menéndez, 2017, p. 117; Bobić, 2017, p. 1409; Tuori, 2018, p. 46; Drinóczi, 2020, p. 107).[29] As M. Claes points out, the national identity review is transformed into a proportionality test to avoid "potentially explosive content" (Claes, 2013, p. 134). Despite the form of the review carried out being based on a proportionality test, the "intensity" of the review remains unclear (Cloots, 2015, p. 273). Some argue national identity is applicable only where the identity is significantly affected, which is ascertained by applying the proportionality test (Burchardt, 2019, p. 100), as national identity is not a measure of "absolute defence" (Dobbs, 2014, p. 322). This clause is applied by the ECJ, testing the proportionality against other EU values (Lenaerts, 2014, p. 156; Bogdandy, Schill, 2011, pp. 1442–1443) establishing limits for the application of national identity (Bobić, 2017, p. 1408) and assuring mutual tolerance (Fabbrini, Sajó, 2019, p. 14). These opinions allow us to conclude that the more national identity is expressed, the more it is affected, the bigger the priority over EU law it will have. A question might arise at this point: how does the ECJ balance elements of national identity presented by the Constitutional Courts and EU law?

In fact, the ECJ uses the technique of "conversion", transforming national (constitutional) law norms into the equivalent EU law norms, and assessing the situation as a conflict of two EU norms (Cloots, 2015, p. 269). This is exactly the reason national Constitutional Courts are so important for substantiating proportionality (Dobbs, 2014, p. 332) and

---

29 Examples of the proportionality test could be the following jurisprudence of the ECJ: C-416/13, para 45; C-683/16 para 49; C-611/17, para 56. For more on the proportionality test, see Menéndez, 2017, pp. 123–125.

submitting arguments as to why the implementation of EU norms is impossible or unproportionally complicated, or affects other vital interests (Davies, 2012, p. 281). To summarise, when applying the national identity clause, the ECJ uses the proportionality test. National elements, explained by the national Constitutional Court, are converted to the equivalent of EU law and then the balancing of the two principles is carried out. It is important to mention that, due to the circumstances of each case, even though the same principles are balanced, the outcome of each case might be different.

However, it is very important to note a reservation. As was explained, the Constitutional Court is perceived by scholars as an interlocutor of the ECJ in the national identity case. This is, however, just a purely theoretical model, which has not had a chance to be implemented (yet). In practice, national Constitutional Courts have very few opportunities to refer a request for a preliminary ruling for the ECJ. This is done by national common courts, functioning as decentralised EU courts, empowered by the ECJ (Mayoral, Wind, 2016, p. 1). In the case of a potential national identity controversy, an ordinary court might not properly identify the challenge that faces it. And even if the ordinary court properly estimates the potential national identity issue, it still has the flexibility to send a request for the preliminary ruling to the ECJ directly, or to send a request to the national Constitutional Court. It is hardly possible to disallow a national court from making simultaneous references (Velaers, 2012, p. 341). In such situations, the French *QPC*[30] seems like a safeguarding solution, which was acknowledged by the ECJ as compliant with EU law, albeit under certain conditions (Preshova, 2019, p. 62).[31] However, even the *QPC* model would not be sufficient since the concept of a "national court" in EU law is different[32] than in national law. Therefore, it is possible that

30 La question prioritaire de constitutionnalité.

31 See the ECJ *Melki and Abdeli* decision (joined cases C-188/10 and C-189/10), para 57.

32 Because the notion of "court" is broader under EU law. See, for example, the ECJ decisions in case C-385/09, where the Tax Disputes Commission under the Government of the Republic of Lithuania was acknowledged as a "court" in the framework of EU law. For more examples, see cases C-549/13, para 21, and C-363/11, para 18.

the reference to the ECJ will be submitted by the "court", which (hypothetically) may not assume it acts in the "area" of national identity. Such a probability is much higher if the national Constitutional Court had not established the doctrine of national identity in its jurisprudence regarding certain constitutional structures.

The referral of a case to the ECJ by a court (or by a "court" under EU law) presupposes the risk of potential tensions between the ECJ and national Constitutional Courts, if the referring court does not properly point out the feasibility of the national identity situation. However, this risk cannot be limited to the national courts only. It also applies to the same extent to the Government which represents a Member State before the ECJ. An illustrative example of such a possibility is the *Landatova* case,[33] where the Government took the side of the Supreme Administrative Court of Czechia, openly opposing the jurisprudence of the Czech Constitutional Court (Priban, 2015, pp. 344–345; Zemánek, 2016, p. 131). This significantly contributed to the follow-up *ultra vires* decision *Holubec* of the Czech Constitutional Court.[34] Since a reference to the ECJ has been addressed, some observations are required regarding this procedure.

3.3. Preliminary reference procedure

Article 267 TFEU is a procedural norm to implement the norm of substantial law, Article 4(2) TEU (Mayer, 2009, p. 431), seeking an exemption from EU law (Murphy, 2017, p. 117). The instrument of preliminary ruling ensures dialogue in the environment of multilevel constitutionalism (Wendel, 2011, p. 104). Therefore, national courts, invoking the national identity clause, should always refer questions to the ECJ, explaining the reasons (Claes, 2012, p. 232). However, a reference does not necessarily mean a cooperative attitude (Baraggia, 2015, p. 69) and might even be a sign of the application of the *controlimiti* doctrine. However, preliminary rulings continue to be the only avenue for direct dialogue (Murphy, 2017,

33 Thw ECJ *Landatova* decision (case C-399/09).
34 31/01/2012 decision of the Constitutional Court of the Czech Republic (*Ústavní Soud*) PL. ÚS 5/12: *Slovak Pensions*.

p. 117), significantly reducing the possibility of plausible judicial conflict (Bogdandy, Schill, 2011, p. 1450).

The preliminary ruling focuses on cooperation (Bogdandy, 2012, p. 765). However, the connection between national Constitutional Courts and national courts is weakened by judicial decentralisation. It would not have had a significant impact if it did not have one significant flaw. Although national courts (and "courts") have a possibility or even an obligation to refer a preliminary reference to the ECJ, the former lacks any such instrument. Within the current structure of Treaties, the ECJ has no proper means of referring certain questions to the national Constitutional Court. The "reversed preliminary reference" would be a truly desirable model from the perspective of constitutional pluralism. The only currently applicable instrument from a purely legal (formalistic) point of view could be considered Article 70 of the Rules of Procedure of the ECJ. However, there is no need to debate that no Constitutional Court would ever accept the role of an expert in the proceedings before the ECJ. It seems also highly unlikely that the ECJ could be seen as a proponent of "reversed preliminary", especially considering the procedure of amendment of the Rules of Procedure foreseen in Article 253 TFEU. It could be argued that the Treaties do not foresee such a "reversed" form of dialogue. A response to these arguments could be the national identity clause itself, which, as argued earlier, is binding on the EU, including the ECJ itself.

The novelty of the national identity clause is represented by a tiny number of cases – only thirteen in total. Such insignificant use of the clause might also show some alternative possibilities: first, the reluctance of the parties to substantiate their positions on the national identity clause, apprehending that the outcome of the case might affect national constitutional law. Second, the preliminary reference procedure does not constitute a true dialogue between the courts, as the partners in this dialogue are probably not in the tantamount position.

As the national identity clause might be a basis for constitutional judicial dialogue, defining national identity becomes inevitable (Rodin, 2011, pp. 20–21). National identity is not a "stylistic device" but refers to "deep and inherent elements of the culture and history" of the Member State (Burgorgue-Larsen, 2013, p. 304). However, the provisions of national Constitutions are only an initial indication of what could be regarded as a national identity. No less important is the jurisprudence of national Constitutional Courts, especially the one establishing the relation between national constitutional law and EU law (Bogdandy, Schill, 2011, p. 1433). It is not the case that national identity must be defined in constitutional law or jurisprudence (Van de Heyning, 2012, p. 202). The expression of national identity might be much broader (Cloots, 2015, p. 146). Therefore, the question of what national identity is remains open, as the courts "have not been so keen on listing" what could be regarded as national identity and deciding on the matter in particular cases (Preshova, 2012, p. 296). Neither has the ECJ made any definition or doctrine regarding what could be regarded as a national identity. So far, the ECJ has recognised national identity in isolated cases only (Polzin, 2017, p. 1606).

Although it is questionable whether such a pre-defined list would be desirable (Cloots, 2015, p. 13), it would be appropriate to show the elements that have already appeared in the jurisprudence of the ECJ and could be regarded as concerning national identity. Aside from those explicitly established in Article 4(2) TEU as "regional and local self-government",[35] such elements as: the division of competence,[36] internal situations,[37] freedom of expression,[38] freedom of assembly,[39] child protection[40] and language[41] could be considered as constituting national identity. Secondly, certain elements are suggested by the Advocates General, such as diversity in the cultural sector,[42] division of competence within the Member State,[43] composition and distribution of

35 The ECJ *Azores* decision (case C-88/03), paras 58 and 66. See also the *Horvath* decision (case C-428/07), paras 57–58 and *Digibet* decision (C-156/13), para 34.
36 The ECJ *Remondis* decision (case C-51/15), para 40.
37 The ECJ case C-212/06, para 38–39.
38 The ECJ *Familiapress* decision (case C-368/95), para 18.
39 The ECJ case C-112/00, para 69 and 78.
40 The ECJ *Dynamic Medien* decision (case C-51/15), para 42.
41 The ECJ *Las* decision (case C-202/11), para 25. See also the opinion of Advocate General M.P. Maduro in case C-160/03, see point 35, and the opinion of Advocate General J. Kokott in case C-566/10 P, point 87.
42 Opinion of Advocate General J. Kokott in case C-222/07, points 93–94.
43 Opinion of Advocate General J. Kokott in joined cases C-428/06 to C 434/06, point 54, see also the opinion of Advocate General V. Trstenjak in case C-324/07, point 85.

powers,[44] nationality[45] and secularism.[46] Last, there are elements invoked by the Member States to uphold the argument of national identity. The following examples are to be mentioned: the status of judges,[47] the profession of lawyer[48] and the status of the head of state.[49] These elements have a certain meaning and help understand better the notion of national identity. To explore the elements of national identity more thoroughly, select case-law of the European Court needs to be analysed.

4. Examples of application of the national identity clause

There is a difference between "pure" examples of national identity cases and those that are more ambiguous. Solid examples are characterised by three key features. First, there is a significant element of national constitutional law. Second, this element of constitutional law might affect the application of EU law. Third, the element of constitutional law is assessed by the ECJ to a certain extent. Although many researchers interpret the notion of national identity in broad terms, the most comprehensive analysis of the selection[50] of cases based on different linguistic versions and content examination was made by L. Burgorgue-Larsen (Burgorgue-Larsen, 2013, p. 287). Therefore, the work of L. Burgorgue-Larsen is taken as the basis for further analysis.

The concern about national identity might appear in direct actions concerning the legality of acts and EU law enforcement, or indirect actions, by preliminary ruling (Claes, 2013, p. 136). Therefore, it is necessary to briefly overview the existing jurisprudence relevant to the application of the national identity clause.

---

44 Opinion of Advocate General D.R.J. Colomer in case C-205/08, point 47.
45 Opinion of Advocate General M.P. Maduro in case C-135/08, points 24–25.
46 Opinion of Advocate General J. Kokott in case C-157/15, points 31–32
47 The ECJ case C-393/10, paras 47 and 49.
48 The ECJ decision in joined cases C-58/13 and C-59/13, para 58.
49 The ECJ case C-364/10, para 35.
50 With the sole exception of the ECJ's *Bogendorff* decision (case C-438/14), which was given after the publication of the work of L. Burgorgue-Larsen.

4.1. Actions of annulment

An EU act can be invalidated either by direct or indirect actions. What becomes obvious is that in the procedure of Article 263 TFEU, national courts have no means of participating. And that means that the national Constitutional Courts are left "outside" of this procedure. This brings us back to the item discussed above – the relationship between the Government and the national Constitutional Court. On the substance of the procedure of Article 263 TFEU, it is unlikely that the national identity clause will emerge as an autonomous ground for the invalidation of EU acts (Dobbs, 2014, pp. 317–318), since the obligation of the EU to respect national identities does not determine the outcome of cases (Konstadinides, 2013, p. 8). However, under exceptional circumstances, where "clear abuse" takes place, the national identity clause could be applicable (Panara, 2015, p. 62). Maintaining objectivity, one must point out that the ECJ has yet to confirm yet that the national identity clause might be an autonomous ground for invalidating EU acts. However, such a suggestion could be found in the opinion of the Advocate General.[51] Perhaps the national identity clause will not appear as a ground for invalidation since it will be addressed in the phase of legislative procedure. However, national identity might appear only in the process of applying the act (Faraguna, 2017, p. 1640). Nevertheless, one should consider the position of the Member State in legislative pipeline matters, especially where acts are adopted unanimously[52] (Dobbs, 2014, p. 323).

When summarising the case-law relevant to the examination of the role of the national identity clause under Article 263 TFEU, some observations

51 Opinion of Advocate General Y. Bot in the Melloni case (C-399/11), point 139: "A Member State which considers that a provision of secondary law adversely affects its national identity may therefore challenge it on the basis of Article 4(2) TEU."

52 See the ECJ *Melloni* decision (case C-399/11), para 62: "That framework decision effects a harmonisation of the conditions of execution of a European arrest warrant in the event of a conviction rendered in absentia, *which reflects the consensus reached by all the Member States regarding the scope to be given under EU law* to the procedural rights enjoyed by persons convicted in absentia who are the subject of a European arrest warrant" (*emphasis added*).

can be made. First, there is a sole case before the ECJ itself, namely C-344/01, where Germany contested the decision of the European Commission to apply financial corrections to the support for the agricultural sector for the whole of Germany after the checks were performed and risks established in several Lander. It must be noted that the argument of national identity was invoked reasonably, however, in the horizontal situation, as the Commission's decision also applied for Belgium, Spain, France, Ireland, Italy, and Portugal. Only Spain and Greece also tried to contest the decision, but without reference to national identity. Second, the subject of the dispute was not a regulatory provision, but the implementing practice. Therefore, there was no dispute on values. Third, no arguments about national constitutional law are present in the decision.[53] This case also shows that the argument of national identity depends on the "geographical factor" – the more Member States are linked to such a situation, the less likely it is that such an argument will be accepted by the court (Bogdandy, Schill, 2011, p. 1446).

As there is a sole case in this group before the ECJ, as an exception, it is advisable to observe the case-law of the General Court. A national language, a "true" element of national identity, was present before EGC in case T-185/05. However, this argument was not developed in the decision of the EGC, since the contested decision of the European Commission was annulled on other grounds. Still, it is plausible to suppose that national identity could be a supporting reason.

Another case to mention is T-267/08, where regional self-governments of France sought the annulment of a decision regarding their exclusion from the state aid procedure started by the European Commission. The applicants reasonably supported their position with an argument of national identity. The EGC addressed the arguments of the applicants, however, noting that under the procedure for reviewing state aid, only the Member States are interested parties.

53 However, it would be logical to assume that arguments on constitutional law were presented before the ECJ, and reasonable to assume that the ECJ was not convinced by these arguments.

The last case is T-453/10, where the argument of national identity is obviously the weakest within this group of cases. The applicant, the Department of Northern Ireland, contested a European Commission's decision regarding the exclusion of certain expenses from the agricultural support scheme. According to the applicant, referring to national identity, regional institutions should be regarded as having the same *locus standi* under Article 263 TFEU as a Member State. This argument was dismissed by the EGC.

What is common in all these cases is a lack of arguments of constitutional law substantiated by the jurisprudence of the national Constitutional Court. Perhaps within the cases on the annulment of the EU act, so far there has been neither a "real" case where national identity could be used as a properly supportive argument, nor a case of significant importance for the development of the national identity doctrine.

4.2. Actions for failure to fulfil obligations

Another group of cases to be discussed is those dealing with EU law infringement procedure. To the same extent as the action of annulment, this procedure before the ECJ (and Commission) also involves the Government only, leaving national courts aside. This leads to a sufficiently sensitive situation, as EU law infringements can be of two types. The absolute majority are "ordinary" EU law infringements and only isolated "constitutional" EU law infringements are linked to the decisions of national Constitutional Courts applying the *controlimiti* doctrine regarding EU law. The latter is most likely outside the limits of the national identity clause and (so far) is considered to not fall within this article.

The "ordinary" EU law infringement procedure is initiated after a Member State has not respected or implemented EU law effectively. Article 4(2) TEU establishes the limits of application of EU acts even when such application is possible (Rodin, 2011, p. 41). Therefore, the national identity clause might serve as the basis for reasoning regarding a failure to fulfil its obligations under EU secondary law without questioning the legality of an EU act itself (Bogdandy, Schill, 2011, p. 1444). Such reasoning must be coherent and well-motivated, and should establish the purpose rather than just a reference to the national identity clause.[54] However, EU law infringement might also occur because of an administrative practice of national institutions[55] or even courts.[56] It was argued that national identity might not be properly indicated in the legislative procedure but appear in the stage of implementation or application. In such a case, negotiations with the Commission are mandatory, nonetheless, the outcome might be a procedure before the ECJ. If the case is sent to the ECJ, the Court is left with two alternatives – to establish the exemption based on the national identity clause or decide that a Member State had not fulfilled its obligations under EU law. In the latter case, there is a potential tension if national identity is established by the national Constitutional Court and the position of a Member State is well-grounded on such jurisprudence. The same lack appears as with the annulment procedure; as already explained, the ECJ has no tools for direct dialogue with national Constitutional Courts.

There are three cases before the ECJ within this group. The first one is the *Luxembourg* decision,[57] which contains the first-ever mention of national identity in the jurisprudence of the ECJ (Reestman, 2009, p. 376). The subject matter is freedom of movement for workers within the Community to pursue activities as employed persons without differential treatment based on their nationality. Certain exemptions were interpreted restrictively by the ECJ. Luxembourg argued that the profession of teacher should fall within the exception of public service because of the need to transmit traditional values. Luxembourg's position was strengthened by provisions in the Luxembourg Constitution stating that only Luxembourg nationals may hold civil and military positions. Luxembourg argued that since such an exemption is based on the Constitution, it prevents the ECJ from establishing the infringement of EU law. The ECJ admitted that the preservation of national identities is a legitimate aim and, therefore,

54 See for example ECJ case C-165/08, paras 51–52.
55 See for example ECJ case C-416/07, para 24.
56 See for example ECJ case C-416/17, para 107.
57 ECJ case C-473/93 (Commission of the European Communities v Grand Duchy of Luxembourg).

should be respected, but the interests of Luxembourg could be safeguarded without an unjustified general exemption.[58]

However, in his opinion, Advocate General P. Léger argued that, while the general exemption was deemed unjustified, a more narrow scope exclusion was possible. He argued that such an exemption could apply to certain categories of teachers, such as national language, literature, and history teachers, who are undeniably capable of "fostering and preserving national identity."[59] The ECJ, referring to its *Internationale Handelsgesellschaft* decision, also rejected the Luxembourg argument based on constitutional law. Therefore, in the *Luxembourg* decision, national identity played a symbolic role, more like a cultural peculiarity (Claes, 2013, p. 117).

The second case within this category is also Luxembourg "based" and has similar circumstances to the first *Luxembourg* proceedings.[60] Here, the criterion of nationality was established for notaries. Luxembourg argued notaries exercise official authority because of the characteristics of their functions. According to the ECJ, the authentication of documents and all other functions scrutinised by courts do not involve a direct connection with the exercise of official authority. Therefore, the nationality requirement established by Luxembourg legislation is discriminatory. As in the first *Luxembourg* case, the argument of national identity was used for support of the position. Luxembourg argued that the Luxembourgish language is required to perform notarial duties, and therefore, the requirement of nationality should ensure national identity. The Court, referring to the first *Luxembourg* case, reiterated that national language can be safeguarded otherwise than by a general exclusion.[61]

The last case to be discussed is that of *Gibraltar*.[62] The reason this case attracts attention might not be just the argument of national identity but also the legal proceedings, as the action for EU law infringement was

58 See particularly, paras 35–36 of case C-473/93.

59 See the opinion of Advocate General P. Léger in case C-473/93, points 134, 137–138.

60 ECJ case C-51/08 (*European Commission* v. *Grand Duchy of Luxembourg*).

61 See particularly, para 124.

62 ECJ case C-145/04 (*Kingdom of Spain* v. *United Kingdom of Great Britain and Northern Ireland*).

brought by another Member State.[63] The dispute has arisen because of the status of Gibraltar and a UK decision allowing qualifying Commonwealth citizens (QCC) to vote in the election of the European Parliament. Spain claimed that the status of a QCC could not be assimilated to the status of EU citizenship. The UK argued that its decision is based on historical reasons and the grant of the right to vote for QCCs is one of the constitutional traditions. The position of the UK regarding constitutional traditions was supported by the European Commission and was accepted by the ECJ. The Court stated that the European Parliament comprises representatives of the peoples of Member States, and the term "peoples" might have different meanings in the Member States, therefore the UK decision is not contrary to EU law.[64]

Several comments could be made regarding the *Gibraltar* case. Most importantly, in the *Gibraltar* case, national identity was not explicitly mentioned (Faraguna, 2016, p. 508). The UK substantiated its position by using the argument of constitutional traditions. The notion of "constitutional traditions" might be attributed either to the national identity clause or to Article 6(2) Nice Treaty, stating that the EU respects fundamental rights as they result from constitutional traditions common to the Member States. On top of that, the UK's decision to grant voting rights to QCCs was an implementation of the ECHR decision.[65] Finally, the ECJ did not use its technique of conversion from national law to EU law nor the application of the proportionality test to balance the principles. Therefore, there are grounds for some doubts about whether *Gibraltar* could be considered as a "pure" national identity case. Scientists consider this case as an example of national identity jurisprudence. To support such a stance, first, arguments about historical circumstances could be used, since the status of Gibraltar stems from the Utrecht treaty of 1713. Second, the decision of the UK affects a few residents of Gibraltar, just 200 people. Finally, the ECHR decision could also be considered as a supporting element of national identity.

63 This procedure currently is foreseen by Article 259 TFEU.
64 See particularly, para 63.
65 The ECHR decision *Matthews* v. *United Kingdom*, No. 24833/94.

However, the *Gibraltar* case is remarkably different from the *Luxembourg* cases. In the *Luxembourg* cases, the argument of national identity was not "sincere", which was properly noted by the ECJ and the Advocate Generals. Second, national identity in the *Luxembourg* cases was invoked to support the restrictive national measures. Third, the national identity clause was addressed in the circumstances of double-horizontal situations. Primarily, for certain professions with no differentiation throughout Luxembourg, horizontally. Furthermore, the same restrictions were present in other Member States and none of them referred to national identity. This circumstance is identical to that in the previously discussed case C-344/01. Moreover, in the *Luxembourg* cases, provisions of constitutional law do not seem to be very convenient. Meanwhile, the *Gibraltar* case clearly has an individual character, and the identity argument serves to enhance fundamental rights. Therefore, an exemption in the *Gibraltar* decision seems properly supported and practically inevitable.

4.3. References for preliminary rulings

The last group of cases to be analysed in order to explain the national identity clause are those originating from indirect action, preliminary ruling. This is the biggest group compared to the previous ones. The first example is slightly ambiguous because the concept of national identity was mentioned in jurisprudence even before the Maastricht Treaty, and that is even before the first *Luxembourg* case.

However, the *Groener* case[66] is widely considered as an example of the scope of national identity. The pivot point is the Irish language as a requirement to apply for the position of teacher in Ireland. The ECJ had to evaluate whether such a condition for employment was not discriminatory. It was highlighted that such a requirement applied without distinction of nationality because of the "special linguistic situation" and Article 8 of the Irish Constitution. Ireland sought to promote the use of the Irish language as an expression of culture and national identity. The ECJ stressed that such promotion should not be disproportionate, however, given the importance of education and the role of teachers, such a

66 The ECJ *Groener* decision C-379/87.

requirement is reasonable. The logic applied by the ECJ is most evident in the opinion of Advocate General M. Darmon, who assessed whether the element of national identity meets its aim and whether it was strictly necessary to achieve that aim. The provision of the Irish Constitution was considered as evidence that major importance is attributed to the Irish language. The logic of the *Groener* later applied in the *Vardyn* case. Therefore, it is another argument to add that even though *Groener* could not be considered *de jure* as a national identity case, *de facto* it qualifies with no major doubts.

The second example is the *Grogan* case[67] concerning the dissemination of information in Ireland regarding medical pregnancy termination in the United Kingdom, which was also decided on before the Maastricht Treaty. The referring court noted that Article 40(3) of the Irish Constitution establishes that the state acknowledges the right to life of the unborn. This constitutional provision was construed by national jurisprudence as precluding assisting pregnant women in Ireland to travel abroad to get abortions, even by informing them of the identity and location of a specific clinic or clinics. The ECJ gave an answer explaining that the provision of information of general character should be regarded not as a limitation of economic activity, but as a limitation of freedom of expression. As a result, the prohibition on the distribution of information on pregnancy termination was determined not to violate Community law. Additionally, it should be noted that Advocate General W. Van Gerven's opinion acknowledged that such a prohibition is general and is not discriminatory. Moreover, such a prohibition is established in the Irish Constitution and should be regarded as a basic principle of society, a fundamental value to which a nation adheres. Finally, referring to the *Groener* case, the Advocate General applied the proportionality test and concluded that such a prohibition is not contrary to Community law. Furthermore, the Advocate General substantiated his opinion with an argument based on a fundamental constitutional principle. The latter aspect was missing in the ECJ decision. However, one question remains open: what would be the ECJ's answer if the information distributed had been not of general nature,

67 The ECJ *Grogan* decision C-159/90.

but an intentional advertisement for a particular clinic established in the United Kingdom?

The third case to be discussed is the *Omega* decision.[68] The circumstances relate to a laser sports installation used for the imitation of firing upon humans, in other words, "playing at killing." German police suspended such activity as it simulated homicide. It was considered as infringing human dignity. The referring court noted that under national law, such a prohibition is reasonable on the basis of the German Constitution, but there are some doubts regarding the compliance with EU law provisions on freedom to provide services. The ECJ noted national restrictions are independent of any links to the nationality of the providers or recipients of the services. This restriction was placed to protect human dignity as a fundamental value established in the German Constitution and was also confirmed by national courts. The Court confirmed that EU law allows restrictions justified for reasons of public policy. As fundamental rights form an integral part of the general principles of law, human dignity should be considered as a general principle compatible with EU law. After such "conversion", the ECJ assessed the proportionality of the restriction, establishing that it corresponds to the level of protection of human dignity under the German Constitution. As the Court stated, this prohibition "did not go beyond what is necessary in order to attain the aim pursued." It is also important to note the conclusion of the ECJ in *Omega* that the restrictive measure should not be a "conception shared by all Member States."

Some words about the opinion of Advocate General C. Stix-Hackl should be added. The Advocate General noted that the restriction on EU market freedoms "cannot immediately be justified by the protection of specific fundamental rights", even if guaranteed by the Constitution. The validity of EU law cannot be based on constitutional law or determined unilaterally. Even though Member States have some discretion, a restriction must be justified under EU law and under the control of EU institutions.

The Omega decision could be looked at from several perspectives. Unlike the *Groener* and *Grogan* cases, the *Omega* decision was issued after

68 The ECJ *Omega* decision C-36/02.

the establishment of national identity in the Treaties. Despite this change, the ECJ did not invoke the notion of national identity explicitly. The technique of the Court remained unaffected. A national constitutional principle was "converted" to the EU principle, and a proportionality test was carried out, and the exemption was justified on public policy grounds. The *Omega* decision illustrates that derogation is possible if a legitimate interest exists (Claes, 2015a, p. 209) and shows openness towards national identity (Martinico, 2012, pp. 223–224).

The fourth case is the *Sayn-Wittgenstein* decision[69] which could be considered as the second most important decision within the domain of the national identity clause, with the first being the *Vardyn* decision. This case concerns the Austrian citizen Ilonka Fürstin von Sayn-Wittgenstein, who was adopted in Germany and given the family name of her adoptive father. This family name was registered in the Austrian register of civil status, and an Austrian passport was issued. In 2003, the Austrian Constitutional Court adopted a decision in a case with similar circumstances, declaring that the abolition of nobility precludes acquiring a family name, which includes a nobility title. Austrian regional authorities adjusted the family name to Sayn-Wittgenstein. Judicial proceedings were started, referring to freedom of movement guaranteed under EU law. The ECJ noted a name is a constituent element of a person's identity and private life. However, Sayn-Wittgenstein only had an Austrian passport, therefore the issuing of that document fell within the exclusive competence of Austrian institutions. The Austrian government invoked the argument of national identity, and such a position was also supported by the European Commission. The Court stated that restrictions on market freedoms can be justified only if they are proportionate and pursue legitimate objectives. It was also stated that national identity may be taken into consideration when balancing legitimate interests. The ECJ went on to argue that Austrian constitutional regulation should be interpreted as reliance on public policy and followed the same judicial logic as in the *Omega* case, converting constitutional provisions on the abolition of nobility to the EU principle of equal treatment. Finally, the Court decided that

69 The ECJ *Sayn-Wittgenstein* decision C-208/09.

national regulation is not disproportionate and does not unjustifiably undermine freedom of movement. As the ECJ thoroughly assessed proportionality (Kröll, 2012, p. 113), *Sayn-Wittgenstein* may appear to be like other decisions. However, it was the first time the ECJ referred to (Mohay, Tóth, 2017, p. 36) and leaned upon the national identity clause (Tatham, 2013, p. 296; Konstadinides, 2011, p. 202), although in the opinion of Advocate General E. Sharpston this clause is not mentioned (Besselink, 2012, p. 674). This decision was the first post-Lisbon national identity case (Lenaerts, 2014, p. 156) and it was issued slightly more than a year after the Lisbon Treaty came into force (Bogdandy, Schill, 2011, p. 1423). However, the reference to national identity was secondary (Mohay, Tóth, 2017, p. 36), extra (Faraguna, 2016, p. 512), and subsequent (Toniatti, 2013, p. 70).

The *Vardyn* decision,[70] according to the subjective assessment of the present author, is the most significant example from among the national identity group of cases. *Vardyn* could be considered as a post-Lisbon version of *Groener* (Burgorgue-Larsen, 2013, p. 288) and as a successor of the *Groener* decision (Faraguna, 2016, pp. 510–511). The *Vardyn* decision also has quite a few references to the *Sayn-Wittgenstein* case. In his speech before the Supreme Court of Lithuania in 2016, K. Lenaerts singled out *Vardyn* as one of the three most important cases "originating" in Lithuania ever, because of its "crucial constitutional importance." The circumstances of this case are related to the marriage of Malgožata Runevič, a Lithuanian citizen, and Łukasz Paweł Wardyn, a Polish citizen. Although the husband's surname in the marriage certificate was written as "Wardyn", the surname of Malgožata Runevič appeared as "Vardyn", *i.e.* without the letter "W" as this letter does not exist in the Lithuanian alphabet and therefore cannot be used, according to national legislation and the ruling of the Lithuanian Constitutional Court. The ECJ argued that, with a marriage between citizens of different Member States, the spelling of family names according to national rules cannot be regarded as less favourable and does not constitute a restriction of free movement. As a result, EU law does not preclude refusing entry of family names in their original form

70 The ECJ *Vardyn* decision C-391/09.

and amending them following national rules governing official language spelling. The Court stated that the objective pursued by national rules is legitimate and, therefore, is justified, and these restrictions could be weighed against the rights of freedom of movement and residence. However, the ECJ stressed that such restrictions are justified only as far as they are necessary, and the aim cannot be attained by less restrictive measures.

Some characteristics that make the *Vardyn* decision exceptional should be analysed. First, only *Sayn-Wittgenstein* and *Vardyn* were the first post-Lisbon cases where explicit reference to Article 4(2) TEU was made, although this reference is more to cultural identity than to constitutional structures (Claes, 2013, p. 133). However, despite explicit reference, the notion of national identity was not analysed in either *Sayn-Wittgenstein* or *Vardyn* (Burchardt, 2019, pp. 100–101). In both *Sayn-Wittgenstein* and *Vardyn* no arguments could be found regarding national constitutional law as a basis for exemption from EU law (Van de Heyning, 2012, p. 200). Second, *Sayn-Wittgenstein* and *Vardyn* were the only "successful attempts" based on national identity (Claes, Reestman, 2015, p. 937). Third, there are only three cases – both the *Luxembourg* decisions and *Vardyn* – where reference to the notion of national identity is made in the decisions of the Court and in the opinions of Advocates General (Burgorgue-Larsen, 2013, p. 282). Fourthly, in the *Vardyn* case, there is no reference to public policy, as the notion of national identity becomes an autonomous ground for the exception (Dobbs, 2014, p. 321; Preshova, 2019, pp. 190–191). Finally, *Vardyn* is the first decision within the national identity category, where the ECJ establishes what should be assessed by the national court. No freedom for national courts was left in previous decisions (Guastaferro, 2012, p. 292; Preshova, 2019, pp. 190–191). Therefore, the margin of appreciation given in national identity cases, is another novelty of *Vardyn* (Cebulak, 2012, p. 490). However, it must be noted that these academic observations were made prior to the *Bogendorff* decision, which introduced certain adjustments to the general assessment.

The last case to observe is the *Bogendorff* decision.[71] The facts are related to a German citizen who left for the United Kingdom and, while

71 The ECJ *Bogendorff* decision C-438/14.

retaining German citizenship, also acquired British citizenship and changed his name to Peter Mark Emanuel Graf von Wolffersdorff Freiherr von Bogendorff. However, in Germany, he was refused the change of name on his birth certificate because of incompatibility with the essential principles of German law and the abolishment of titles of nobility. The ECJ rejected the arguments that the change of name was intentional and that the name itself was too complex. According to the Court, these arguments cannot justify the restrictions on freedom of movement. However, the argument of the constitutional abolition of privileges and the prohibition of titles of nobility was accepted as a ground for such a restriction, since registration of names would create the appearance of a new title of nobility. The ECJ concluded that the abolition of privileges should be considered as Germany's constitutional choice and therefore as an element of national identity and interpreted as a ground relating to public policy. This argument was also supported by the EU principle of equal treatment. The ECJ concluded that, in each case, the assessment of proportionality should be carried out by the national court. The *Bogendorff* decision, being the latest in the category of national identity cases, does not bring any unique novelty. To a large extent, it is based on the *Sayn-Wittgenstein* case, with the ECJ returning to its conversion technique, which was absent in the *Vardyn* case. However, the margin of appreciation and delegation of assessment of proportionality are novelties of the *Vardyn* decision, which were replicated in the *Bogendorff* decision. As in the *Vardyn* decision in *Bogendorff*, the ECJ relied on Article 4(2) TEU directly, but the formula is different. The ECJ stated in *Vardyn* that "the goal pursued by national rules constitutes, in principle, a legitimate goal for justifying restrictions", whereas in *Bogendorff*, it "may be taken into account as an element justifying a restriction." Therefore, the national identity clause was a secondary argument in the Courts' reasoning (Mohay, Tóth, 2017, p. 37).

To summarise, it could be said that the national identity clause is being cautiously explored by the ECJ. The elements of national constitutional law and the jurisprudence of national Constitutional Courts are duly respected and more visible than in EU law infringement or EU law annulment cases. If the national identity clause is secondary and supporting in the *Sayn-Wittgenstein* and *Bogendorff* decisions, it is the primary reason in the *Vardyn* case. The *Vardyn* and *Bogendorff* decisions illustrate that the margin of appreciation and assessment of proportionality could be delegated to national courts.

5. National profile: Lithuania

In major scientific publications on national identity, sections on Lithuania seem to be missing. This is perhaps because the national identity clause has attracted the attention of only two Lithuanian legal scholars: I. Jarukaitis (Jarukaitis, 2014) and E. Jarašiūnas (Jarašiūnas, 2019). It is to be noted that the Constitutional Court of Lithuania, in two of its rulings[72] has only mentioned the national identity clause *obiter dicta*.

When speaking of the national identity clause, it is important to mention that this clause is reflected in the Constitution of Lithuania. The accession of the Republic of Lithuania to the EU required amendments to the Constitution. These amendments were drafted and adopted as a separate Constitutional Act "On Membership of the Republic of Lithuania in the European Union", which is a constituent part of the Constitution. The preamble of this Act notes that the EU "respects the national identity and constitutional traditions of its Member States." Therefore, the respect for national identity is mutually established in Article 4(2) TEU and the Lithuanian Constitution. Moreover, the respect for national identity is a national precondition for Lithuania's membership in the EU. The analysis of *travaux préparatoires* and an interview conducted with the then Chair of the Working Group on Adjustments of Legislation on the Parliament's Work after Membership in the EU, V.P. Andriukaitis, leave little doubt that the notion of national identity established in the Act directly corresponds to the concept of national identity then being drafted in Article I-5 of the Constitutional Treaty. While the wording "constitutional traditions" in the Constitutional Act shows part of the *controlimiti* doctrine, it is not analysed in this article.[73]

---

72 20/10/2017 Ruling of Constitutional Court of Lithuania in Case 40/03, para 27.1 and 08/11/2019 Ruling of Constitutional Court of Lithuania in Case 10/2018, para 14.1.

73 However, I argue that the Constitutional Act establishes a basis for all three types of constitutional review of EU law. More on *controlimiti* in Lithuania can be found for example in: Claes, 2015a, p. 190; Horsley, 2018, p. 224; Sadurski,

Although the notion of national identity has not been interpreted by the Constitutional Court, the above-mentioned wording of the preamble of the Act, I argue, obliges all national institutions, including courts, to "activate" the clause of national identity if needed. Such "activation" is a measure to ensure (or at least seek) the balance between two autonomous legal systems in the environment of constitutional pluralism. Equally important is the perspective from the positions of national constitutional law, as judicial dialogue on values might be a measure to achieve the "special rule" (exemption). The feasibility of such a "special rule" is of paramount importance, as it creates an alternative to the amendments to the Lithuanian Constitution. This is a very important aspect because the Constitutional Court of Lithuania established that if the Constitution and international law obligations are incompatible, the incompatibility must be removed by "renouncing the international obligations [...] or by making the necessary amendments to the Constitution"[74]. Such a "special rule" becomes a salient element in avoiding constitutional amendments and therefore ensuring the stability of the Constitution[75].

However, with Lithuania, in a situation involving national identity the national court has a limited right to apply to the Constitutional Court. It should substantiate such an application if legal acts[76] are seen to be in conflict with the Constitution. The Government would face the same challenge as a national court, whereas a "court" does not have any – even theoretical – possibility of applying to the Constitutional Court. Even if

2012, pp. 104–105. See also 28/03/2006 Ruling of Constitutional Court of Lithuania in Case No. 33/03.

74 18/03/2014 Ruling of Constitutional Court of Lithuania in Case No. 31/2011-40/2011-42/2011-46/2011-9/2012-25/2012, part IV, para 5.3.

75 28/03/2006 Ruling of Constitutional Court of Lithuania in Case No. 33/03, para 13 establishes: "the stability of the Constitution is a great constitutional value. The Constitution should not be altered, if it is not legally necessary."

76 Within the scope of this article, it is sufficient to mention that, according to Article 105 of the Constitution, the Constitutional Court has the jurisdiction to consider whether the laws or other acts adopted by Parliament, acts of the President, or acts of the Government are in conflict with the Constitution. The mandate of the Constitutional Court, defined in Article 105 of the Constitution, is broader but not relevant to the thematic of this analysis.

the notion of national identity appears in the jurisprudence of the ECJ in isolated cases only, it would undoubtedly be beneficial to consider whether broader debate is required to enhance the role of the Lithuanian Constitutional Court in the domain of national identity, for example, by introducing the possibility of consultative opinion. The debates could be heated, but hardly anyone denies that such national practise has the potential to "re-centralise" national courts after they have been "decentralised" by the fundamental principles of EU law.

There might be a place for some reluctance or even fear of empowering national Constitutional Courts, but in the end, such empowerment is a way forward for the dialogue on values in the world of constitutional pluralism. Acknowledging the implied concerns over the strengthening role of national Constitutional Courts, one might be more emphatic and consider whether national Constitutional Courts will not have some disquiet about leaving their usual jurisprudential habitat and entering almost unchartered waters. On the other hand, such discussion is meaningful only assuming the ECJ is also willing to accept the arguments of national Constitutional Courts, as it takes two to tango. Suggestions of indirect dialogue from positions of constitutional patriotism, whether based on the primacy of EU law or the supremacy of the national Constitution, are an undesirable alternative to direct dialogue based on the values of constitutional pluralism.

The "Lithuanian" *Vardyn* case could be used to illustrate the deficiencies previously discussed in this article. The "decentralised" national court of first instance, in submitting a preliminary reference to the ECJ just before the Lisbon Treaty entered into force,[77] hardly knew or could understand the novelty of the national identity clause. However, in the application, the Lithuanian court sufficiently clearly showed core elements of the jurisprudence of the Constitutional Court of Lithuania.[78] From the

77 The application of national court was lodged on 02/10/2009.

78 In the application the national court refers to 21/10/1999 Ruling of Constitutional Court of Lithuania (*Konstitucinis Teismas*) in Case No. 14/98 on the spelling of names and family names in the passports of citizens of the Republic of Lithuania and the 11/06/2009 petition of Seimas (Parliament) requesting the construction of the Ruling of the Constitutional Court.

constitutional law perspective, such a request in *Vardyn* was unnecessary, to say the least. In the *Vardyn* case, an instrument like *QPC* could have acted as a safeguard valve. It is worthwhile to mention that the *Vardyn* case, being one of the most-notorious ECJ decisions based on the national identity clause, could have developed into full-scale judicial warfare if the ECJ had followed the opinion of Advocate General N. Jääskinen. The Advocate General suggested that, under the circumstances of the *Vardyn* case, national law does not constitute an adequate and necessary means of achieving the objective of protecting the national language.[79]

Although the *Vardyn* decision is widely regarded as the most important decision based on the national identity clause, the outcome could not be regarded as a success or mutually acceptable judicial compromise from the purist perspective of national constitutional law. The jurisprudence of the Constitutional Court of Lithuania regarding the spelling of names and surnames is based on the constitutional status of the state language.[80] Undoubtedly, the *Vardyn* decision clearly created a loophole[81] in the jurisprudence of the Constitutional Court, enabling the ordinary courts to

79 See points 80–81, 84, 87 and 101–102 of the opinion.

80 Constitutional Court of Lithuania, Case No. 14/98, see para 4: "under Article 14 of the Constitution, Lithuanian shall be the state language. The establishment of the status of the state language in the Constitution means that Lithuanian is a constitutional value. The state language preserves the identity of the nation, it integrates a civil nation, it ensures the expression of national sovereignty, the integrity and indivisibility of the state, and the smooth functioning of the state and municipal establishments."

81 See the operative part of the *Vardyn* decision: "Article 21 TFEU must be interpreted as not precluding the competent authorities of a Member State from refusing, in circumstances such as those at issue in the main proceedings and pursuant to those same rules, to amend the joint surname of a married couple who are citizens of the Union, as it appears on the certificates of civil status issued by the Member State of origin of one of those citizens, in a form which complies with the spelling rules of that latter State, on condition that that refusal does not give rise, for those Union citizens, to serious inconvenience at administrative, professional and private levels, this being a matter *which it is for the national court to decide*. If that proves to be the case, *it is also for that court to determine* whether the refusal to make the amendment is necessary for the protection of the interests which the national rules are designed to secure and is proportionate to the legitimate aim pursued" (*emphasis added*).

circumvent it, despite the strict limits established by the Constitutional Court itself.[82] To tackle this loophole, the Constitutional Court could use an approach similar to that of the Italian Constitutional Court in the *Taricco* saga,[83] thus establishing that the Constitutional Court is the only national court that can take a decision and, by its decision, re-establish the supremacy of the Constitution. However, this aspect has not – as yet – been discussed even in national academic works, as the stance of the Constitutional Court in the last decade could be perceived as "full friendliness" towards EU law and the ECJ.

6. Conclusions

In summary, some final conclusions could be drawn. The origin of the national identity clause, established in Article 4(2) TEU, determines that this clause is binding on the EU and all of its institutions, the ECJ included. Although national identity is an autonomous principle of EU law, it is subordinated to the EU values, entrenched in Article 2 TEU. There are opinions that national identity overcomes the primacy of EU law, but such an approach lacks sufficient reasoning. Although the national identity clause does not modify the primacy principle significantly, this clause could serve as a basis to establish a "special rule" from the uniform application of EU law, and therefore to some extent, the principle of primacy is variably affected, depending on the circumstances of the case. There is no doubt that the national identity clause is a category of EU law. Consequently, the institution adopting an exemption from the uniform application of EU law is inevitably the ECJ.

However, the approach suggesting that national identity overcomes EU law primacy stems from the theoretical background, assuming an equation

82 28/03/2006 Ruling of Constitutional Court of Lithuania in Case 33/03, para 15.4: "Constitutional Court's rulings, conclusions and decisions by which a constitutional justice case is finished, i.e., final acts of the Constitutional Court, are obligatory to all State institutions, courts, all enterprises, establishments and organisations, as well as officials and citizens, including the Constitutional Court itself."

83 10/04/2018 decision of Constitutional Court of Italy (*Corte Costituzionale*) *Taricco II*, No. 115/2018

of two separate concepts: national identity and constitutional identity. Although such an approach could be considered more common, it is argued in the article that those two notions should be understood as detached one from another as they represent (or imply) different instruments of judicial review. A national identity review is to be performed by the ECJ, while a constitutional identity review is to be carried out by the national Constitutional Court.

National identity refers to fundamental constitutional structures and therefore requires "composite jurisdiction", elements of national constitutional law to be interpreted by the national Constitutional Court, and the final evaluation of such interpretation by the ECJ. This evaluation was done by the ECJ applying the technique of "conversion", converting national interpretation to the categories of EU law, and balancing it against EU principles, by using a proportionality test in each case. The ECJ is reluctant to establish a general framework to define what constitutes national identity and instead interprets this notion in a case-by-case manner.

However, there is a very tiny probability that the national Constitutional Court will submit an evaluation of national identity to the ECJ. Such a situation might lead to judicial tensions, as the ECJ has no instrument for direct communication with the national Constitutional Court. Therefore, direct two way judicial dialogue between the apex courts remains theoretical aspiration. A "reversed preliminary ruling" could be an instrument completing the creation of what would be tantamount to judicial dialogue in the environment of constitutional pluralism.

Nonetheless, the constitutional law arguments and jurisprudence of national Constitutional Courts receive proper attention from the ECJ. However, there are only a few individual cases where national identity is given attention by the parties or by the Court. There are even fewer "authentic" cases, where national identity is given the role of "true" argument. Furthermore, national identity remains a "secondary" argument with the sole exception of the *Vardyn* case.

The *Vardyn* case is of "Lithuanian" origin, and it illustrates both the effectiveness of the national identity clause and its weaknesses and dangers. It also gives an opportunity to present the Lithuanian stance on national identity briefly, as academic attention is scarce in this area.

Bibliography

Arnaiz, A.S., Llivina, C.A. (2013), *Why Constitutional Identity Suddenly Matters: A Tale of Brave States, a Mighty Union and the Decline of Sovereignty*, [in:] A.S. Arnaiz, C.A. Llivina (eds.), *National Constitutional Identity and European Integration*, Intersentia, pp. 1–15.

Arnull, A. (2012), *Judicial Dialogue in the European Union*, [in:] J. Dickson, P. Eleftheriadis (eds.), *Philosophical Foundations of European Union Law*, Oxford University Press, pp. 109–133.

Auby, J.-B. (2018), *Global Constitutionalism and Normative Hierarchies*, [in:] M. Belov (ed.), *Global Constitutionalism and Its Challenges to Westphalian Constitutional Law*, Hart Publishing, pp. 3–12.

Avbelj, M. (2011), *Supremacy or Primacy of EU Law – (Why) Does it Matter?*, "European Law Journal", vol. 17, no. 6, pp. 744–763.

Baquero Cruz, J. (2018), *What's Left of the Law of Integration? Decay and Resistance in European Union Law*, Oxford University Press.

Baraggia, A. (2015), *Paths of Dialogue Between the ECJ and Constitutional Courts on Fundamental Rights Protection: A Still-Puzzling Scenario*, "Tulane Journal of International & Comparative Law", vol. 24, no. 1, pp. 65–95.

Besselink, L.F.M. (2010), *National and constitutional identity before and after Lisbon*, "Utrecht Law Review", vol. 6, no. 3, pp. 36–49.

Besselink, L.F.M. (2012), *Case C-208/09, Ilonka Sayn-Wittgenstein v. Landeshauptmann von Wien, Judgment of the Court (Second Chamber) of 22 December 2010, nyr.*, "Common Market Law Review", vol. 49, no. 2, pp. 671–694.

Bobić, A. (2017), *Constitutional Pluralism Is Not Dead: An Analysis of Interactions Between Constitutional Courts of Member States and the European Court of Justice*, "German Law Journal", vol. 18, no. 6, pp. 1395–1428.

de Boer, N. (2013), *Addressing Rights Divergences under the Charter: Melloni*, "Common Market Law Review", vol. 50, no. 4, pp. 1083–1104.

de Boer, N. (2018), *The False Promise of Constitutional Pluralism*, [in:] G. Davies, M. Avbelj (eds.), *Research Handbook on Legal Pluralism and EU Law*, Edwards Elgar Publishing, pp. 199–222.

Bofill, H. (2013), *What is not Constitutional Pluralism in the EU: National Constitutional Identity in the German Lisbon Judgment*, [in:] A.S. Arnaiz, C.A. Llivina (eds.), *National Constitutional Identity and European Integration*, Intersentia, pp. 221–242.

von Bogdandy, A. (2009), *Founding Principles*, [in:] A. von Bogdandy, J. Bast (eds.), *Principles of European Constitutional Law*, Hart Publishing, pp. 11–54.

von Bogdandy, A. (2012), *Neither an International Organization nor a Nation State: The EU as a Supranational Federation*, [in:] E. Jones, A. Menon, S. Weatherill (eds.), *The Oxford Handbook of the European Union*, Oxford University Press, pp. 761–776.

von Bogdandy, A., Schill, S. (2011), *Overcoming Absolute Primacy: Respect for National Identity Under the Lisbon Treaty*, "Common Market Law Review", vol. 48, no. 5, pp. 1417–1454.

von Bogdandy, A. et al. (2015), *A European Response to Domestic Constitutional Crisis: Advancing the Reverse-Solange Doctrine*, [in:] A. von Bogdandy, P. Sonnevend (eds.), *Constitutional Crisis in the European Constitutional Area. Theory, Law and Politics in Hungary and Romania*, Hart Publishing, pp. 235–253.

Burchardt, D. (2019), *The Relationship Between the Law of the European Union and the Law of its Member States – A Norm-based Conceptual Framework*, "European Constitutional Law Review", vol. 15, no. 1, pp. 73–103.

Burgorgue-Larsen, L. (2013), *A Huron at the Kirchberg Plateau or a Few Naive Thoughts on Constitutional Identity in the Case-law of the Judge of the European Union*, [in:] A.S. Arnaiz, C.A. Llivina (eds.), *National Constitutional Identity and European Integration*, Intersentia, pp. 275–304.

Callies, C., van der Schyff, G. (eds.), *Constitutional Identity in a Europe of Multilevel Constitutionalism*, Cambridge University Press.

Callejon, F.B. (2012), *The Relations Between the EU Court of Justice and the Constitutional Courts of the Member States*, [in:] H.-J. Blanke, S. Mangiameli (eds.), *The European Union after Lisbon. Constitutional Basis, Economic Order and External Action*, Springer, pp. 251–278.

Cebulak, P. (2012), *Inherent Risks of the Pluralist Structure: Use of the Concept of National Constitutional Identity by the Polish and Czech*

Constitutional Courts, "Croatian Yearbook of European Law and Policy", vol. 8, pp. 473–504.

Chalmers, D., Davies, G., Monti, G. (2014), *European Union Law*, Cambridge University Press.

Claes, M. (2012), *Negotiating Constitutional Identity or Whose Identity it is Anyway?*, [in:] M. Claes et al. (eds.), *Constitutional Conversations in Europe: Actors, Topics and Procedures*, Intersentia, pp. 205–233.

Claes, M. (2013), *National Identity: Trump Card or up for Negotiation?*, [in:] A.S. Arnaiz, C.A. Llivina (eds.), *National Constitutional Identity and European Integration*, Intersentia, pp. 109–139.

Claes, M. (2015a), *The Primacy of EU Law in European and National Law*, [in:] D. Chalmers, A. Arnull (eds.), *The Oxford Handbook of European Union Law*, Oxford University Press, pp. 178–211.

Claes, M. (2015b), *Luxembourg, Here We Come? Constitutional Courts and the Preliminary Reference Procedure*, "German Law Journal", vol. 16, no. 6, pp. 1331–1342.

Claes, M., Reestman, J.-H. (2015), *The Protection of National Constitutional Identity and the Limits of European Integration at the Occasion of the Gauweiler Case*, "German Law Journal", vol. 16, no. 4, pp. 917–970.

Cloots, E. (2015), *National Identity in EU Law*, Oxford University Press.

Cloots, E. (2016), *National Identity, Constitutional Identity, and Sovereignty in the EU*, "Netherlands Journal of Legal Philosophy", vol. 45, no. 2, pp. 82–98.

Craig, P., de Búrca G. (2011), *EU Law: Text, Cases, and Materials, EU Law: Text, Cases, and Materials*, Oxford University Press.

Davies, G. (2012), *Constitutional Disagreement in Europe and the Search for Pluralism*, [in:] M. Avbelj, J. Komárek (eds.), *Constitutional Pluralism in the European Union and Beyond*, Hart Publishing, pp. 269–283.

Dicosola, M., Fasone, C., Spigno, I. (2015), *Constitutional Courts in the European Legal System After the Treaty of Lisbon and the Euro-Crisis*, "German Law Journal", vol. 16, no. 6, pp. 1317–1330.

Dobbs, M. (2014), *Sovereignty, Article 4(2) TEU and the Respect of National Identities: Swinging the Balance of Power in Favour of the*

Member States?, "Yearbook of European Law", vol. 33, no. 1, pp. 298–334.

Drinóczi, T. (2020), *Constitutional Identity in Europe: The Identity of the Constitution. A Regional Approach*, "German Law Journal", vol. 21, no. 2, pp. 105–130.

Drinóczi, T., Mohay, Á. (2017), *The Preliminary Ruling Procedure and the Identity Review*, [in:] *Procedural Aspects of EU Law*, Krešendo, pp. 192–209.

Fabbrini, F., Sajó, A. (2019), *The Dangers of Constitutional Identity*, "European Law Journal", vol. 25, no. 4, pp. 457–473.

Faraguna, P. (2015), *A Living Constitutional Identity: The Contribution of Non-Judicial Actors*, "Jean Monnet Working Paper Series", no. 10/15.

Faraguna, P. (2016), *Taking Constitutional Identities Away from Courts*, "Brooklyn Journal of International Law", vol. 41, no. 2, pp. 491–578.

Faraguna, P. (2017), *Constitutional Identity in the EU – A Shield or a Sword?*, "German Law Journal", vol. 18, no. 7, pp. 1617–1640.

Flynn, T. (2019), *The Triangular Constitution. Constitutional Pluralism in Ireland, the EU and the ECHR*, Hart Publishing.

Gamba, B.D., Lentzis, D. (2017), *Crafting Constitutional Identity in the Era of Migration and Financial Crises – The Case of Greece*, "German Law Journal", vol. 18, no. 7, pp. 1683–1701.

Gérard, P., Verrijdt, W. (2017), *Belgian Constitutional Court Adopts National Identity Discourse*, "European Constitutional Law Review", vol. 13, no. 1, pp. 182–205.

Gisbert, R. (2013), *National Constitutional Identity in European Constitutionalism: Revisiting the Tale of the Emperor's New Clothes in Spain?*, [in:] A.S. Arnaiz, C.A. Llivina (eds.), *National Constitutional Identity and European Integration*, Intersentia, pp. 75–91.

Grabenwarter, C. (2009), *National Constitutional Law Relating to the European Union*, [in:] A. von Bogdandy, J. Bast (eds.), *Principles of European Constitutional Law*, Hart Publishing, pp. 83–129.

Gragl, P. (2018), *Legal Monism*, Oxford University Press.

Grewe, C. (2013), *Methods of Identification of National Constitutional Identity*, [in:]A.S. Arnaiz, C.A. Llivina (eds.), *National Constitutional Identity and European Integration*, Intersentia, pp. 37–48.

Groussot, X. (2012), *Constitutional Dialogues, Pluralism and Conflicting Identities*, [in:] M. Avbelj, J. Komárek (eds.), *Constitutional Pluralism in the European Union and Beyond*, Hart Publishing, pp. 319–342.

Guastaferro, B. (2012), *Beyond the Exceptionalism of Constitutional Conflicts: The Ordinary Functions of the Identity Clause*, "Yearbook of European Law", vol. 31, no. 1, pp. 263–318.

Halmai, G. (2018), *Concluding Remarks*, "Italian Journal of Public Law", vol. 10, no. 2, pp. 477–484.

Van de Heyning, C. (2012), *The European Perspective: from lingua franca to a common language*, [in:] M. Claes et al. (eds.), *Constitutional Conversations in Europe: Actors, Topics and Procedures*, Intersentia, pp. 181–203.

Horsley, T. (2018), *The Court of Justice of the European Union as an Institutional Actor. Judicial Lawmaking and its Limits*, Cambridge University Press.

Jarašiūnas, E. (2019), *Konstitucinis tapatumas: sąvokos vartojimo prasmingumo klausimas*, "Jurisprudencija", vol. 26, no. 1, pp. 6–39.

Jarukaitis, I. (2014), *Pagarba valstybių narių nacionaliniam tapatumui kaip bendrasis Europos Sąjungos teisės principas*, [in:] G. Švedas, V. Nekrošius, J. Machovenko (eds.), *Europos Sąjungos teisės įtaka Lietuvos teisinei sistemai*, Vilniaus universiteto Teisės fakultetas, pp. 557–600.

Kellerbauer, M., Klamert, M., Tomkin, J. (2019), *Commentary on the EU: Treaties and the Charter of Fundamental Rights*, Oxford University Press.

Klamert, M. (2014), *The Principle of Loyalty in EU Law*, Oxford University Press.

Koncewicz, T.T. (2015), *The European Comity of Circumspect Constitutional Courts. Searching for Constitutional Reason, Relevance and Voice*, [in:] K. Budziło (ed.), *IX World Congress of Constitutional Law (Oslo, 16–20 June 2014). Contributions By Polish Scholars*, Biuro Trybunału Konstytucyjnego, pp. 51–85.

Konstadinides, T. (2011), *Constitutional Identity as a Shield and as a Sword: The European Legal Order within the Framework of National Constitutional Settlement*, "Cambridge Yearbook of European Legal Studies", vol. 13, pp. 195–218.

Konstadinides, T. (2013), *The Constitutionalisation of National Identity in EU Law and its Implications.*

Kosta, V. (2009), *European Court of Justice: Case C-213/07, Michaniki AE v. Ethniko Simvoulio Radiotileorasis, Ipourgos Epikratias*, "European Constitutional Law Review", vol. 5, no. 3, pp. 501–516.

Kovács, K. (2017), *The Rise of an Ethnocultural Constitutional Identity in the Jurisprudence of the East Central European Courts*, "German Law Journal", vol. 18, no. 7, pp. 1703–1720.

Kröll, T. (2012), *The European Court of Justice, a Guardian ('Hüter') of the Republican Principle of the Austrian Federal Constitution?*, "Vienna Journal on International Constitutional Law", vol. 6, no. 1, pp. 110–121.

Kumm, M. (2012), *Rethinking Constitutional Authority: On the Structure and Limits of Constitutional Pluralism*, [in:] M. Avbelj, J. Komárek (eds.), *Constitutional Pluralism in the European Union and Beyond*, Hart Publishing, pp. 39–66.

Kumm, M., Comella, V.F. (2005), *The Primacy Clause of the Constitutional Treaty and the Future of Constitutional Conflict in the European Union*, "International Journal of Constitutional Law", vol. 3, no. 2–3, pp. 473–492.

Lenaerts, K. (2014), *EU Values and Constitutional Pluralism: The EU System of Fundamental Rights Protection*, "Polish Yearbook of International Law", pp. 135–160.

Maduro, M.P. (2003), *Europe and the Constitution: What if this is as Good as it Gets?*, [in:] J.H.H. Weiler (ed.), *European Constitutionalism Beyond the State*, Cambridge University Press, pp. 74–102.

Martí, J.L. (2013), *Two Different Ideas of Constitutional Identity: Identity of the Constitution v. Identity of the* People, [in:] A.S. Arnaiz, C.A. Llivina (eds.), *National Constitutional Identity and European Integration*, Intersentia, pp. 17–36.

Martinico, G. (2012), *The Tangled Complexity of the EU Constitutional Process: On Complexity as a Constitutional Theory of the EU*, "Yearbook of European Law", vol. 31, no. 1, pp. 198–226.

Martinico, G. (2013), *What Lies Behind Article 4(2) TEU?*, [in:] A.S. Arnaiz, C.A. Llivina (eds.), *National Constitutional Identity and European Integration*, Intersentia, pp. 93–108.

Martinico, G. (2018), *Constitutional conflicts and agonistic pluralism: what can we learn from political theory?*, [in:] G. Davies, M. Avbelj (eds.), *Research Handbook on Legal Pluralism and EU Law*, Edward Elgar Publishing, pp. 78–94.

Mayer, F. (2009), *Multilevel Constitutional Jurisdiction*, [in:] A. von Bogdandy, J. Bast (eds.), *Principles of European Constitutional Law*, Hart Publishing, pp. 399–439.

Mayer, F. (2011), *Rashomon in Karlsruhe: A Reflection on Democracy and Identity in the European Union*, "International Journal of Constitutional Law", vol. 9, no. 3–4, pp. 757–785.

Mayer, F. (2014), *Rebels Without a Cause? A Critical Analysis of the German Constitutional Court's OMT Reference*, "German Law Journal", vol. 15, no. 2, pp. 111–146.

Mayer, F. (2017), *The Transformation of Europe: Loyalty Lost, Democracy Lost?*, [in:] M.P. Maduro, M. Wind (eds.), *The Transformation of Europe: Twenty-Five Years On*, Cambridge University Press, pp. 274–288.

Mayoral, J.A., Wind, M. (2016), *Introduction: National Courts Vis-À-Vis EU Law. New Issues, Theories and Methods*, [in:] B. de Witte et al. (eds.), *National Courts and EU Law: New Issues, Theories and Methods*, Edward Elgar Publishing, pp. 1–11.

Menéndez, A.J. (2017), *Constitutional Review, Luxembourg Style: A Structural Critique of the Way in Which the European Court of Justice Reviews the Constitutionality of the Laws of the Member States of the European Union*, "Contemporary Readings in Law and Social Justice", vol. 9, no. 2, pp. 116–145.

Menéndez, A.J. (2011), *From Constitutional Pluralism to a Pluralistic Constitution? Constitutional Synthesis as a MacCormickian Constitutional Theory of European Integration*, [in:] A.J. Menéndez, J.E. Fossum (eds.), *Law and Democracy in Neil MacCormick's Legal and Political Theory: The Post-Sovereign Constellation*, Springer, pp. 211–241.

Mohay, Á., Tóth, N. (2017), *Nobility Titles and Free Movement: Case C-438/14 Nabiel Peter Bogendorff von Wolffersdorff*, "Pécs Journal of International and European Law", vol. 1, pp. 30–38.

Murphy, N. (2017), *Article 4(2) TEU: A Blow to the Supremacy of Union Law?*, "Trinity College Law Review", vol. 20, pp. 94–121.

Panara, C. (2015), *The Sub-national Dimension of the EU*, Springer International.

Paris, D. (2018), *National and Supranational Courts as Battleground and Meeting Ground of Constitutional Adjudication*, "Italian Journal of Public Law", vol. 10, no. 2, pp. 205–225.

Pérez, A.T. (2012), *The Dual System of Rights Protection in the European Union in Light of US Federalism*, [in:] E. Cloots, G. de Baere, S. Sottiaux (eds.), *Federalism in the European Union*, Hart Publishing, pp. 110–130.

Pérez, A.T. (2013a), *The Challenges for Constitutional Courts as Guardians of Fundamental Rights in European Union*, [in:] P. Popelier, A. Mazmanyan, W. Vandenbruwaene (eds.), *The Role of Constitutional Courts in Multilevel Governance*, Intersentia, pp. 49–76.

Pérez, A.T. (2013b), *Constitutional Identity and Fundamental Rights: The Intersection between Articles 4(2) TEU and 53 Charter*, [in:] A.S. Arnaiz, C.A. Llivina (eds.), *National Constitutional Identity and European Integration*, Intersentia, pp. 141–157.

Pérez, A.T. (2014), *Melloni in Three Acts: From Dialogue to Monologue*, "European Constitutional Law Review", vol. 10, no. 2, pp. 308–331.

Pernice, I. (2011a), *Does Europe Need a Constitution? Achievements and Challenges After Lisbon*, [in:] A. Arnull (eds.), *A Constitutional Order of States? Essays in EU Law in Honour of Alan Dashwood*, Hart Publishing, pp. 75–98.

Pernice, I. (2011b), *Motor or Break for European Policies? Germany's New Role in the EU after Lisbon-Judgement of its Federal Constitutional Court*, [in:] Nomos (ed.), *Europe's Constitutional Challenges in the Light of Recent Case Law of National Constitutional Courts*, pp. 355–389.

Pollicino, O. (2010), *The New Relationship between National and the European Courts after the Enlargement of Europe: Towards a Unitary Theory of Jurisprudential Supranational Law?*, "Yearbook of European Law", vol. 29, no. 1, pp. 65–111.

Polzin, M. (2017), *Constitutional Identity as a Constructed Reality and a Restless Soul*, "German Law Journal", vol. 18, no. 7.

Popelier, P. (2012), *Judicial Conversations in Multilevel Constitutionalism. The Belgian Case*, [in:] M. Claes et al. (eds.), *Constitutional*

Conversations in Europe: Actors, Topics and Procedures, Intersentia, pp. 73–99.

Preshova, D. (2012), *Battleground or Meeting Point? Respect for National Identities in the European Union – Article 4(2) of the Treaty on European Union*, "Croatian Yearbook of European Law and Policy", vol. 8, pp. 267–298.

Preshova, D. (2019), *On the Rise While Falling. The New Roles of Constitutional Courts in the Era of European Integration*, PhD thesis, Universität zu Köln.

Priban, J. (2015), *Constitutional Sovereignty in Post-Sovereign Jurisprudence of the Czech Constitutional Court: from the Lisbon Judgments to the Landtová Ultra Vires Controversy*, [in:] M. Bobek (ed.), *Central European Judges Under the European Influence: The Transformative Power of the EU Revisited*, Hart Publishing, pp. 323–348.

Reestman, J.-H. (2009), *The Franco-German Constitutional Divide Reflections on National and Constitutional Identity*, "European Constitutional Law Review", vol. 5, no. 3, pp. 374–390.

Rodin, S. (2011), *National Identity and Market Freedoms After the Treaty of Lisbon*, "Croatian Yearbook of European Law and Policy", vol. 7, pp. 11–41.

Rosas, A., Armati, L. (2018), *EU Constitutional Law: An Introduction. Third revised edition*, Hart Publishing.

Rugge, G. (2017), *The Italian Constitutional Court on Taricco: Unleashing the normative potential of 'national identity'?*, "Questions of International Law", vol. 37, pp. 21–29.

Sadurski, W. (2012), *Constitutionalism and the Enlargement of Europe*, Oxford University Press.

Safjan, M. (2015), *Central and Eastern European Constitutional Courts Facing New Challenges: Ten Years of Experience*, [in:] M. Bobek (ed.), *Central European Judges Under the European Influence. The Transformative Power of EU Revisited*, Hart Publishing, pp. 375–389.

Sarmiento, D. (2013), *The EU's Constitutional Core*, [in:] A.S. Arnaiz, C.A. Llivina (eds.), *National Constitutional Identity and European Integration*, Intersentia, pp. 177–204.

Schnettger, A. (2020), *Article 4(2) TEU as a Vehicle for National Constitutional Identity in the Shared European Legal System*, [in:] C. Callies, G.

van der Schyff (eds.), *Constitutional Identity in a Europe of Multilevel Constitutionalism*, Cambridge University Press, pp. 9–37.

van der Schyff, G. (2016a), *Exploring Member State and European Union Constitutional Identity*, "European Public Law", vol. 22, no. 2, pp. 227–241.

van der Schyff, G. (2016b), *EU Member State Constitutional Identity: A Comparison of Germany and the Netherlands as Polar Opposites*, "Heidelberg Journal of International Law", vol. 76, no. 1, pp. 167–191.

Tatham, A.F. (2013), *Central European Constitutional Courts in the Face of EU Membership*, Martinus Nijhoff Publishers.

Toader, T., Safta, M. (2016), *The Dialogue of Constitutional Judges*, Peter Lang.

Toniatti, R. (2013), *Sovereignty Lost, Constitutional Identity Regained*, [in:] A.S. Arnaiz, C.A. Llivina (eds.), *National Constitutional Identity and European Integration*, Intersentia, pp. 49–73.

Tremps, P.P. (2013), *National Identity in Spanish Constitutional Court Case-law*, [in:] A.S. Arnaiz, C.A. Llivina (eds.), *National Constitutional Identity and European Integration*, Intersentia, pp. 263–274.

Tuori, K. (2015), *European Constitutionalism*, Cambridge University Press.

Tuori, K. (2017), *The Pluralism of European Fundamental Rights law*, [in:] S. Douglas-Scott, N. Hatzis (eds.), *Research Handbook on EU Law and Human Rights*, Cheltenham, pp. 35–57.

Tuori, K. (2018), *From Pluralism to Perspectivism*, [in:] G. Davies, M. Avbelj (eds.), *Research Handbook on Legal Pluralism and EU Law*, Edward Elgar Publishing, pp. 39–56.

Velaers, J. (2012), *The Protection of Fundamental Rights by the Belgian Constitutional Court and the Melki-Abdeli Judgment of the European Court of Justice*, [in:] M. Claes et al. (eds.), *Constitutional Conversations in Europe: Actors, Topics and Procedures*, Intersentia, pp. 323–342.

Voßkuhle, A. (2013), *The Cooperation Between European Courts: The Verbund of European Courts and its Legal Toolbox*, [in:] The Court of Justice of the European Union (ed.), *The Court of Justice and the Construction of Europe: Analyses and Perspectives on Sixty Years of Case-Law*, Asser Press, pp. 81–98.

Wendel, M. (2011), *Lisbon before the Courts: Comparative Perspectives*, [in:] J.M. Beneyto, I. Pernice (eds.), *Europe's Constitutional Challenges in the Light of the Recent Case Law of National Constitutional Courts: Lisbon and Beyond*, Nomos, pp. 65–106.

Wendel, M. (2013), *Comparative reasoning and the making of a common constitutional law: EU-related decisions of national constitutional courts in a transnational perspective*, “International Journal of Constitutional Law”, vol. 11, no. 4, pp. 981–1002.

Wendel, M. (2014), *Exceeding Judicial Competence in the Name of Democracy: The German Federal Constitutional Court's OMT Reference*, “European Constitutional Law Review”, vol. 10, no. 2, pp. 263–307.

Wilkinson, M.A. (2017), *Constitutional Pluralism: Chronicle of a Death Foretold?*, “European Law Journal”, vol. 23, no. 3–4, pp. 213–233.

de Witte, B. (2011), *Direct Effect, Primacy and the Nature of the Legal Order*, [in:] *The Evolution of EU Law, Second Edition*, Oxford University Press, pp. 323–362.

Wójtowicz, K. (2014), *Constitutional Courts and European Union Law*, Uniwersytet Wrocławski.

Zemánek, J. (2016), *An 'Entirely-Specific' Situation or a Routine Limitation of the National Autonomy? Slovak pensions XVII of the Czech Constitutional Court*, [in:] R. Arnold (ed.), *Limitations of National Sovereignty through European Integration*, Springer.

Anna Kalisz[2]

The Margin of Appreciation – a Safety Anchor for Constitutional Identity in Semiotic and Legal Contexts[1]

Abstract

Multicentrism has recently been one of the leading paradigms describing legal reality. This not only reshapes the classic concepts and paradigms of law and challenges legal theory and practice, but also puts the emphasis on blurring the lines between legal systems in Europe, rather than on specifying their boundaries. Multilevel protection of human rights may serve as a great illustration of the diversity of interpretative communities.

However, recent political and social trends prove that there is a need for an alternative form of building European identity. Multiculturalism, pluralism and multicentrism are no longer the prevailing perspectives for bolstering Europe's identity, and the concept of human rights has been weakened by contemporary populism and nationalism, as well as their outcomes. In such circumstances it is necessary to address the grassroots process of building a European identity through shaping and strengthening citizens' constitutional consciousness, as well as through integrating them around the principles and values that the constitution is based on. Since

1 This essay is the result of research project no. 2017/27/L/HS5/03245, "Constitutional Consciousness as a Remedy for the Crisis of Discourse and Democracy Deficit in the European Union", financed by the National Science Center (dec. no. DEC-2017/27/L/HS5/03245).

2 Anna Kalisz – is an associate professor at the Marie Curie Sklodowska University in Lublin; attorney-at-law (legal counsel), member of the Bar Association of Attorneys-at-Law, former court-mediator. Currently an expert in European and human rights law in the Judicial Bureau at the Supreme Administrative Court of Poland. Her academic work consists of approximately 90-100 *scholarly publications*. Academic interests to date can be split into several clear fields. They cover not only theory and philosophy, but also consider the issues of legal interpretation (mainly of the European Union law); human rights (especially the general clauses concerning and limiting human and/or fundamental rights); and *Alternative Dispute Resolution* (particularly mediation).

"Europe" concerns more than 500 million EU citizens, the process of building a European identity requires partial stages and elements, and naturally involves both individual and national identities.

The "margin of appreciation" may serve not only as an example of multicentric judicial dialogue, but also as a positive response to the aforementioned sort of needs. However, there is the question of whether it is a tool for providing and protecting the "constitutional identity", or whether it is rather proof that the ECHR has reached a dead end due to the lack of a core European consensus on the delicate matter of social values.

The main goal of this essay is to present the margin of appreciation as being far from the latter. This doctrine (and practical legal tool) links proportionality with subsidiarity within the European space of human rights protection, which means that the state should decide democratically what is appropriate in the domestic environment. This strengthens the above-mentioned dialogue between the ECHR and the domestic courts. The ECHR's main – and growing – role is a constant supervision of national solutions undertaken in order to ensure that the rights laid down in the Convention are not interfered with unnecessarily. This means that the ECHR is approaching the position of sui generis "constitutional court", which, in turn, may also empower European integration. In the area of human rights protection it may help to achieve the convergence in a consensual manner, in spite of ongoing challenge.

The essay *is divided into three sections and gradually narrows* its scope. It starts with a introductory section covering a brief overview of the linguistic, philosophical and practical dimensions of identity per se, European/constitutional identity, and constitutional consciousness – issues which mutually affect and limit each another. The second section covers a brief depiction of the margin of appreciation as an example of a limit on the ECHR's jurisdiction emerging from constitutional identity, and as a legal tool created long before European integration entered into the present multileveled crisis. The last section deals with a case-study that serves as an illustration for the previous considerations.

Keywords: human rights protection, margin of appreciation, multicentrism, alternative identities, European identity, constitutional identity, constitutional consciousness, judicial dialogue, semiotics of law, case-study

In varietate concordia

1. Introduction

The following considerations have been *divided into three mutually connected but separate sections and the scope of the essay gradually narrows*. It starts with an introductory section which provides a brief overview of the linguistic, philosophical and practical dimensions of identity *per se*, as well as European/constitutional identity and constitutional consciousness – issues which mutually affect and limit one another in a multicentric legal world. The second section offers a brief depiction of the margin of appreciation as an example of a limit on the ECHR's jurisdiction, emerging from constitutional identity, and as a legal tool created for mediating the contradictions between "European" and "domestic" identity long before European integration entered into the present multileveled crisis. The last section deals with a case-study based on the jurisdiction of the ECHR and Polish administrative courts, which serves as an illustration for all the previous considerations.

2. Identity issue

2.1. Multicentrism is nowadays perceived as one of the leading paradigms describing legal reality. Multi-level legal systems and legal orders are linked to each other on both the legislative and decisional dimensions. This does not solely reshape the classic concepts and paradigms of law and challenge legal theory and practice, but it also puts emphasis on blurring the lines between legal systems in Europe,[3] rather than on specifying their boundaries.

The multilevel protection of human rights may serve as a great **illustration** of a multicentric legal solution. It is provided not only on the domestic and European level, but it has also been aspiring to cover the global level (though not with complete success). Hence, human rights may be considered an appropriate area for examining both the **advantages** and the

3 "Europe" is hereinafter understood in terms of membership of the European Union and the Council of Europe – as a legal community – rather than in terms of geography *stricto sensu*.

"**traps**" (arising from diversity of interpretations) of the multicentrism phenomenon, as well as the notion of European and constitutional identity.

2.2. "European identity", in turn, is a complex issue. The first issue concerns the concept as such. In spite of the "inspiration from the cultural, religious and humanist inheritance of Europe, from which have developed the universal values of the inviolable and inalienable rights of the human person, freedom, democracy, equality and the rule of law",[4] it is undeniable that remarkably different things were inherited from European history – not just Athenian democracy, Roman law and Judeo-Christendom. There were numerous violations of human rights, such as wars, tyrannies, oppression, slavery, intolerance and inequalities, which also constitute part of the European "inheritance" forming European civilization. Constitutionalizing selective values leads to the question of whether there has ever been – at any time – anything like one European identity, a common "European dream" based on the quoted principles, apart from the current "European project" of Community law within the European Union that certain European states have enjoyed for 6 decades at the most. Furthermore, since Europe in this sense concerns more than 500 million EU citizens, the process of building a European identity requires partial stages and various elements, and it also involves, naturally, individual and national identities.

Identity itself in its practical aspect has an individual **component of choice** coupled with a collective component whereby individuals orient themselves to aggregate groups or collectives. In semiotic and philosophical aspects it has a twofold meaning. The first covers the identification of particular characteristics and peculiarities that distinguish a certain object from the others – a **selfhood,** while the second meaning also covers qualitative identity (of the same nature and characteristics) – a **sameness.** *Ergo*: identity may be viewed as either *sameness* or *selfhood*. According to the philosopher Paul Ricoeur,[5] an individual's identity is their (his or her)

---

4 Preamble to the Treaty of European Union (Lisbon Treaty version, consolidated version) available *via*: https://eur-lex.europa.eu/resource.html?uri=cellar:2bf140bf-a3f8-4ab2-b506-fd71826e6da6.0023.02/DOC_1&format=PDF

5 P. Ricoeur, *Oneself as Another*, Chicago–London 1992, pp. 2–3, 29, 32, 36–37. Ricoeur places a threefold approach which converge in the question of

narrative identity that is characterized by the dialectic of sameness and selfhood. Selfhood implies otherness to such an extent that selfhood and otherness cannot be separated. On the other hand – sameness may denote a numerical identity, such as unity (opposed to plurality) and/or an uninterrupted continuity or a lack of variation and lack of diversity. Thus, they seem to be contradictory to each other, to some extent.

Apart from the linguistic and philosophical analysis (briefly covered for the purposes of this essay), European identity is undeniably linked to the collective **“domestic” identity** – as both its constituent component and, at the same time, balancing counterpoint. “Domestic” identity can be, in turn, regarded in national or constitutional terms, which also leads to analogous uncertainties – is there any unique essence that distinguishes one nation from all the others and that remains common for the majority and also unchanged during history? Or is it rather the question of constitutionalizing selective principles and rules that are considered to be worthy? If so, another issue that arises concerns the creation of such a catalogue and exercising a certain amount of discretion in this process. In particular, when trying to outline identity in a legal manner, it finally comes to the same catalogue as in the European *quasi*-constitutional law. The same principles and values are covered by both the EU’s “constitution” (in its unwritten sense – as treaty law and the general principles) and by the constitutional acts as well as the non-codified[6] constitutions of all European democratic states of law. This suggests that European identity is not necessarily mutually exclusive with national identities in their constitutional sense. But there is also something that differentiates one legal system and the society it serves from another.

The concepts of **constitutional identity** (and also constitutional consciousness as its source) have not been defined in legal science, let alone legal provisions, and they are used in a field of sociology that has not

---

selfhood: a polarity of “self-sameness” and “selfhood” and a polarity of selfhood and otherness.

6 The British example of an unwritten constitution, more: R. Blackburn, *Britain’s Unwritten Constitution* [in:] *Magna Carta Today*, 2015, retrieved from: https://www.bl.uk/magna-carta/articles/britains-unwritten-constitution (accessed: 10.10.2019).

provided a precise definition of the notion either. It is an unclear, abstract and relatively dynamic issue, which also makes it questionable. It also brings back the questions – perennial for legal philosophy – about the nature and origins of law and stresses the discursive elements of law. However, the term became more and more attractive and recognizable[7] and seems to be gaining in importance in public discourse – both on domestic and European levels, particularly due to the tensions and contradictions between them. Constitutional identity arises from the provisions and meta-norms serving as the basis for the entire legal order. The level of awareness regarding law as well as such meta-norms has been defined as **constitutional consciousness.** For the purpose of this essay, the "consciousness"-aspect refers to the constitution as such (constitutional awareness) as well as to the area of individual rights (human rights awareness). This determines their civic, universal and democratic nature.

2.3. Recent political and social trends prove that nowadays there is a **need for alternative** forms of building a European identity.[8] The proposal of outlining such an identity – arising from both the European Union and the Council of Europe – has been challenged by the **de-multi-centralist tendencies** which have arisen throughout Europe today. Leaving the liberal narrative in the times of the "twin-revolution"[9] in bio-tech and info-tech, multiculturalism, pluralism and multicentrism, which have been strictly associated with European identity for decades, are **no longer the prevailing perspectives** that characterize European countries, and the concept of human rights has been weakened by contemporary populism. What we are now witnessing in some European countries is a great return to ideas which combine a mixture of nationalist sentimental attachments

---

7 Within a constitutional science further reading recommended: M. Rosenfeld, *The Identity of the Constitutional Subject: Selfhood, Culture, and Community*, New York, 2010; G. Jacobson, *Constitutional Identity*, Cambridge, 2010; A.S. Arnaiz, C.A. Llivina (eds.), *National Constitutional Identity and European Integration*, Cambridge, 2013.

8 Cf.: L. Rorato, A. Saunders (eds.), *The Essence and the Margin. National Identities and Collective Memories in Contemporary European Culture*, Rodopi, 2009.

9 "*...twin revolutions* of *infotech* and *biotech could reconstruct not just economics* and *societies but our very bodies* and *minds*" – N.Y. Harari, *21 lessons for 21st Century*, London, 2018, p. 7.

with religious traditions, and with anti-democratic and anti-integration resentments. To rephrase the issue in the terms defined earlier: **sameness has encountered selfhood.**

In this sense, sameness, identity understood as unity, **co-creates the common European identity** that arises – *inter alia* – from the elements belonging to the constitutional traditions (constitutional identities) of each European state. In contrast, selfhood – self-identity that implies otherness, asserts the divergence from the others. Contemporary changes to social, cultural and economic reality have not been well received and are perceived by some parts of European society as a great danger to the identity that has been in place until now. In other words, we are probably also witnessing a conflict between the "old" and "new" Europe based on the dialectical conflict between **imitated identity** and **genuine identity,**[10] with the "**struggle for recognition**"[11] in its background.

The question that follows is whether is it possible to encounter the current social emotions and needs (such as fear of losing the narrow, intuitively-known national identity to a broader though not-exactly-known European identity[12]) without reentering the nationalist narration.

---

10 According to Ivan Krastev, "…the transformation [after 1989 – A.K.] that took place was based on the idea […] should imitate the West. Some of the crises we currently see in Eastern Europe express a revolt against imitation. A part of the problem you see in […] Poland is a return to tradition. […] This is the case in many Eastern European states." – available *via*: https://www.dw.com/en/get-ready-for-the-end-of-the-eu-as-we-know-it-says-ivan-krastev/a-48462082 – 24.04.2019 (accessed: 15.08.2019). See also: https://www.journalofdemocracy.org/articles/explaining-eastern-europe-imitation-and-its-discontents-2/ (accessed: 20.09.2019). Cf. also: D. Dolenec, *Democratic Institutions and Authoritarian Rule in South East Europe*, Colchester, 2013, *passim* and I. Krastev, S. Holmes, *The Light that Failed*, London, 2019, *passim*.

11 Cf.: A. Honneth, *Struggle for Recognition* (first published as *Kampf um Anerkennung. Zur moralischen Grammatik sozialer Konflikte*, Frankfurt am Main, 1992), *passim*.

12 Another question worth being pursued in such aspect is: are there any existing European concepts or instruments to support such development or is the "constitutional identity" purely a downward tendency or even it shall be considered as utopian in its nature.

With regard to the **democracy crisis in the process of European integration** (meaning not only the EU system, but also – and for the purpose of this essay mainly – the European system of human rights protection), the issue that needs to be addressed is the possibility of building European identity through shaping and strengthening citizens' constitutional consciousness, as well as through integrating them around the principles and values that serve as the foundation of the constitution (instead of ethnic factors alone). The current "democracy deficit"/"public legitimacy crisis" – which refers to a perceived lack of accessibility to the ordinary citizen and/or lack of representation for the ordinary citizen, as well as lack of accountability of the EU bodies and institutions[13] – may be examined not solely from a European perspective, but also from an individual one. The level of social consciousness about the role of public institutions (mainly in the area of human rights protection) corresponds with the level of constitutional identity. Even though – given the limited scope of this essay – more profound examination of the identity issue seems superfluous, it is worth concluding that in the current situation of European turbulence, constitutional identity may **mediate** between national and European identity.

3. The margin of appreciation as a limiting tool

3.1. The contradictions in question, as well as axiological divergence across Europe, become apparent in different contexts. In the context of human rights they can be illustrated by the term in the title – the margin of appreciation.

The concept of human rights tends to derive its grounds from *dignitas humana,* the very essence of human identity. Multi-centric human rights protection, in turn, involves the discourse on universal (pan-human) identity, and especially on advanced European and national identities, all of which are related to the system of certain values and result from it. Such

13 The European Union has been criticized for its "democratic deficit" since 1979, the year when David Marquand used this expression for the first time – https://www.thenewfederalist.eu/the-questionable-democratic-deficit-of-the-european-union (accessed: 15.09.2019).

discourse implies the need for a tool to mediate inevitable semiotic and cultural differences.

This essay attempts to present the margin of appreciation not only as a doctrine that responds to the necessity to resolve **hard cases**[14] involving such delicate matters as principles and values, but also as a mechanism that takes care of a space where the sameness of the common European identity and community of values encounters the selfhood of local traditions within the area of human rights.[15] The **margin of appreciation may be considered as an expression of constitutional identity**. Both of these terms – the practical tool of margin of appreciation and the abstract concept of constitutional identity – are strictly related in the sense of balancing principles and values[16] concerning human rights with their legitimate and proportional limits. Therefore, they both serve to define the permitted level of divergence in human rights protection.

3.2. Regarding the diverse cultural and legal traditions embraced by each state, it has been difficult to identify and consolidate common European standards – the more delicate and disputable matter they concern, the more difficult this is. Yet, the entire project of European integration is voluntary and based on respect for the culture and sovereignty of each particular state. Thus, the process of establishing the uniform standard of human rights protection in Europe is – and must be – gradual and flexible, like the convergence process as a whole.

The differences, in the meantime, have the **potential to result in conflicts of laws** – not only in terms of legal norms, but also legally binding decisions – on the European and national levels. This potential is being increased by the fact that the European Convention on Human Rights and

---

14 The cases in which the decisional result is not clearly dictated by the legal provisions and norms, which leads to exercising the judicial discretion. R. Dworkin, *Hard Cases*, "Harvard Law Review" 1975, vol. 88, no. 6, pp. 1057–1109.

15 Cf. on the concept itself: G. Letstas, *Two Concepts of The Margin of Appreciation*, Oxford Journal of Legal Studies, 2006, vol. 6, no. 4 (26), pp. 705–722.

16 The concept of such balance see: R. Alexy, *The Theory of Constituional Rights*, Oxford, 2002, *passim*.

Fundamental Freedoms (The Convention[17]) is of a very general, "open-texture" nature, crowded with minimally clarified general clauses in its substantive part. All the clauses refer to common values, but their content may vary from one legal system to another, and the problem seems to increase together with the number of signatory states.

Regarding those, the states within the system of the Convention were equipped by the case-law of the European Court of Human Rights' (ECHR)[18] with a **practical legal tool** – the **margin of appreciation.**[19] This term – also known as the margin of **state discretion** – refers in its essence to the permitted degree of latitude and certain space for manoeuvre that is provided for the national authorities (domestic courts), in fulfilling their obligations under the European law (the Convention).[20] Defining the exact scope of the doctrine, however, is not possible, as can be observed with the

---

17 The text of the Convention available *via*: https://www.echr.coe.int/Pages/home.aspx?p=basictexts&c=

18 *Vide inter alia*: judgments of ECHR – judgment of 7.12.1976, *Handyside* v. *U.K.*, no. 5493/72; judgment of 26.04.1976, *The Sunday Times* v. *U.K.*, no. 6538/74; judgment of 13.06.1979, *Marckx* v. *Belgium*, no. 6833/74; judgment of 22.10.1981, *Dudgeon* v. *U.K.*, no. 7525/76; judgment of 28.11.1984, *Rasmussen* v. *Denmark*, no. 8777/79; judgment of 21.02.1986, *James* v. *U.K.*, no. 8793/79; judgment of 24.05.1988, *Müller* v. *Switzeland*, no. 10737/84; judgment of 29.10.1992, *Open Door and Well Woman* v. *Ireland*, no. 14234/88; judgment of 24.09.1993, *Informationsverein* v. *Austria*, no. 13914/88, 15041/89, 15717/89, 15779/89, 17207/90; judgment of 20.09.1994 *Otto Preminger Institute* v. *Austria*, no. 13470/87; judgment of 24.08.1998, *Lambert* v. *France*, 88/1997/872/1084; judgment of 21.02.2002, *Matyar* v. *Turkey*, no. 23423/94; judgment of 8.07.2003, *Hatton* v. *U.K.*, no. 36022/97; judgment of 22.05.2008, *Petrov* v. *Bulgaria*, no. 15197/02, etc.

19 The legal basis of such doctrine may be found in jurisprudence, particularly that of the French *Conseil d'état*, which has used the term *marge d'appréciation*, although most sophisticated and complex doctrines of administrative discretion have been developed in Germany – G. Nolte, *General Principles of German and European Administrative Law – A Comparison in Historical Perspective*, Modern Law Review Limited, Blackwell Publishing, Oxford, 1994, *passim*.

20 S. Greer, *The Margin of Appreciation: Interpretation and Discretion under the European Convention on Human Rights*, Council of Europe, 2000, p. 5. On the evolution of this doctrine, see also: https://www.coe.int/t/dghl/cooperation/lisbonnetwork/themis/echr/paper2_en.asp (accessed: 15.09.2019.

Strasbourg case-law. Due to the lack of an abstract definition, the margin of appreciation is thus, like constitutional identity, "context dependent", and its limits can be drawn only within a specific case.[21] Notably, at the level of international law such a margin is reached as well as the references to it within the ECHR's rulings co-created the *acquis conventionnelle.*

The margin of appreciation provides the flexibility sufficient to prevent turning potential conflicts of laws into real ones, which can lead to confrontations that are damaging for the process of implementing unified standards of human rights protection in Europe. The sovereignty question has been stressed in this context, since the ECHR is not only obliged to interpret the European Convention, but is also obliged to respect the autonomy of particular states.

The fundamental role of the mechanism in question is to enable balancing not only particular principles, but – extensively – the sovereignty of member states and their **autonomous culture** with the unifying role of the ECHR rulings. The margin of appreciation permits applying the Convention in accordance with the states' own unique legal traditions without flouting the ultimate objective and purpose of the Convention. In such manner it plays a **mediating role** between national and European identity. It does not only strengthen the **judicial dialogue** between the ECHR and domestic courts on the Convention as a "living document", but also empowers a **dialogue between sameness and selfhood**, serving the voluntary integration within the area of human rights protection.

2.3. Hard cases, arising from the confrontation between the ECHR and the national systems (including the role played therein by domestic courts) are reduced – in the light of primacy of the Convention – to the **balance of principles** and values, since constitutional identity is not a term employed by the ECHR. On the one hand the states occasionally view the application of their EHCR obligations differently, but on the other the margin of appreciation allows the smooth functioning of the organs and institutions of the states in relation to the ECHR.

21 N. Lavender, *The Problem of the Margin of Appreciation*, "European Human Rights Law Review", 1997 no. 4, p. 382.

However, there must exist certain principled criteria for the application of the margin of appreciation doctrine. These criteria have been developed in the Strasbourg jurisprudence as: subsidiarity of the Convention (to the national system of effective human rights protection); state interferences prescribed in accordance with law, the pursuit of legitimate and necessary aims in democratic society; and the proportionality of state actions.

Thus, the doctrine of the margin of appreciation links proportionality with subsidiarity within the European sphere of human rights protection, which means that the **state shall decide** democratically what is appropriate in the domestic environment determined by constitutional identity. It may serve as a great example of a solution and **a positive response** to the aforementioned sort of challenges and needs in Europe-state relations – one created long before the European integration fell into crisis.

All this leads to the conclusion that the margin of appreciation should be considered as a sort of **limit for the ECHR's jurisdiction, which emerges from constitutional identity** and the local axiology of a particular state (society).

4. A (Polish) case study – an illustration

The following section presenting "**a margin of appreciation case study**" aims to shed some light on the remit of the doctrine in question and how it is exercised in the Polish legal context.

The ECHR's recent rulings concluding that a particular country has breached the Convention, will reveal a great deal about what the condition of the legal culture in such a state. One of the recent, hot and recurrent issues raised before Polish administrative courts today concerns the citizenship status of persons born in same-sex marriages, when at least one of the spouses is granted Polish citizenship.

The cases concerning **citizenship registration/confirmation** fall under the jurisdiction of both domestic administrative courts and the ECHR, in the latter case – as an element of a right to the protection of private life (**Art.** 8) and of the principle of non-discrimination (**Art. 14**). The basic principle covering that question is ***jus sanguinis***, which can be traced back to Roman law and is currently still common to all the civil law systems in continental Europe, including Poland. It states that a person acquires citizenship at birth – through their parents or a parent or other ancestors. The fact of parenthood had been mostly uncomplicated to confirm up to now. The aforementioned "**twin revolution**" in bio-tech and info-tech not only has been restructuring the economy, society and even the human body and mind, but also causes unforeseeable consequences and brings great changes to the legal area, including the matter in question. One of these unpredicted consequences is the quite recent possibility of same-sex couples bearing biological children. Gamete donation, *in vitro* fertilization, gestational *surrogacy* – though not widely accepted within all legal systems, traditions and religions – make it nowadays entirely possible for **a person in a non-heterosexual relationship**. Therefore, some states have consequently introduced major changes to domestic family law, adjusting the "*mater sempre certa est (pater quem nuptiae demonstrant)*" principle, which goes back to Roman times, and recognizing same-sex couples as parents. Other states did not do this, or only did so partially, employing very sophisticated legal mechanisms to recognize only certain and selected effects. Some are still in the process of establishing their case-law on this matter, since social and scientific advances are almost always ahead of the legislation.

Regarding the Polish *casus* examined below, the **conflict of laws** is governed by: (1) Polish administrative and family law regulations (not recognizing either same-sex marriages or same-sex parents); (2) international private law (which is also, in spite of its confusing name, a Polish regulation) with its unclear "**public order clause**" and – last but not least – (3) international public law (namely, the Convention on the Rights of the Child[22] as well as (4) regional international law (the European Convention along with *acquis conventionnelle*) in conjunction with EU law (and *acquis de l'Union*).

Case no. 56846/15 and 56849/15, ***Schlittner-Hay versus Poland***[23] arose as a consequence of Polish administrative courts' rulings IV SA/

22 The text of the Convention available *via*: https://www.ohchr.org/en/professionalinterest/pages/crc.aspx

23 The summary (in French) is available *via*: http://media.aclj.org/pdf/Schlittner-Hay-contre-Pologne,-Observations-%C3%A9crites-ECLJ,-23-juillet-2019.pdf. Brief depiction (in English) of the cases concerning gestational surrogacy arrangements pending before the ECHR – *via*: https://www.echr.coe.int/Documents/FS_Surrogacy_ENG.pdf 18 (accessed: 18.08.2019).

Wa 925/13 and II OSK 2372/13.[24] The case involves Applicants who are minor children of a same-sex couple. The male twins were carried by and born to a surrogate mother in the State of California (USA), where the same-sex married couple – the intended parents – were also declared officially in the twins' birth certificate "the natural, joint and equal parents" by a Californian court. One of the male spouses – the genetic father of the twins – is a Polish citizen, granted also with Israeli citizenship. The children, after applying to Polish public authorities, were refused Polish citizenship and the appeals were dismissed. In their decisions, the Polish authorities argued that the surrogacy agreement was not valid in the Polish legal system, therefore accepting the judgment of the Superior Court of California would be against the principles of the Polish legal order and the public order clause (derived from international private law provisions), and in consequence the birth certificate could not have any legal effect.

The Applicants complained under Article 8 taken alone and together with Article 14 of the European Convention,[25] arguing that the Polish authorities had breached their rights under the Convention. According to the applicants, the decisions of the Polish authorities were based on considerations relating to the sexual orientation of their legal parents, which abuse the non-discrimination principle. They claim that Poland breached their rights to private and family life by refusing to recognize the family ties to their parents. The case is still pending[26] before the European Court of Human Rights – along with 5 analogous Polish cases concerning this issue.

The main legal problem in question is twofold:

> – whether the ECHR requires its signatory states to recognize the links already legally and factually established among the members of a family in another country

and

> – whether domestic courts exercised their discretion in accordance with the *acquis conventionnelle*, or misused the public order clause and exceeded their margin of appreciation.

24 The case-law (in Polish) available *via* http://orzeczenia.nsa.gov.pl/cbo/query
25 Application communicated to the Polish Government on 26 Feb. 2019.
26 September 2019.

The crucial issue concerns merely permitting the continuation – on the legal level – of the factual parent-child relationship already established and enjoyed between children and their (legal) parents.

The issue had already been partly covered by the **advisory opinion of the ECHR,**[27] concerning the recognition in domestic law of a legal parent-child relationship between a child born through a surrogacy arrangement made abroad and the intended parent (in that case – a mother). The opinion also referred to the margin of appreciation doctrine.

The advisory opinion was requested by the French *Cour de Cassation.* In that case two children were also born in California through a gestational surrogacy arrangement, and their intended parents had difficulties in obtaining recognition in France of the parent-child relationship legally established between them in the United States. In the judgment *Mennesson v. France* (no. 65192/1, ECHR 2014) the Court held there had been a violation of the children's right to respect for their private life, since *"everyone should be able to establish details of their identity as individual human beings, which include[d] the legal parent-child relationship."* This argument, read together with paragraph 100 of the *Mennesson* judgment, regarding *"the importance of biological parentage as a component of identity"*, seems to constitute sufficient grounds for anticipating the forthcoming judgment of the Strasbourg Court.

For the purpose of this essay, the issue of greater importance than the final ruling itself is the question of the permissible margin of discretion. In its opinion, the ECHR deliberated whether Article 8 of the Convention requires domestic law to provide a possibility of recognizing the relationship between a child and the intended parent and whether there is any space for state discretion. In the Court's opinion, two factors carry particular weight: the **child's best interests** and the **scope of the margin of appreciation** available to the states. As regards the latter – *"the scope of the States' margin of appreciation will vary according to the circumstances, the subject matter and the context; in this respect one of the relevant factors may*

---

27 The very first opinion issued in reference to the new Protocol No. 16 of the European Convention that entered into force from 1 Aug 2019 – The Advisory Opinion P16-2018-001, delivered on 10 Apr 2019, available *via*: https://hudoc.echr.coe.int/eng#{"itemid":["003-6380464-8364383"]}

*be **the existence or non-existence of common ground between the laws of the [...] States. Thus, where there is no consensus within the member States** of the Council of Europe, either as to the relative importance of the interest at stake or as to the best means of protecting it, particularly where the case raises sensitive moral or ethical issues, **the margin of appreciation will be wide**. The [...] comparative-law survey* [conducted in §§ 22 – 24 of the opinion – A.K.] *shows that, despite a certain trend towards the possibility of legal recognition of the relationship between children conceived through surrogacy abroad and the intended parents, **there is no consensus in Europe on this issue**"* [§ 43]. Thus, "*[...] a child born abroad through a gestational surrogacy arrangement **requires** that domestic law provide a possibility of recognition of a legal parent-child relationship [...]* **though it "*falls within the States' margin of appreciation*"** [§ 51] and "***Article 8 of the Convention does not impose a general obligation on States to recognise*** **ab initio** ***a parent-child relationship*** *[...]. What the child's best interests – which must be assessed primarily* in concreto *rather than* in abstracto *– require is for recognition of that relationship, legally established abroad, to be possible at the latest when it has become a practical reality.*" Approaching the conclusion, the Court points out that "*[i]t is in principle not for the Court but first and foremost for the national authorities to assess whether and when, in the concrete circumstances of the case, the said relationship has become a practical reality.*" The existing biological and genetic liaison between the child and the intended parent (both in *Mennesson* as well as *Schlittner-Hay* cases) entails that "*the need to provide a possibility of recognition of the legal relationship [...] applies with even greater force.*"

Therefore, the margin of appreciation available to states entails that **the choice of means, alternatives ways of registering as a parent may be acceptable** in so far as the procedure laid down by domestic law ensures that they can be implemented promptly and effectively, **in accordance with the child's best interests**. In other words: "*the child's right to respect for private life within the meaning of Article 8 of the Convention requires that domestic law provide a possibility of recognition of a legal parent-child relationship [...]*", **but** it "*does not require such recognition to take the form of entry in the register of births, marriages and deaths of the details of the birth certificate legally established abroad; another means [...], may* *be used provided that the procedure laid down by domestic law ensures that it can be implemented promptly and effectively, in accordance with the child's best interests."*

The quoted opinion provides fair balance between the autonomy of domestic legal solutions derived not only from statutory acts, but also – in their more profound legal sources –from constitutional identity (a selfhood) and the unified solutions (a sameness), in order to protect the standards arising from *acquis conventionnelle*.

5. Conclusions

From the perspective of the European Convention, the margin of appreciation may be regarded as a notion consistent with constitutional identity.[28] In this context, the doctrine balances not only a "sameness-selfhood" liaison, but also the perspectives of the state and the individual.

Prior to the Convention, which was the first stage on the modern path of European integration, the states had complete power and discretion regarding the protection of human rights at the domestic level. The Convention was endorsed as a minimum standard and the states had the possibility to ensure a higher level of human rights protection as well as the obligation not to decrease such a standard. In this manner the states relinquished a considerable part of their sovereignty, which lead to empowering sameness at the expense of selfhood. This may – and did – generate some tension that, in turn, creates a need to establish a fair balance between two disparate values and interests: the states' interest in maintaining their power and discretion *versus* the individual's interest in benefiting from a high level and a unified standard of rights protection.

Such a legal mechanism as the margin of appreciation may serve as a **tool for mediation** between national identity (domestic traditions and superstitions at times conflicting with the constitutional values) and European identity (understood, *inter alia,* as unified human rights standards). The given case-study is an *exemplum* of such mediation, particularly significant in Polish circumstances, where – mainly for historical grounds – a

28 *Vide*: A. Legg, *The Margin of Appreciation in International Human Rights Law: Deference and Proportionality*, Oxford, 2012, *passim*.

strong sense of national liberty and identity encounters a relatively underdeveloped sense of individual freedom.

However, the question arises of whether it is a tool for providing and protecting "constitutional identity", or it is rather proof that the ECHR has reached a dead end due to the lack of a core European consensus on delicate matters of social values (such as public order, morals or religion values). The margin of appreciation seems to fall into the latter definition as it **creates some room for selfhood within sameness.** While the issue of **deference to the sovereignty of each member state** continues to be raised, the enforcement of the Strasbourg authorities' undertakings ultimately **depends on the good faith and continued cooperation** of each state. With regard to the "open-texture" nature of the Convention, the margin of appreciation may help with this cooperation.

Nonetheless, the margin of appreciation cannot serve solely as a **safety anchor** and a limit for the ECHR's jurisdiction emerging from constitutional identity. It is important to emphasize that it **does not prevail over the minimum standards** arising from the Convention and *acquis conventionnelle.* In this context the limiting tool is also limited itself, which was illustrated in the given case-study.

The illustration of the advisory opinion of 10th April seems to prove that **the margin of appreciation**, despite – or rather as a result – of tension between subsidiarity and universality, **is gaining in importance** at the time of the semiotic crisis in understanding of European common values. Judicial dialogue is particularly significant at the times of abrupt social change, when legal regulations lag behind and it is left to the courts to address the new reality.

The case-study is not only an illustration of multicentric judicial discursive practices – a *sui generis* mediation between European and domestic identity, but also relatively optimistic proof that, in times of turbulence and crisis, *Potestas Iudicandi* shall continue to give more weight to the sophisticated constitutional *acquis* than to the tempting "short-cuts" lined with political and traditional resentments. The ECHR's main and growing role is a consistent and constant supervision of national solutions undertaken in order to ensure that the rights laid down in the Convention are not interfered with unnecessarily. This means that the ECHR – equipped with the competence to pass advisory opinions – is gradually approaching the position of *sui generis* "constitutional court",[29] which, in turn, may also strengthen European integration in the area of human rights protection in a consensual manner, in spite of the ongoing conflict and challenge. And the doctrine of the "margin of appreciation" performs the important function of ensuring that – as stated in the ECHR jurisprudence – "the international protection of human rights and sovereign freedom of action are not contradictory, but complementary."

29 Which had been notice long before Protocol XVI to the Convention was worded and enforced, *vide, inter alia*: R. Harmsen, *The European Court of Human Rights as a 'Constitutional Court': Definitional Debates and the Dynamics of Reform*, [in:] J. Morison, K. McEvoy, G. Anthony (eds.), *Judges, Transition and Human Rights*, Oxford University Press, Oxford, 2007. pp. 33–53.

Bibliography

Alexy, R., *The Theory of Constituional Rights*, Oxford, 2002.

Arnaiz, A.S., Llivina C.A. (eds.), *National Constitutional Identity and European Integration*, Cambridge, 2013.

Blackburn, R., *Britain's Unwritten Constitution*, [in:] *Magna Carta Today*, 2015, https://www.bl.uk/magna-carta/articles/britains-unwritten-constitution

Convention on the Rights of the Child: https://www.ohchr.org/en/professionalinterest/pages/crc.aspx

Dolenec, D., *Democratic Institutions and Authoritarian Rule in South East Europe*, Colchester, 2013.

Dworkin, R., *Hard Cases*, "Harvard Law Review" 1975, vol. 88, no. 6.

ECHR, *Gestational surrogacy*, https://www.echr.coe.int/Documents/FS_Surrogacy_ENG.pdf

ECHR, *The Advisory Opinion P16-2018-001*, https://hudoc.echr.coe.int/eng#{"itemid":["003-6380464-8364383"]}.

European Centre for Law and Justice, *Observations écrites soumises à la Cour européenne des droits de l'homme dans l'affaire Schlittner-Hay contre Pologne*, http://media.aclj.org/pdf/Schlittner-Hay-contre-Pologne,-Observations-%C3%A9crites-ECLJ,-23-juillet-2019.pdf

European Convention on Human Rights, https://www.echr.coe.int/Pages/home.aspx?p=basictexts&c=

Greer, S., *The Margin of Appreciation: Interpretation and Discretion under the European Convention on Human Rights*, Council of Europe, 2000.

Harari, N.Y., *21 lessons for 21st Century*, London, 2018.

Harmsen, R., *The European Court of Human Rights as a 'Constitutional Court': Definitional Debates and the Dynamics of Reform*, [in:] J. Morison, K. McEvoy, G. Anthony (eds.), *Judges, Transition and Human Rights*, Oxford, 2007.

Honneth, A., *Kampf um Anerkennung. Zur moralischen Grammatik sozialer Konflikte*, Frankfurt am Main, 1994.

Jacobson, G., *Constitutional Identity*, Cambridge, 2010.

Knipp, K., *Fear of the future' has EU in turmoil*, https://www.journalofdemocracy.org/articles/explaining-eastern-europe-imitation-and-its-discontents-2/

Krastev, I., Holmes S., *The Light that Failed*, London, 2019.

Lavender, N., *The Problem of the Margin of Appreciation*, "European Human Rights Law Review" 1997, no. 4.

Legg, A., *The Margin of Appreciation in International Human Rights Law: Deference and Proportionality*, Oxford, 2012.

Letstas, G., *Two Concepts of The Margin of Appreciation*, "Oxford Journal of Legal Studies" 2006, vol. 6, no. 4 (26).

Nolte, G., *General Principles of German and European Administrative Law – A Comparison in Historical Perspective*, Oxford, 1994.

Porchez, M., *The questionable "democratic deficit" of the European Union*, https://www.thenewfederalist.eu/the-questionable-democratic-deficit-of-the-european-union.

Ricoeur, P., *Oneself as Another*, Chicago–London, 1992.

Rorato, L., Saunders A. (eds.), *The Essence and the Margin. National Identities and Collective Memories in Contemporary European Culture*, Rodopi, 2009.

Rosenfeld, M., *The Identity of the Constitutional Subject: Selfhood, Culture, and Community*, New York, 2010.

The Margin of Appreciation, https://www.coe.int/t/dghl/cooperation/lisbonnetwork/themis/echr/paper2_en.asp

Milena Korycka-Zirk[2]

The Political Versus Proportionality – Methods of Justifying Conflicts of Constitutional Values[1]

Abstract
The main purpose of the paper is to confront the individualistic conception of resolving conflicts between constitutional values with the non-individualistic conception. This is done by drawing on ideas from political philosophy and legal concepts of interpretation that concern principles of law. These pre-existing premises of constitutional conflicts can result in different interpretative presuppositions in methods of solving collisions of constitutional principles. Different methods have different justifications: on the one hand, the principle of proportionality implies a preference for broadening the scope of protection of individual rights, and on the other, the concept of "the political' expresses a preference for constitutional order (which reflects "political unity").

Keywords: principle of proportionality, the political, constitutionality of law, constitutional, rights and liberties

1. Introduction

The polarisation of political-legal discourse between liberal constitutionalism and its antithesis, i.e. the position asserting the supremacy of

---

1 This article is a result of the research project no. 2017/27/L/HS5/03245, "Constitutional Consciousness as a Remedy for the Crisis of Discourse and Democracy Deficit in the European Union", financed by the National Science Center (dec. no. DEC-2017/27/L/HS5/03245).

2 Milena Korycka-Zirk – Professor at the Nicolaus Copernicus University in Torun (Faculty of Law and Administration). She received a PhD degree (2006) and doctor habilitatus of legal sciences degree (2017) in Law. The field of her scientific interest: significance of analytical method and logic in scrutinizing law, theory of principles of law, constitutional review, philosophical implications for the test of the principle of proportionality.

constitutional unity, is a confrontation, from a philosophical-legal perspective, between two methods for resolving conflicts of values – in relationships between individuals, or an individual's relationship with a social group. While pointing out that a potential conflict of values can be resolved by non-individualistic argumentation, in the sense that one can consider the conflict as a collision between an individual and a group, which is not accepted in liberal doctrines, I suggest that aggregative argumentation, i.e. perceiving the group to be the holder of constitutional values, is accepted in non-liberal theories, such as the idea of the supremacy of constitutional unity (which I propose is the antithesis of constitutional discourse based on the application of the principle of proportionality). Liberal constitutionalism, which is based on the assumption that the constitutional norm can function as a defence shield for the individual and protect them against values that gain the support of the majority in legislative discourse, and which draws extensively on argumentative theories of law,[3] is founded on the assumption that in constitutional discourse (i.e. the procedure for controlling the constitutionality of an act of the legislature) any value is relevant if it protects the autonomy of the individual, as long as this is not precluded by the principle of harm.[4] The consequence of this assumption is, firstly, that the idea of constitutionalism is based on a plurality of substantive constitutional norms (the vast majority of legal principles) justified by different individual interests constituting the determinants of the content of sub-constitutional norms, and secondly, that this assumption has the effect of shifting the evaluation of the potential relation of compliance of a substantive constitutional norm with a sub-constitutional norm, to a

3 R. Alexy's theory of practical discourse or J. Habermas's theory of communicative action are relevant here. On the former see: R. Alexy, *Theorie der Juristischer Argumentations. Die Theorie des Rationalen Diskurses als Theorie der Juristishen Begrundung*, Suhrkamp, Frankfurt am Main, 2001, p. 259 ff., on J. Habermas' conditions of correct communication ("presupositions of argumentation speech") see: J. Habermas, *Communication and the Evolution of Society* (trans. T. McCarthy), Beacon Press, Boston, 1979, p. 23.

4 On the harm principle see: J.S. Mill, *On Liberty*, Pennsylvania State University, Electronic Classics Series, Faculty ed. Jim Manis, Hezleton, PA, 1998, p. 13. As Mill puts it, the basis for limiting individual autonomy can only be to "prevent harm to others".

norm or norms of a procedural nature. In liberal constitutionalism, such a role is played by the principle of proportionality, in supranational law the terms limitation clauses or limiting clauses are used (with the proviso that the conflict of substantive norms primarily concerns declaratively defined human rights and freedoms), while in American constitutionalism, on the other hand, the notion of tests is used (e.g. strict scrutiny[5]). Irrespective of the terminology, the essence of resolving conflicts of values framed in the form of substantive norms is shifted to procedural presuppositions. The principle of proportionality, by its nature a very specific procedure within the premises of argumentation theory, is consequently constructed for these theories to ensure the ethical correctness of a discourse in which the constitutionally relevant values coming into conflict *in concreto* – i.e. when a concrete regulation of a legislative act is juxtaposed with the constitution – are subjected to a weighing procedure in a manner appropriate to the requirements of discourse. In other words, the test of the proportionality of the limitation of one value in favour of another must meet the ethical requirements of discourse – based on the requirement of coherence with the essence of liberal constitutionalism. Such requirements are an interpretive presumption of preference for the right and freedom of the individual when confronted with a value protecting the public interest; relevance for the discourse of values protecting the individual, although unsupported by the statutory discourse as the one that exemplifies in principle the will of the majority (this is a consequence of parliamentarism as a representation of the will of the majority of voters); furthermore, the public interest should be a representation not of an abstractly assumed will or will understood aggregatively, but of the individual interest, and as such should receive the support of public authority. The principle of proportionality is thus a consequence of the recognition of the relevance of

5 For more on the rigor of "strict scrutiny" see e.g.: R.G. Spece, D. Yokum, *Scrutinizing Strict Scrutiny*, "Vermont Law Review" 2015, vol. 40, pp. 285–351. The authors identify the constitutional hierarchy of values as a consequence of applying a particular type of constitutionality test (p. 287). On the three types of rigor (tests) of the constitutionality of the law, see e.g.: N. Kilasonia, *Constitutionality of Differential Approach in Electoral Disputes – scrutiny tests*, "Constitutional Law Review" 2016, no. 9, pp. 80–82 (78–95).

each individual interest through its inclusion in constitutional discourse, and through its requirements it creates assumptions for the balancing of values consistent with those of liberal constitutionalism.

A contrary position on the subject of conflicts of values fundamental to the constitutional order is presented by the concept of the test of "the political" for the choice of a preferred value. The archetype for this position is Schmitt's theory of the "political unity" of the constitutional order. The test of "the political" for constitutional disputes is an emanation of illiberal constitutionalisms, be they constitutions based on a rejection of these assumptions or, more often, through a process of interpreting constitutional substantive norms in an illiberal direction or rejecting, in the process of applying the principle of proportionality, the ethical principles of the correctness of constitutional discourse (balancing values based on the preference of individual interest) indicated above.

What actually is the essence of "political unity"? First and foremost, it is the assumption of the constitutional irrelevance of arbitrarily defined values and then directing constitutional discourse in a direction devoid of argumentation through this procedure. The irrelevance of certain substantive norms, i.e. based on the conclusion that they are not essential to the constitutional order, is primarily the result of a negative test of the "unity" of these norms. In other words, they do not gain, in a political sense, the title of norms that exemplify national unity. This negative evaluation may result either simply from being a value not supported by the majority (exposing a lifestyle, views, customs not shared by the majority of society), or, in a more regime-like form, it may result from the suppression of forms of life that do not fit into the public morality imposed by the ruling party in acts of the legislature. The expression of unity is thus the sovereign, understood as the majority, or the Schmittian subject with supreme power (not necessarily taking the will of the majority into account). Most importantly, the will of the sovereign, possibly understood in both these ways, is not limited.

The inevitability of the need to resolve conflicts of constitutional values, beyond the reflection of political science, is originally a theoretical-legal issue. It engages the notion of an intrinsically non-conclusive principle as a constitutional norm.

In both types of justification for the ways of resolving conflicts of principles, the specificity of the functioning of the principles becomes apparent at a different constitutional moment. In the application of the principle of proportionality, the non-definitive character of the principles as norms materially open to balancing will be activated in the procedure of proportion assessment. This means that, essentially, a principle can be weighed (optimized) in its application only at the moment of a conflict. In the application of the test of the political, the non-absolute character of a norm taking the form of a constitutional principle is exposed even before it comes into conflict with another value. The political narrative is directed to excluding the need to assess the legal and factual possibility of limiting the application of the principle through a narrative exposing the thesis of the need for primary elimination of the conflict. Either the elimination of the need to resolve the value dispute occurs by interpreting the substantive norm in a way that eliminates its essence (eliminating the core of the right or freedom that does not acquire the characteristic of political "unity") so that no conflict with the value gaining the support of the public-political interest arises at all, or the exclusion of the principle occurs through a deformed application of the principle of proportionality in constitutional jurisprudence. This deformation consists in the rejection of the requirements of the ethical correctness of constitutional discourse, i.e. the rejection of the requirements of the application of the principle of proportionality coherent with the assumptions of liberal constitutionalism (as outlined above).

This thesis of the article, already covered quite extensively in this introduction, concerns the possible juxtaposition in contemporary constitutionalism of two methods of justifying disputes over constitutional values, namely the test of proportionality and the test of the political. In the remainder of the study, this thesis will primarily be subjected to an analysis aimed at identifying its philosophical-legal archetypes and the assumptions underlying the theoretical-legal concepts.

2. Proportionality

The principle of proportionality – which takes the form of a limiting clause, the literal wording of which manifests the established constitutional order of preferences, where the protection of rights and freedoms is the principle and their limitation the exception – is a consequence of the philosophical-legal assumptions of liberal constitutionalism. It thus entails highlighting a constitutional principle that materially declares the protection of an individual right or freedom as a model for sub-constitutional legislation. It is a declaration of liberal democracy, i.e. the majority that expresses its will in sub-constitutional acts is subject to limitations with regard to this will. At the same time, the importance of protecting the constitutional autonomy of each individual potentially opens up the problem of conflict – the collision of these principles. Constitutional principles or the principle of proportionality in their constitutional formulation (reinforced by their genesis, i.e. the political philosophy of individualism inherent in liberalism) create an order of preference – the priority of the protection of rights and freedoms in conflict with the interest exposed in the sub-constitutional regulation, and at the same time determine the procedure of its limitation (the correctness of constitutional discourse). The *pro libertate* preference for constitutional protection and the formulation of the conditions for the correctness of the limitation procedure must be mutually coherent and not negate the essence of liberal constitutionalism – i.e. that the constitutional norm is treated as a protective barrier against the unrestricted will of the majority or of the rulers. Determining the weight of a constitutional principle in the value-balancing procedure (applying the principle of proportionality) is an *in concreto* assessment of constitutional jurisprudence and the application of limitation clauses by the international judicial bodies established to protect rights and freedoms.[6] Firstly, this

6 Within the jurisprudence of the European Court of Human Rights *in concreto*, the assessment of value relations additionally takes into account another factor: the so-called margin of appreciation, i.e. the interpretation and assessment of the limitation of the enjoyment of rights is made to some extent on the basis of the cultural specificities of a particular state. For the leading cases in the creation of this construction see: *Cossey* v. *U.K.* 1990, *Caskey, Jaggard, Bron* v. *U.K.* 1997, *Marckx* v. *Belgium* 1979, *Johannes* v. *Norway* 1996, *Otto-Preminger Institute* v. *Austria* 1994, and *Lehideux and Isorni* v. *France* 1998. For more on the application of the principle of proportionality in the case-law of the European Court of Human Rights see: *Zasada proporcjonalności na tle orzecznictwa Europejskiego Trybunału Prawa Człowieka*, [in:] D. Bunikowski,

means there is a sphere wherein the content of the rights and freedoms of the individual are not determined by the text of the constitution or an international protection document, resulting in the actual protection of a specific constitutional right or freedom (even if the text is understood declaratively with regard to the inherent nature of the right and freedom, the concept of constitutional rights and freedoms is thus possibly understood more broadly; or if common constitutional traditions and the sharing of common values declared in documents of international protection of individual rights[7] and freedoms are taken as the object of the declaration of protection, the order of preference and the boundaries of limitation is an open question). Secondly, this opens up the problem of continuity or discontinuity with respect to the earlier jurisprudence of the so-called core or essence of rights and freedoms – that is, the jurisprudential continuity of the interpretative determination of such limits of a right, the breaching of which by a sub-constitutional act implies the absence of its constitutional or treaty protection. The latter two factors constitute a margin that, with the preference for the political in constitutional discourse, are used to mask the actual rejection of the interpretative presumption *pro libertate* in constitutional jurisprudence.

The essence of the application of the principle of proportionality in jurisprudence – underpinned by the theory of the principles of law and thus developed extensively on the grounds of legal theory[8] – boils down

R. Musiałkiewicz (eds.), *Koncepcje integracji w Europie w XX i XXI wieku*, Toruń, 2008, pp. 89–105.

7 The leading cases in the case-law of the Court of Justice of the European Union in this regard are *Erich Stauder* v. *City of Ulm*, *Internationale Hendelsgesellschaft GmbH* v. *Einfuhr und Vorratsstelle fur Getreide und Futtermittel*, *J. Nold, Kohlen und Baustoffgrosshandulung* v. *European Commission*. For more detailed discussion see: M. Korycka-Zirk, *Teorie zasad prawa a zasada proporcjonalności*, LexisNexis, Warszawa, 2012, pp. 158–162.

8 I would consider R. Dworkin's texts the most representative texts in this regard, in particular *The Model of Rules*, "The University of Chicago Law Review" 1967–68, vol. 35, no. 14, pp. 14–46, as well as the work of R. Alexy, in particular *A Theory of Constitutional Rights* (trans. J. Rivers), Oxford University Press, Oxford, 2002. Both these concepts are based, firstly, on the assumption that constitutional rights and freedoms are norms that take the form of legal principles and that this is essentially a type of norm that is differently applied.

to the substantive-legal aspect (of course, the formal aspect examined in the framework of the application of the principle of proportionality is also important, i.e. the requirement to maintain an appropriate type of sub-constitutional act for the possibility of introducing a limitation of a constitutional right or freedom, and the related requirement to maintain appropriate principles of decent legislation in this respect, which, however, does not create a margin of appreciation on the grounds of which the possibility of applying a limitation clause in a manner that "masks" an action in compliance with constitutional or treaty regulations is clearly revealed). This can be reduced to two problems. The first is how to justify the constitutional correctness of the application of the proportionality test, i.e. the collision of principles-norms defined in a very general way, even while specifying jurisprudentially and theoretically what the test is actually supposed to mean. Within civil law culture, the prevailing theory in this respect is that of Robert Alexy, developed on the basis of the case-law of the German Federal Constitutional Court, which, firstly, does not differentiate the application of the principle of proportionality with regard to the type of constitutional right subject to limitation; and secondly, asserts that the effect of the positive proportionality test, i.e. finding a limitation consistent with the constitution, contains the assumed element of recognition resulting from the application of the sub-principle of the proportionality test, defined as the proportionality test in the strict sense, which is only an assessment of the so-called legal possibilities of limiting the right resulting from assessments that fall outside the cause-and-effect reasoning

---

Within legal theory, the only controversy is whether the difference between a legal principle as a norm and another type of norm (legal rule) is a logical difference. A. Aarnio refers to this controversy as the dispute between the so-called strong and weak demarcation thesis; for more detailed discussion, see: A. Aarnio, *Taking Rules Seriously*, ARSP Stuttgart, 1990, pp. 180–181. Here it should be noted that the definition of principles as norms is made (especially after the doctrinal acceptance of the work of R. Dworkin) by showing the otherness of their application in relation to legal rules, hence the indispensable use of the work of H. Hart, in particular *The Concept of Law*, Oxford Clarendon Press, Oxford, 1961. This is also noted by J.R.T. Muñiz, see: J.R.T. Muñiz, *Legal Principles and Legal Theory*, "Ratio Juris" 1997, vol. 10, no. 3, September, p. 269.

(instrumental rationality). These features of the proportionality test are somewhat different in American constitutional jurisprudence, where they are characterised by a difference in the application of the proportionality test in accordance with the type of right to be restricted and, secondly, by a difference in the discretion allowed and the degree of discretion held by the court in assessing proportionality.[9]

However, returning to the analysis of the sub-principles constituting the principle of proportionality, which is of key importance for the civil law system, and proceeding to their characteristics, one should also note a very important cultural factor affecting the application of the principle of proportionality, i.e. the attachment to interpretative textualism, even when the interpreted text is the constitution, and its effect and cause, i.e. a specific reduction of constitutional interpretation consisting in the elimination, in the process of applying the law, of philosophical and legal considerations, is present as a preconception of the constitutional text. In other words, the tendency to interpret only the linguistic text of the constitution is an effect, but it also entails, in the application of the principle of proportionality, the elimination (visible in the justifications of the judgements of constitutional courts) of non-textual considerations that are important for the understanding and interpretation of individual sub-principles of the principle of proportionality (i.e. especially the requirement to interpret *pro libertate*, and the unconstitutionality of aggregative reasoning – i.e. assuming that it is possible to assess the necessity to limit constitutional law through utilitarian argumentation; in other words, that when assessing proportionality, the majority argumentation typical of parliamentary discourse can be used as an argument – i.e. the situation of protecting the rights of a greater number of people, even if this right were to be touched less drastically by the protection of an individual constitutional right, it

9 American constitutionalism differentiates between strict scrutiny, intemediate scrutiny and rational basis scrutiny in the application of assessing the preservation of the proportionality of a limitation of a constitutional right. For a broader discussion, see: M. Korycka-Zirk, *Rodzaje testów judical review a zasada proporcjonalności*, "Archiwum Filozofii Prawa i Filozofii Społecznej" 2022, no. 2(31), pp. 54–69 and the literature cited therein.

can be used as an argument that prevails for constitutional settlement in the application of the principle of proportionality).

In its constitutional application, the principle of proportionality consists of three tests (sub-principles) which the constitutional court evaluates when assessing whether a sub-constitutional regulation is constitutional: the principle of effectiveness (the "factual requirement", meaning that its assessment entails the necessity of using cause-and-effect arguments typical for empirical evaluations; so in the assessment of this test, the sub-constitutional regulation is evaluated in terms of whether it is able to achieve its goal); the principle of necessity (the "factual-legal" requirement, meaning that the court examines whether the sub-constitutional regulation limiting the constitutional right is necessary, in the sense of whether the same effect can be achieved in another way, by encroaching less on the constitutional right; here the reduction of the constitution to a mere text, without the basis of liberal constitutionalism, allows the use of utilitarian argumentation, i.e. the necessity for the group, by virtue of its greater representation, to be able to prevail over the more important constitutional interest, but not the one with greater social representation); and the principle of proportionality *sensu stricto* (the "legal requirement", which essentially means evaluating and weighing only constitutionally significant values supported by the law).

The principle of proportionality thus understood can create a trap for itself, i.e. for its individualistic assumptions. Above all, the jurisprudence has not laid down precise criteria for a possible limitation of a constitutional right in accordance with the type of right. In other words, with a right that is particularly sensitive in terms of the preservation of individual autonomy, e.g. freedom of speech, developing particular strictures in the application of the sub-principles of the principle of proportionality could result in the practical impossibility of its limitation by a sub-constitutional act. Constitutional jurisprudence limiting such a fundamental right would not only *in concreto* have to justify the correctness of the application of the principle of proportionality, which is not difficult in a situation where the interpretation of the constitution is reduced to the text and leaves some discretion in the application of the principle of proportionality *sensu stricto*, but such a ruling would have to undermine the procedural requirements developed in the case-law for the strict assessment of proportionality in a situation where a right recognised as essential in the case-law is involved (this process of assessing the sharpening of proportionality requirements and limiting discretion in this respect can be observed in the application of strict scrutiny in American case-law). Strengthening the protective effect should also be achieved by redefining the assumption of the constitutionality of sub-constitutional acts. In this case as well, drawing on the American constitutionalism focused on jurisprudence and legislation, one should – in accordance with the textual wording of the limitation clauses – treat the protection of the right as a principle, and not its limitation, and conclude that, at least with regard to rights and freedoms of importance for the autonomy of the individual, the argumentation should be reversed and the procedure for the application of the proportionality test should be based on the presumption of the unconstitutionality of a limitation of a right or freedom of importance for the autonomy of the individual. Furthermore, the assessment of the legal weight of conflicting principles in a strongly textual legal culture makes it possible to justify applications of the principle of proportionality that are not consistent with legal constitutionalism as constitutional effects. These are the fundamental pitfalls that allow the argumentation of the antithesis of liberal constitutionalism to be introduced into institutions that arose from the achievements of individualist thought, i.e. the essential protection of individual autonomy and the need to create a counterbalance to parliamentary discourse within constitutional jurisprudence.

3. The political

The Schmittian "unity" of the constitution[10] is currently taking on the role of a very strong standard that is based on a revision of liberal constitutionalism. The focus of this critique is the collision of constitutional norms, a notion which is central to the present work. For since all interests are taken to be equally important, each having a claim to be taken into account within the procedures of governance (as limitations on the content of the

10 In analysing this theory, I draw on my earlier research included in the paper: M. Korycka-Zirk, *Filozoficznoprawny wymiar kontroli konstytucyjności*, TNOiK, Toruń, 2017.

law), the essence of constitutionalism is necessarily the effort to balance and protect these interests, based on the procedure of the co-application of conflicting interests. The liberal pluralism of constitutionally protected values implies the need for a procedure for the proportional resolution of conflicting laws protecting these interests. A consequence of liberal pluralism is the multiplicity and complexity of constitutional discourse; hence the conclusion is that the constitution does not express unity, entailing that an entity is needed to eliminate this collision *in concreto*. Parliament was the original entity that eliminated collisions, and it still fulfils this function, but it has nevertheless proved to be a body that often only articulates goals and aspirations that gain majority legitimacy. Individual rights and freedoms that failed to attract this support appeared to lack political and, consequently, legal representation. The development of constitutionalism, in realising the liberal demands encoded at its core, thus assigned the role of guardian of liberal rights and values to the judiciary (either a universal court, e.g. in the United States, or a constitutional court, being a model more common in Europe). Democracy itself (understood as majority rule without the definition "liberal" or the institutional guarantee of the realisation of this adjective) did not realise the essence of constitutionalism. The relationship between the sovereign-people and the constitution was defined by the judiciary – as the institution which is able to resolve the conflict of a multiplicity of potentially conflicting constitutional principles objectively, i.e. without the representation of political interest.

In the theory of the political, the multiplicity of core constitutional interests subject to constitutional protection and inevitably coming into conflict *in concreto* is seen as a threat to the identity of the nation and as a denial of the individual's natural need for clarity and sense that there is homogeneity in the expressed essence of law, including the constitution. The political, i.e. the way of eliminating constitutional conflict presented in the Schmittian vision of the constitution, is thus based on the need to eliminate ambiguity in the constitution's determination of how a conflict of constitutional values is to be resolved. Underlying this assumption is, of course, a particular vision of power and law. The former is justified politically, not legally; the latter is not supposed to give rise to potential legitimacy for non-political power, i.e. one not representing a political interest, and this is the nature of the judicial power. This means that the political, as a form of justification for the elimination of conflicts of constitutional values, rather than the means of resolving them, is opposed to the transfer of any conception of power to the judiciary, especially that of a discretionary nature. As an emanation of the concept of the political, Schmittian unity therefore links the essence of the constitution to the closure of the content of the constitution rather than to its complexity and openness. In Schmitt's conception, this is justified by the assumption that the political will constitutes the constitution, i.e. its text, as an expression of the power establishing the constitution.[11] Consequently, then, the guarantor of unity thus understood is the subject with supreme political power. The latter, in Schmitt's terminology, has the necessary legitimacy to be the sovereign. Thus, if the constitution is to express the will of the sovereign, it expresses the will of the politically strongest holder of state power. This is not parliament (and on this issue the theory of liberal constitutionalism and Schmitt's theory agree) but the supreme sovereign, the one who is actually able, within the complex structure of governance, to enforce this unity. Schmitt thus relocates the holder of sovereignty from the people to the de facto sovereign revealed in crisis, in conflict. In terms of the assessment and legitimation of power, the political can be described as temporarily revealing a lack of unity, and uncertainty, and thus defining *in concreto* who the sovereign is. It transpires that the authority acquiring its constitutional justification may be as undetermined by the content of the constitution as the potential way of resolving conflicts of principles protecting individual rights. The political, then, is a form of complete definition of the position of the individual (supported by the constitution understood as an enforcing unity), and a complete form for the determination of the form of governance. The guarantor of the unity of the constitution is potentially the one who determines this unity and his authority and legitimacy to perform this function are based on the argument of power, i.e. the possibility of the actual realisation of unity.

Threats to unity are determined in fact and not in law: specific formal decisions by state bodies declaring that there is a lack of unity – a state of

11 C. Schmitt, *Nauka o konstytucji* (trans. M. Kurkowska, R. Marszałek), Fundacja Świętego Mikołaja, Redakcja "Teologii Politycznej", Warszawa, 2013, p. 54.

exception – are not necessary. A state of exception, potentially also a collision of constitutional values, falls within the scope of the situations that can occur in the state.[12] The holder of sovereignty can consider everything and nothing as realising the characteristics of such a state.[13] Pluralism, the multiplicity expressed by liberal constitutions, is directed against the state, since it relativises the state. Unity is the concrete reality of the state, loss of unity discredits the state, undermines its supremacy, the law in the theory of the political (based on the preference of the state over law – MKZ) is not able to function in the abnormal situation it is in when the state does not express this unity.[14] Unity is a necessary element of law, and also of the constitution – this is the conclusion to be drawn from Schmitt's theory. The control of constitutionality thus aims at the preservation of unity, and this unity cannot be realised by judicial bodies whose activity is based on the settlement of disputes. For Schmitt it is not the guarantor of the constitution that is called upon to eliminate the dispute between constitutional values; it is strictly a body that exercises control with regard to the excesses of parliament when it creates laws that undermine unity. At the same time, the state of exception, that is, the state of departure from normal circumstances, is not precisely defined, just as unity is not precisely defined; it is a situation of opposition between law and order.

The state in the theory of liberal constitutionalism is identified with the constitution; the constitution expresses the limits for the state (i.e. its power) and thus provides guarantees for the autonomy of the individual confronted with it. The control of the constitutionality of the law is therefore external to the organs of power – the political subjects of power. In contrast, since in the theory of unity the essential function of the constitution is the protection of the state, the subject of control cannot be external to power – it must be the centre of power, and the strongest centre, because only such a subject is able to reveal its sovereignty i.e. supreme power. The judicial function must not be jeopardized; for example, according to Schmitt (in the framework of the theory of the political) if the courts

12 *Idem*, *Teologia polityczna i inne pisma*, Wydawnictwo Aletheia, Warszawa, 2012, p. 45.
13 *Ibidem*, pp. 233–234.
14 See *Ibidem*, pp. 227–228, 232.

became organs of power by exercising control of constitutionality, they would lose their judicial function.[15] A constitutional court would create a semblance of justice, the adjudication of the constitution would politicise the administration of justice, thus a better solution would be, according to Schmitt, the judicialisation of politics,[16] i.e. the transfer of the function of the guardian of the constitution to an essentially political body.

The concept of the political is based on the assumption that there is a social need for authority, understood as a strong centre of power. Since liberalism opens up disputes, it is therefore seen as not generating authority.

In Schmitt's conception of the political, the unified state does not express its will through the ruling majority, for democratic majority procedures do not express the principle of identity, i.e. the identification of the people with the political unity, since this is only reflected in direct democracy.[17] For Schmitt, the undermining of the role of the law in political discourse opened the way to a "new" concept of the sovereign, i.e. one with actual power in states of exception. Similarly, he viewed the courts as being unable to express unity due to their lacking sovereign power.

The different positioning of the sovereign subject in the theory of the political (i.e. as the supreme power with the most political instruments), not linked to the people, is justified in two ways: firstly as a non-decision-making subject (except in situations of direct democracy) it does not express its will politically, and secondly it is not in itself a factual unity, for it expresses very different individual interests. Therefore, in Schmitt's theory, the concept of the "people" is reduced to an abstract concept, rather than a factual-political entity. It is thus defined as a unified aggregate, an abstract will, and as such can be seen to express political unity.[18] Characteristically, the people are not seen as a class of identical individual interests protected constitutionally, but are viewed as an abstract, assumed entity, the vehicle of political unity, the engine of the constitutional act – the essence of the constitution. The abstraction becomes a higher form than

---

15 D. Dyzenhaus, *Legality and Legitimacy: Carl Schmitt, Hans Kelsen and Hermann Hellee in Weimar*, Oxford University Press, Oxford, 1999, pp. 110–111.
16 C. Schmitt, *Nauka...*, p. 210.
17 *Ibidem*, p. 347.
18 See: C. Schmitt, *Nauka...*, pp. 31, 36.

the text of the constitution, it is an abstract form to which the subject actually exercising political power can refer in order to justify a particular understanding of the text of the constitution. For the will expressing unity is prior to the text. Political unity is indivisible, the representation of this unity through constitutionally regulated centres of power is always a representation of – and not a substitute for – this unity. The constitutional act as an act of granting does not arise from nature but is the result of convention, in which the sovereign subject plays a key role.[19] The genesis of the constitution thus lies in the political power of a subject independent of any other power. In this way, Schmitt accepts the definition of the sovereign as precisely one whose power is not derived from another power, with one aspect of this power being constitutive power.[20] Nevertheless, he notes, firstly, that the constitutive power[21] is not bounded by the constitutive text and, secondly, that the sovereign power understood as indicated above is an abstract concept that acquires reality in states of exception.[22] Actual sovereignty is inextricably bound up with the state of exception. Thus, a situation in which political unity is threatened reveals the sovereign and at the same time has a self-defining nature, since identifying the essence of the constitution necessitates defining the sovereign. The constitution, as a vehicle of unity, is always an act of power, of the one who wields political power.

Therefore, the guardian of the constitution, i.e. of political unity, firstly requires a situation of conflict that threatens the unity of the state (and thus the constitution) and, secondly, an authority that can be identified as possessing supreme political power. The theory of the political argues that such an authority finds its justification in the need to eliminate conflict and restore the state of unity. The constitution, in this theory, first and foremost constitutes an organisation[23] that maintains political unity

19 R. Cristi, *Carl Schmitt on Sovereignty and Constituent Power*, "Canadian Journal of Law and Jurisprudence", vol. X, no. 1, 1997, p. 195.
20 *Ibidem*, p. 190.
21 *Ibidem*, p. 198.
22 *Ibidem*, p. 190.
23 Cf.: C. Schmitt, *Dyktatura*, Biblioteka Kwartalnika Kronos, Warszawa, 2016, p. 278.

by creating public order in the state and ensures a state of normality. The preference is for a constitutional norm of an organisational nature rather than a substantive norm expressing a declaration of individual autonomy. Public order and security are treated as synonyms of unity.

Amendments and repeals of constitutional provisions are the result of the functioning of the constitution, expressing the stability and continuity of the legislative power, and thus do not threaten political unity.[24] Hence a state of exception is not brought about by a change being made to the provisions of the constitution – an amendment of the constitutional laws in Schmitt's terminology – or even if the constitution is abolished, that is, if the constitution is repealed without the removal of the legislative power, for instance in order to define the subjects of political power differently.[25] A constitution is not a constitution by virtue of its content, but because it is the expression, in the highest form, of the unity of the constituting political power. The constitution is thus the effect and at the same time the source and ultimate goal of the unity and hence the identity of the state. It is an absolute value that requires protection and justifies violations even of specific constitutional provisions in order to restore the constitution as a whole, the absolute constitution – that which constitutes unity.[26]

The essence of the constitution, understood as unity, is only revealed in states of exception, when there are grave conflicts of interest. When there is a severe threat to public unity, order and security, this is treated as the state in which the sovereign is revealed. A state of exception shows who has supreme political power in the state. Schmitt does not posit who must be the sovereign subject in the normal functioning of the state – the monarch, the people, or a powerful group in the state,[27] instead he points out that since the source of the constitution is not an abstract norm or state of nature but a concrete constituting power, and that the constitution itself is a decision about the type and form of political unity, this is a value to

24 *Idem*, *Nauka...*, p. 170.
25 *Ibidem*, p. 179.
26 *Ibidem*, p. 62.
27 R. Cristi, *Carl...*, p. 198.

be protected.[28] If this is the case, then the constituting power can change its holder. This is how Schmitt's concept of the sovereign should be understood: when there are crucial conflicts of interest, the sovereign is he who reveals himself to be the representative of the constituting power.

Schmitt's vision of constitutionalism and the entire conception of the political are based on the assumption of a discontinuity of political thought rather than its historical continuity.[29] This is also a fundamentally different basis from that on which the concept of liberal constitutionalism is grounded. The latter, through the inherent need for a continuation of the liberal foundations of constitutionalism, provides a material basis for the use of preferences to protect the individual interest in the application of the constitutional principle of proportionality. In contrast, the theory of the political locates preference in the abstract assumption of the existence of the will of the people, which needs unity and consequently a guardian. As such it can only be an entity wielding strong political power, because only in this way can it ensure order and security, and this gives rise to the social authority of government. Viewing the constitution as an effect of the realisation of political power, i.e. revealing the unity of the state, does not imply, as in liberal constitutionalism, the specific content of the constitution. The consequence of political unity seen in this way, and the openness to changes in the content of constitutional provisions, is the mobility of the subjective location of sovereignty – i.e. the supreme centre of power. In constructing the concept of the sovereign, Schmitt adopts effectiveness as the key assumption: it is effectiveness that ensures political unity in a situation of constitutional emergency.

Thus, since sovereignty manifests itself as the authority to make the final decision on a state of exception,[30] i.e. a state in a state of emergency, it is necessary to clarify when the authority must manifest itself, that is,

---

28 E.W. Böckenförde, *The Concept of Political: A Key to Understanding Carl Schmitt's Constitutional Theory*, "Canadian Journal of Law and Jurisprudence" 1997, vol. X, no. 1, p. 11 (5–19).

29 J. Seitzer, *Carl Schmitt's Internal Critique of Liberal Constitutionalism: Verfassungslehre as Response to Weimar State Crisis*, "Canadian Journal of Law and Jurisprudence" 1997, vol. X, no. 1, p. 216 (203–224).

30 E.W. *Böckenförde, The Concept...*, p. 9.

when a state of conflict occurs (i.e. when the state of unity is in danger) and why it is undesirable.

Schmitt sees the sovereign as a subject empowered to save the endangered political unity of society,[31] but what does this mean? Pluralism is a threat to the state, the exclusion of political unity i.e. the integrity of the state.[32] Similarly, in Schmitt's conception of the political, the threat is posed by closure through the legal norm or non-political judicial power, the domination of the factual, of ad hoc political judgements over the legal text. Such phenomena are seen as eliminating efficiency, in the sense of agile decision-making, and introducing uncertainty that threatens public order and security (political unity). Pluralism,[33] as a situation wherein the idea of unity is not expressed through political and legal institutions, threatens the concept of the constitution as an effect of the fusion of society and state, i.e. unity. In the theory of the political, the constitution is the state, whereas in the concept of proportionality the constitution is a barrier to the state. Extra-constitutionality, i.e. an abstractly assumed will for the unity of the people as different as possible from the text of the constitution, is the inviolable core of constitutionalism in the theory of the political. Its principles are those that that determine the unity of the people or those on the basis of which social conflicts can be resolved. This substantive (content) core should not be subject to amendment, at most only the constitution can be amended, and this unity can be expressed differently. The aim of unity is to protect the constitutional order from political crises. The guardian of the constitution is he who protects the

31 *Ibidem.*

32 D. Leydet, *Pluralism and the Crisis of Parliamentary Democracy*, "Canadian Journal of Law and Jurisprudence", vol. X, no. 1, 1997, p. 53.

33 As D. Leydet notes, in Schmitt's view, the liberal state is subordinated to the pursuit of the interests of the ruling party, whose members in parliament are obliged to vote in a certain direction. This implies a lack of realisation of the interests of the people and this in itself is not the norm. See: D. Leydet, *Pluralism...*, pp. 53–54.

constitutional order from particular political crises, but also the one who is able to charismatically articulate the constitutional order.[34]

4. Conclusion

Juxtaposing the two types of justifications for the protection of specific constitutional values – the more legally focused proportionality test and, on the other hand, the concept of unity based on political discourse, one must first of all conclude that the focus of academic research on illiberal concepts does not imply their acceptance as alternatives for resolving conflicts of constitutional values, but it does imply an awareness of the fragility and ease of undermining the foundations of constitutionalism and the constitutional act, properly understood. The theory of constitutional unity is based on the basic social and psychological need for security and certainty. Around such political-legal argumentation, a vision of the constitution and its guardian is created which is fundamentally different from that of liberal constitutionalism. "Ambivalence" is seen to threaten the constitution in the declaration whose constitutional value is important. Being considered as subject to and constituting the value of the constitution, rights and freedoms inevitably come into conflict and require *in concreto* weighing in the procedure of assessing the constitutionality of sub-constitutional acts (which often also express a constitutionally protected value). In contrast, the concept of unity diminishes the constitution by claiming that it is in essence an empty act (i.e. the text of the constitution is of that nature), and arguing that the constitutional court – a body that does not represent the people (the nation) – decides what the constitution actually is. This argument can be strengthened if the weighing process employed in the application of the principle of proportionality lacks transparency. Liberal constitutionalism is thus confronted with a situation of dissonance, of a painstakingly developed legal culture based to a large extent on what Ronald Dworkin called political morality, i.e. on the assumption that successive generations of lawyers merely add more

34 J.P. McCormick, *The Dilemmas of Dictatorship: Carl Schmitt and Constitutional Emergency Powers*, "Canadian Journal of Law and Jurisprudence" 1997, vol. X, no. 1, p. 163 (163–187).

chapters to the same book, thus preserving the essence of the book's narrative. This unfolds in the context of a hostile political environment and often when there is unwillingness in legal circles to continue the narrative. Thus, an elaborated method of applying the principle of proportionality with directed recognition assumed in its application is not sufficient in a situation where, firstly, this directedness is no longer exposed and, secondly, the application of sub-principles of the principle of proportionality, especially of proportionality *sensu stricto*, i.e. balancing constitutionally relevant values, makes it possible to justify results that are revolutionary in relation to the existing political morality. At the same time, the analysis of these two radically different models for resolving constitutional disputes leads one to reflect on the difficulty of emancipating legal discourse from political discourse. In turn, in a way that is even potentially imperceptible, this poses a danger to the foundations of the rule of law: legalism in the application of the principle of proportionality, understood as creating an undirected *pro libertate* recognition of the body applying the laws, actually implies anti-constitutional conceptions. If we are dealing with an anti-constitutional understanding of the constitution, there is, in turn, the anti-legalism of the basic link with the declaration of the principle of legality (the basis for the declaration of the legal order as based on the rule of law is the norm of the constitution). The constitution as it is properly understood (i.e. in line with the assumptions of its historical and cultural foundations associated with liberal constitutionalism) is no longer such an act. In this regard, with the use of the same term for fundamentally different concepts, the constitution in the theory of unity is an act that is, on a fundamental level, differently understood, and thus is socially and politically difficult to grasp. The fundamental question remains why non-liberal theoretical positions continue to use the term "constitution"? If they are based on the assumption that individualism is not the optimal form for solutions in a normative system, e.g. law, consequently it should not use the term constitution, as it evokes strictly liberal connotations and above all has value in the political and legal discourse thanks to the doctrine of liberalism (for liberalism takes into account that the individual functions within multiple normative systems: moral, religious, etc. and draws consequences from this multitude – it is not the role of law to duplicate other normative systems; liberal constitutionalism, by declaring the autonomy of the individual, leaves the individual free to follow the guidelines of a particular normative system; the law remains materially reductive towards them, based on the principle of harm and the coexistence of individuals). In other words, the social and psychological perception of the constitution as an act relevant to legal and social culture is the result of Dworkin's aforementioned book, the main narrative of which has been defined by social liberalism, and to deviate from this narrative is no longer to add another chapter to the same book but to start writing a new book with the same title. The logical conclusion to be drawn from this is that non-liberal conceptions are firstly unable to build from the outset (without using concepts developed by liberal doctrines that have accepted values in legal and social culture) their own narrative for legal culture, and secondly they realise that the conception of the constitution constructed in liberal culture has such a high value that an attempt to change it for another, thus the departure from the name "constitution"– rather than basing the understanding of the name constitution on the assumption that it is a homonymously ambiguous name, i.e. it can have extremely different connotations – will leave no illusions as to what consequences the theory of constitutional unity has for the protection of the fundamental rights of the individual. Accordingly, we may observe elements of masking through the use of the term "constitution", which ascribes meaning to aconstitutional provisions. For the actual protection of the fundamental rights of the individual in the model of liberal constitutionalism the principle of proportionality is crucial, so it is important to work out the procedural aspects of its application, i.e. the differentiation of its application depending on the type of right infringed, the reversal of the presumption of constitutionality into a presumption of unconstitutionality with regard to the infringement of particularly important constitutional rights resulting in a change in the burden of proof, so that the non-liberal justifications of the understanding of the constitution are clear in their assumptions.

Bibliography

Aarnio, A., *Taking Rules Seriously*, ARSP Stuttgart, 1990.

Alexy, R., *A Theory of Constitutional Rights* (trans. J. Rivers), Oxford University Press, Oxford, 2002.

Alexy, R., *Theorie der Juristischer Argumentations. Die Theorie des Rationalen Diskurses als Theorie der Juristishen Begrundung*, Suhrkamp, Frankfurt am Main, 2001.

Böckenförde, E.W., *The Concept of Political: A Key to Understanding Carl Schmitt's Constitutional Theory*, "Canadian Journal of Law and Jurisprudence" 1997, vol. X, no. 1.

Cristi, R., *Carl Schmitt on Sovereignty and Constituent Power*, "Canadian Journal of Law and Jurisprudence" 1997, vol. X, no. 1.

Dworkin, R., *The Model of Rules*, "The University of Chicago Law Review" 1967–68, vol. 35, no. 14.

Dyzenhaus, D., *Legality and Legitimacy: Carl Schmitt, Hans Kelsen and Hermann Hellee in Weimar*, Oxford University Press, Oxford, 1999.

Habermas. J., *Communication and the Evolution of Society* (trans. T. McCarthy), Beacon Press, Boston, 1979.

Hart, H., *The Concept of Law*, Oxford Clarendon Press, Oxford, 1961.

Kilasonia, N., *Constitutionality of Differential Approach in Electoral Disputes – scrutiny tests*, "Constitutional Law Review" 2016, no. 9.

Korycka-Zirk, M., *Filozoficznoprawny wymiar kontroli konstytucyjności*, TNOiK, Toruń, 2017.

Korycka-Zirk, M., *Rodzaje testów judical review a zasada proporcjonalności*, "Archiwum Filozofii Prawa i Filozofii Społecznej" 2022, no. 2(31).

Korycka-Zirk, M., *Teorie zasad prawa a zasada proporcjonalności*, LexisNexis, Warszawa, 2012.

Leydet, D., *Pluralism and the Crisis of Parliamentary Democracy*, "Canadian Journal of Law and Jurisprudence" 1997, vol. X, no. 1.

McCormick, J.P., *The Dilemmas of Dictatorship: Carl Schmitt and Constitutional Emergency Powers*, "Canadian Journal of Law and Jurisprudence" 1997, vol. X, no. 1.

Mill, J.S., *On Liberty*, Pennsylvania State University, Electronic Classics Series, Faculty ed. Jim Manis, Hezleton, PA, 1998.

Muñiz, J.R.T., *Legal Principles and Legal Theory*, "Ratio Juris" 1997, vol. 10, no. 3, September.

Schmitt, C., *Dyktatura*, Biblioteka Kwartalnika Kronos, Warszawa, 2016.

Schmitt, C., *Nauka o konstytucji* (trans. M. Kurkowska, R. Marszałek), Fundacja Świętego Mikołaja, Redakcja "Teologii Politycznej", Warszawa, 2013.

Schmitt, C., *Teologia polityczna i inne pisma*, Wydawnictwo Aletheia, Warszawa, 2012.

Seitzer, J., *Carl Schmitt's Internal Critique of Liberal Constitutionalism: Verfassungslehre as Response to Weimar State Crisis*, "Canadian Journal of Law and Jurisprudence" 1997, vol. X, no. 1.

Spece, R.G., Yokum D., *Scrutinizing Strict Scrutiny*, "Vermont Law Review" 2015, vol. 40.

Zasada proporcjonalności na tle orzecznictwa Europejskiego Trybunału Prawa Człowieka, [in:] D. Bunikowski, R. Musiałkiewicz (eds.), *Koncepcje integracji w Europie w XX i XXI wieku*, Toruń, 2008.

Martin Škop[2]

The Indifference of Law to Literature[1]

Indifference to others and indifference to the fate of the whole is precisely what opens the door to evil.[3] (Václav Havel)

Abstract

The chapter focuses on the importance of literature in the construction of legal consciousness and legal identity. In the text, these concepts merge because their meaning is the same from the perspective of literary narrative. It will therefore focus on three areas in which the possible contribution of fiction to the formation of legal consciousness is evident: imagination, interpretation and identity. These are areas related to the conception of law as a social phenomenon embedded in society and exploiting social ties and structures. Literature can therefore be seen as a possible "catalyst" that creates an image of law and possible ways of its reception by society. *Belles-lettres* (sophisticated literature) will not be the dominant institution creating legal meaning. Still, it can influence the change of interpretive frameworks

1 This study is the result of a research activity supported by the Grant Agency of the Czech Republic, Reg. No. GA19-12837S – "Law in Literature: Qualitative Analysis of the Image of Law in Belles-Lettres at the Turn of the 19th and 20th Century". The English version of this article is a result of the research project no. 2017/27/L/HS5/03245, "Constitutional Consciousness as a Remedy for the Crisis of Discourse and Democracy Deficit in the European Union," financed by the National Science Centre (dec. no. DEC-2017/27/L/HS5/03245).

2 Martin Škop is an associate professor at the Department of Legal Theory, Faculty of Law, Masaryk University, Brno, Czech Republic (PhD in 2004 at Masaryk University in *Theoretical Legal Sciences*). As a teacher, he participates in teaching legal philosophy, legal theory, sociology of law, and media law. Critical legal studies, law and literature, and sociology of statutory drafting are among his scientific interests. He has published four monographs in Czech (*Law and Violence; Law in Postmodern Situation; Law and Passion; ...Law, Language, Narrative*) and many peer-reviewed articles. He chaired the *Argumentation* conference organized in Brno every two years with WoS-indexed proceedings. For 2019–2027, he has been appointed to the Dean's office of the Law Faculty.

3 V. Havel, *Speech presented on 8 May 1993*, http://old.hrad.cz/president/Havel/speeches/1993/0805.html

of law, reinforce the related content of values, and (de)legitimize sources of law. These consequences are particularly evident in the literature from the end of the 19th century and the beginning of the 20th century, which shaped – among other things – the legal identity of the contemporary Czech Republic.

Keywords: law and literature, legal identity, literature of the 19th – 20th centuries, legal imagination, legal consciousness

The title of the article is obviously false – misleading, and a caricature. But it is a prompt for law not to be indifferent to its context and the society in which it functions. Law is not indifferent to literature: it regulates it, takes note of its practices, and is partly connected to the same object: the text.[4] Nevertheless, it is clear that literature (belles-lettres) has much more to offer law, even if law does not make sufficient use of it. That is where the indifference of law lies. Literature, in particular with regard to the national or European or international context, is as much a carrier of values as law. Literature is also much freer in expressing values and can therefore work with them explicitly. Moreover, not being bound by formal procedures, it can more freely express the current conception of values in society and shape national or even European identity. Law should therefore pay heed to it: not in the sense of its potential authoritative role. Through its actors, law should be able to draw on the values and cultural anchorage the literature offers.

This chapter therefore turns to literature as a bearer of values and one of the factors that can influence the interpretation of law in the direction of socially shared values and thus help their presence in law as such. Literature is able to respond in a timely manner to the social situation, the hidden currents in society, and possible transformations of values. It is therefore desirable for law to use this source and to be able to deal with how society is developing or what its foundations are. As Kamil Zeidler mentions, literature has the ability to humanize lawyers and, on the other hand, to improve the legal consciousness of non-lawyers.[5] It is a tool for

4 See e.g. K. Zeidler, *Prawo i literatura. Garść uwag spóźnionych*, [in:] J. Kamień, J. Zajadło, K. Zeidler,. *Prawo i literatura*, Wydawnictwo Uniwersytetu Gdańskigo, Gdańsk, 2019, pp. 15–28.

5 *Ibidem*, p. 19.

the dissemination of information about law, but also in law, within the legal community,[6] and not only among lawyers.

According to a study conducted by Kathryne M. Young and Katie R. Billings, there are multiple ways in which the possession of cultural capital is connected to legal consciousness: the greater the cultural capital, the better the ability to navigate law, including the ability to defend one's rights.[7] People with a high level of cultural capital are able to act in the same way as the legal-related elite, or are able to ask for help more often than people with a low level of cultural capital. There is no doubt that cultural capital is partly formed by navigation in the arts, including literature. Patterns rendered through literature are able to reflect the legal environment and influence both its perception by the audience and its use by professionals. Even a legal expert may succumb to the way law is generally interpreted in the literature and begin to see law through this prism.

The situation today is quite different from the one at the turn of the 20th century, when the modern constitutional identity of contemporary Central and Eastern European states was slowly emerging. At the time, belles-lettres was one of the dominant sources through which people gained information about the world around them. About things, phenomena, people and situations they did not know from their everyday life. Including a further transformation of the roots of the national revival that culminated in the Czech lands in the mid-19th century.[8] The images offered by literature could influence not only the general view of the world, but also the premises on which the perception of the world was based. Including, of course, law. The images created by literature may have shaped contemporary legal consciousness. Slowly, indirectly, gently. The importance of literature in the past does not mean, however, that literature could not once again become one of the foundations shaping the contemporary

6 R. Mańko, *W stronę krytycznej filozofii orzekania: Polityczność, etyka, legitymizacja*, Uniwersytet Łódzki, Łódź, 2018, p. 107.

7 K.M. Young, K.R. Billings, *Legal Consciousness and Cultural Capital*, "Law and Society Review" 2020, vol. 54, no. 1, p. 50.

8 For further information see e.g.T.G. Masaryk, *Česká otázka. Snahy a tužby národního obrození*, Pokrok, Praha, 1908.

legal identity, legal consciousness and concept of law in the countries of Central and Eastern Europe.

Undoubtedly, it is very difficult to respond to a kind of universal law: law that is an abstract idea that works in the same way everywhere. Law is life and must necessarily be reflected in the life of a particular society. It depends on a particular social or cultural identity. It is associated, as James Boyd White mentions, with the processes of thought and conversation, or the culture of legal argumentation.[9] If it is to be comprehensible, it must be in harmony with society. Every right is associated with a specific identity that shapes its practical image and creates a "living mechanism" capable of regulating important social conditions. Without a connection to cultural and social identity (in our case both national and European), effective regulation is not possible.

This chapter will focus on the use of literature in law (the use of law). It focuses on the necessity of constitutional (cultural and social) identity and its connection to legal practice. The aim is to present a picture of possible ways of thinking about law as a cultural artefact that both exploits and shapes the identity of a particular community, including the role of literature in shaping constitutional consciousness. For it is only the combination of law with other social institutions that can create an effective framework (context) for its action. Thereby, legal or constitutional consciousness is reinforced. Legal institutes (and institutions) that can be associated with the consciousness existing in society gain social acceptance with greater ease.

1. Law and literature: The formation of identity

Let us be clear about two initial theses: first, law is not causally determined by literature. Second, legal science is capable of absorbing the potential offered to it by the Law and Literature movement. There has already been a great deal of writing in expert literature on the relationship between law and literature, and in my opinion there is no need to defend this thesis.[10]

---

9 J.B. White, *Law as Language: Reading Law and Reading Literature*, "Texas Law Review" 1982, vol. 60, no. 3, p. 436.

10 See e.g. M. Škop, T. Smejkalová, M. Štěpáníková, *Právo a literatura – brněnská spojeni*, "Právník" 2019, no. 1, vol. 158, pp. 67–85; M. Škop, *Law*

Legal science is sufficiently familiar with what belles-lettres (or even literary science) has to offer. At the same time, there is no doubt that belles-lettres is causally incapable of influencing law:[11] it can act as a co-factor in the formation of legal identity and influence the interpretative environment[12] or participate in the (re)interpretation of history.[13] It is, however, not a formal (authoritative) source of law, nor does it ensure the validity or invalidity of legal rules. It would also be wrong to claim that it shapes, directly and in isolation, legal consciousness or legal culture. Nevertheless, it can participate in such formation. Belles-lettres[14] can therefore influence legal culture[15] and shape legal consciousness in conjunction with other impulses. In this sense, literature helps to shape legal identity, legal consciousness and the overall image (and acceptance) of law in society.

We will therefore focus on three areas where the potential contribution of belles-lettres to the formation of legal consciousness is evident: imagination, interpretation and identity. These are all areas related to the concept of law as a social phenomenon embedded in society and drawing on social ties and structures. We can perceive literature as a potential "catalyst" creating an image of law, and therefore the possible ways of its acceptance by society.

Constitutional identity, or constitutional consciousness, is a part of any legal culture. According to David Kosař and Ladislav Vyhnánek, in addition to normative dimensions, social, political and historical dimensions are also a part of constitutional identity.[16] At the same time, they highlight

---

and Literatura – a Meaningful Connection, "Filozofia Publiczna i Edukacja Demokratyczna" 2015, vol. 4, no. 1, pp. 6–20.

11 Cf. J.H. Wigmore, *A List of Legal Novels*, "Illinois Law Review" 1908, vol. 2, no. 9, pp. 577–578.

12 S. Levinson, *Law as Literature*, "Texas Law Review" 1982, vol. 60, no. 3.

13 I. Ward, *Law, Literature and History*, "Law and Critique" 2021, 10.1080/1535685X.2021.1872953.

14 For relevant literature for the Czech Republic see M. Štěpáníková, *List of 50 Legal Literary Fictions in Czechoslovakia*, [in:] M. Štěpáníková, M. Malaník, T. Smejkalová, M. Škop, *Argumentation 2019*, Munipress, Brno, 2019, pp. 39–49.

15 For legal culture see e.g. M. Šejvl, *Kritika Legal Origins Thesis a pojem právní kultury*, "Právník" 2013, vol. 152, no. 5, pp. 425–446, 440.

16 D. Kosař, L. Vyhnánek, *Ústavní identita České republiky*, "Právník" 2018, vol. 157, no. 10, p. 855.

the problem of the split between "legal" and "popular" concepts of constitutional identity. They point to the potential split between the legal approach through the text of the constitution and the traditional narratives at work in society. At the same time, they offer a way out of this problem: education or the strengthening of participation.[17] What is evident from this is that traditional (non-legal) narratives influence legal identity or legal consciousness without necessarily using purely legal conceptions derived from the professional legal environment.

The solution offered by Kosař and Vyhnánek is rational. At the same time, it can be added that literature can play a (minor) role. It is a tool that can strengthen educational mechanisms and help form constitutional consciousness and identity. This does not mean that literature is a propaganda tool of power. Rather, it can reflect the fundamental human themes that make up the basic constitutional narrative. Therefore, it is not about a kind of "reprogramming" the consciousness of the population, but about drawing attention to the existing frameworks and drawing addressees into the "sphere of law." Thus, it has the potential to strengthen their consciousness of law in accordance with authoritative sources.

2. The literary image of legal consciousness

In the last quarter of the 19th century, realism made its way into belles-lettres in the Czech lands of Austria-Hungary. This trend, which also highlighted the social problems and hard lives of people from precarized social groups in both urban and rural areas, or the problems of women, drew attention to people who lived hidden from the eyes of privileged groups. This process – albeit rendered through literature – of drawing attention to social inequalities provided information that strengthened constitutional identity and legal consciousness. It is difficult to build an overall socio-cultural concept of the constitution (in its broadest sense, including political action) without a large group of people, without their ideas and without the ability to reflect on their lives and perspectives. It

17 *Ibidem.*

is only through the combination of legal patterns and everyday interpretive frameworks that the addressees can engage with and accept official narratives.

I do not believe that literature presents a comprehensive solution capable of strongly influencing constitutional identity and consciousness. Such a perspective would be naive. It is, however, one of the tools: one capable of identifying existing social inequalities, and one capable of strengthening the consciousness of constitutionality. Literature, besides pointing out problems, can offer solutions: not necessarily practical ones, but solutions that can be emotionally grasped and that can thus contribute to the realizing of one's role in the process of building a legal (constitutional) identity. Let's take a look at an example.

In 1889, Gabriela Preissová published the short story Gazdina roba (The Farmer's Woman),[18] which she reworked into a dramatic work in 1890.[19] The theatre play shows the life of a woman who decides to follow her love – a married man. The drama shows the hardships that a woman living in an unmarried relationship with a man must face, including a tragic ending. The social condemnation she must face, including the fact that "law" is not on her side. Today it is (hopefully) difficult to put oneself in the situations she had to face and the apparent disdain she was subjected to. Yet it can be understood as a struggle for equality and a struggle for one's own identity. Her fate is subordinated to conservative village life and she has no chance of escaping it. This feminist perspective breaches interpretive frameworks because it shows the inexcusableness of a context in which women do not have the chance to make choices and decisions about their own lives.

Of course, neither rural nor urban life was changed by the picture Preissová rendered. However, it drew attention to situations that were interpreted as obvious and natural, even though they were not and are not. What is important is that the drama Gazdina roba had the chance to influence attitudes towards similar cases and contribute to their

18 G. Preissová, *Obrázky bez rámů*, J. Otto, Praha, 1896, pp. 59–104.
19 G. Preissová, *Gazdina roba: drama o třech jednáních*, F. Šimáček, Praha, 1890.

reinterpretation. There was a chance that the legal elites would realize that equality of law was not real equality.

In Gazdina roba, but also in other similar plays, an image of society is formed that is far from the current concept of human rights and therefore constitutionality, but it is through similar narratives that an awareness of a human and his or her position in society is built. Regardless of his or her social status. It is an element that, with its emotional charge, can show a woman's difficult struggle for her rights: without being aware of the modern concept of human rights. That makes such a story all the more powerful. Its effect is unintentional but makes the audience think – even today – about the inalienable right to self-determination, which is undoubtedly part of the Czech constitutional identity.

3. Imagination as part of the relationship between law and literature

One of the manifestations of the connection between law and society is imagination. Imagination, the functioning of which can be helped by the use of cultural patterns and consciousness expressed also in literature. Law is a complex of relationships, only a part of which (the dominant one) is linked to legal rules and court decisions. For them to work properly, it is necessary to use other resources and tools: values, people's behaviour, social context, etc. Only law closely linked to social identity can work effectively. For this, relevant legal (constitutional) consciousness is necessary. The overall social impact of law is defined by individual legal actors who not only possess formal legal knowledge, but also legal consciousness. Law, for its existence, necessarily needs social patterns connecting it to society.

Knowledge of law is stochastic at any point in time and can only be expressed imperfectly in a system model. The legal system and law as such are fluid and relative, without the need to change normative texts. Kent Greenawalt, for example, considers the possibility of determining law only by examining its formal aspects to be naive, because it makes no sense without a connection to the moral and political values of the actors.[20] However, the value framework of law does not derive from law

---

20 K. Greenawalt, *Law and Objectivity*, Oxford University Press, New York,

alone. Law is not a closed system of values isolated from society and its manifestations. For this complexity and the unattainability of knowing all the sub-elements of law, including its value framework, it is necessary to have a "legal imagination." Without the capability of imagination and the **assumption** that the whole system is capable of ensuring the proper functioning of law in accordance with the dominant values (not always explicitly expressed in the Constitution), its application in practice would be excluded.

James B. White points out that it is essential to imagine the world we describe in the text as the real world.[21] Including all its components: a world composed only of formally impeccable rules cannot work. It must be a world in which one can make one's own decisions, create one's own parallels and, above all, connect it to other worlds created by society. The "world of law" can only be real to the extent that it accepts the transition between itself and other social contexts. It cannot be completely isolated from the life of society and therefore from the shifts that are taking place in it. It is not about abstract symbolism, but about the connection of law to a concrete social context. It is impossible to petrify the interpretive links in law and stabilize its position. It could affect its comprehensibility and consequently its capacity to regulate. This could undermine the identity of law and society or people, so to speak. Law cannot be preserved in time, as this would undermine its operability and make its social application more difficult.

The whole functional complex of relations connected with law is not to be found in legal regulations only. To apply legal rules correctly, it is essential to know how to apply the rule, in what ways it confronts reality. This is done through unwritten legal rules (meta-rules) arising from the use of language, the assumptions of a functioning society and other social patterns. Law is associated with stories that shape its concrete image. It provides information about all the rules binding the artificial and ideal world partially described by the legal norm.

1992, p. 12.

21 J.B. White, *When Words Lose Their Meaning*, University of Chicago Press, Chicago and London, 1985, pp. 8–9.

For the ability to imagine, we require a certain degree of continuity.[22] Frames on the basis of which other variable elements are formed. It is not anarchy, but neither is it causality. By using imagination based on a defined context, we are able to predict consequences and formulate future policies. This framework is also shaped by the values on which law is based and which it shares with society. Values that encapsulate the infinite possibilities of the dynamics and interpretation of the legal text, as well as its very creation and its action. This is not necessarily limited to one cultural pattern, i.e. national and European legal identities do not necessarily come into contrast, for example. It always depends on what is acceptable and what is accepted by society.

If law loses its continuity and connection with society, it loses its visible past and the present becomes fragmented.[23] It cannot establish and legitimise its institutes. One of the negative aspects of the current law is the loss of continuity and getting bogged down in minor details that are only marginally related to the meaning and purpose of legal regulation. Because of this, the ability to predict and reconstruct the legal text is then lost. The number of those who are able to copy repeatedly adopted formulas is increasing and those who are able to create them are vanishing.[24]

Let's contemplate the connection between law and values again. Law cannot meaningfully regulate society without values. When adopting values – often not explicitly included in law – it is necessary to rely on the values shared by society. Not in the sense of sociological analysis, but in the sense of argumentation: what values are capable of legitimising legal instruments. In this respect, culture has been shaped over a long period of time by, among other things, literature, which is a useful guide that shapes state identity and therefore the image of law and the limits of its application.

I believe that in the Czech environment it is impossible to cling to strict formal rules: think of the works of Franz Kafka or Jaroslav Švejk. It is

22 I. Ward, *Law, Literature and History...*

23 J. Baudrillard, *Simulacra and Simulation*, The University of Michigan Press, Ann Arbor, 1994, p. 10.

24 G. Binder, R. Weisberg, *Literary Criticism of Law*, Princeton University Press, Princeton, 2000, p. 11.

impossible to abstract from human ideals of law without further consideration, if we remember what was one of the elements of Karel Čapek's work. And it is also impossible to abandon the absurd image of a totalitarian society capable of prosecuting a person for an ironic text on a postcard, as Milan Kundera described it in his Žert (The Joke). The image of the Czech and Moravian village will only become plastic if we imagine its inhabitants' relationship to law through the prism of the work of Ladislav Stroupežnický (Naši furianti, Our Swaggerers) or Alois and Vilém Mrštík (Rok na vsi, A Year in a Village). This can make it obvious that belles-lettres has the ability to cultivate law and make it more connected to the society and culture in which it is situated. It offers legitimating elements that are not artificial, but which create interpretive frameworks that define the understanding of a particular element. In this way, literature can deepen the ability to interpret and empathize with the perspective of others.[25]

This is not unique to legal interpretation. On the contrary, it is one of the proofs that it is connected to how social interpretative frameworks work. In all cases, values are the source of any interpretation.[26] Legal rules are not the only way in which values are expressed (the standard-setter uses them to express their understanding of the right and desirable conduct), but also an object that will be extracted from the legal text only if the relevant values can be identified.

4. Literature and relationship to the identity of law

The chapter is prefaced with indifference. Ignoring the shared concept of values and grasping (understanding) them in a different way is one of the manifestations of indifference. We already know that legal consciousness is an essential part of the functioning of law. It operates not only through knowledge of law, but also through the acceptance of the values that accompany law and, reciprocally, law helps their transcendence into social relations. Therefore, indifference cannot manifest itself in ignoring their

---

25 J. Gaakeer, *The Future of Literary-Legal Jurisprudence: Mere Theory or Just Practice?*, "Law and Humanities" 2011, vol. 5, no. 1, p. 186.

26 E.D. Hirsch jr., *The Politics of Theories of Interpretation*, "Critical Inquiry" 1982, vol. 9, no. 1, pp. 235–247, p. 235.

content or creating their content artificially for the sole purpose of legal assessment. Neither can it manifest itself in the absence of content. Ergo, the values would represent an empty form only.[27]

If we accept the social role of law, it is clear that the mere general concept of "values" would not do for us. This is enough for an abstract description. For real use, it is not necessary to define them, but it is also not sufficient to work with their labels, i.e. just to name them. It is important to find the content of the values. Such content does not have to be explicitly identified (defined), but it is sufficient for it to be clear. In law, we will certainly encounter the following values: justice, the good, dignity, protection of free will, freedom, certainty (legal certainty), etc. It is essential for the proper functioning of law and the formation of identity that these are those values which both society and those who apply law agree upon and recognise as worthy of legal protection.

It is not possible to use values just by their names. Their names are not enough for us to be able to fully understand them and to know how to use them. In order to have a sufficient understanding of the words, it is necessary to know their content. But is society able to agree on their content? Do lawyers know exactly what they mean when they apply them? Aren't these just empty commonplace phrases, with nothing real to be imagined behind them? These are all questions that need to be answered in order to deal with values objectively. It is a matter of ascertaining whether specific values are really relevant or whether they are merely false ornaments hiding the manipulative essence of a certain ideological legal regulation.

The Italian semiotician Umberto Eco saw no problem in the fact that concepts such as justice or legal certainty have no real (tangible) basis.[28] There are a number of such terms or words in society, and we can still get along reasonably well. In order to deal with law, it is not necessary to insist that the word justice must correspond to some actual phenomenon (for example, the word "dog" should correspond to that kind of phenomenon). However, according to Eco, in these cases it is necessary to

---

27 K. Mannheim, *Ideology and Utopia: An Introduction to the Sociology of Knowledge*, Routledge & Kegan Paul, London, 1966, p. 200.

28 U. Eco, *Teorie sémiotiky*, Argo, Praha, 2009, p. 80.

know which *cultural unit* corresponds to this concept.[29] In order for these abstract concepts to be used successfully in society, it is necessary to link them to the culture, or society, and *determine* how it would be appropriate and correct to understand them. These contents are (should be) present in society. For a legal assessment it is necessary to identify them, which does not require sociological research but an understanding of society. For example, through literature and the adoption of cultural contents.

5. Context of interpretation

We have already seen above that law is also a culture of argumentation and interpretation.[30] Interpretation affects the role of law in society, its authority, and the way in which it influences people's behaviour. Given this position of meanings in law and in the world that law creates around us and with our help, it is essential not to leave interpretation to chance. Every right is associated with a conflict.[31] Manipulation of the meaning of law is more difficult where there is a robust constitutional (legal) identity and a strong legal consciousness. The stability of law also derives from the support given by all-society narratives. The world around us adapts better to legal rules that, despite being man-made, we understand as natural. This does not guarantee rightness or inclination to the good and justice. This process can be used to establish elements hostile to democratic modern society. This is one of the reasons not to underestimate this process, but to make it a part of additional educational and participatory activities, as Kosař and Vyhnánek mention.[32]

Law, in forming identity or consciousness, must share with literature not only the basic narratives but also other abstract procedures: e.g. metaphorical ones. In order to understand value patterns, it is necessary to work towards the same. To be aware of what law is talking about. Of course, the language of a legal regulation, for example, will never be as metaphorical

29 *Ibidem.*
30 J.B. White, *Law as Language...*, p. 436.
31 R. Cover, *Foreword: Nomos and Narrative*, "*Harvard Law Review*" 1983, vol. 97, no. 4, p. 6.
32 D. Kosař, L. Vyhnánek, *Ústavní identita...*

as the language of literature. But the narratives through which individual legal instruments legitimize themselves, on the other hand, must work with them. The position of metaphor in law is therefore partly given by legitimation through historical tradition and partly by appeal to *nature*. History as well as nature can give words, concepts and relations a proper aura of correctness and appropriateness.[33]

Note also that law influences the fictional legal (and legalistic) world created by literature. The expectations of the audience will be different if they identify with the world of the empathetic police and court officials that Karel Čapek offered us in both his *Tales from One Pocket* and *Tales from the Other Pocket*. Different expectations and attitudes will be triggered by the acceptance of the patterns of depersonalised procedures that prey upon Josef K. in *The Trial* of Franz Kafka. The action of metaphor is associated with structural similarity. Therefore, the metaphor of law can tell us as much *about law* as the description itself. Therefore, it can also affect legal consciousness and legal identity, as it creates a fictional world, but one associated with real feelings. The fixation of narrative patterns and expectations can subsequently weaken or, on the contrary, strengthen legitimation and thus the acceptance of legal instruments.

Metaphorically, law and the ideal of the good or justice can be mutually connected. Drucilla Cornell sees this as a way of escaping the conception of law through established and commonly shared meanings. The meanings we obtain from legal interpretation are what must be justified by the connection with the good. It is not enough that these meanings are shared by the majority (the more powerful part) of society; their connection to the idea of the good must be demonstrated.[34] The relationship between the good and its position in society is precisely the appropriate moment when literature can have an impact.

33 See e.g.. M. Šejvl, *Vyobcovaní a vlkodlaci v právu a v mýtech*. [cit. 28/02/2012] Available from: http://leblog.cz/?q=node/292; Ad id. see also M. Šejvl, *Spravedlnost se dělá v posteli*. [cit. 28/02/2012] Available from: http://teoriepr ava.blogspot.com/2008/11/spravedlnost-se-dl-v-posteli_1543.html.

34 D. Cornell, *From the Lighthouse: The Promise of Redemption and the Possibility of Legal Interpretation*, "Cardozo Law Review" 1990, year 11, no. 11, p. 1691.

The interpretation of law is not set in stone. It is a constant process of searching for meaning. Interpretations change depending on the social context. In the case of interpretation of normative texts it is less, while in the case of interpretation of legal facts it is more. Let's look at an example. In 1976, some members of the underground music group Plastic People of The Universe were sentenced to prison terms for the crime of disorderly conduct because "by constantly repeating and emphasizing vulgar expressions, the performers expressed disrespect for society and contempt for its moral principles."[35] The then – horrifyingly absurd – interpretation of the group's texts advocated by official authorities is unimaginable today. The same text presented in public today cannot be prosecuted. The text has remained the same, the social context has changed and values have prevailed that are incompatible with the earlier interpretation.

6. Conclusion

In the relationship between literature and legal (constitutional) consciousness and identity, it is necessary to take into account multiple actors who operate outside the official authorities and influence the way in which law operates.[36] Legal consciousness is connected with cultural schemes operating in society in general and influencing participation in officially shared legal patterns.[37] Literature is one of the tools that can be used to influence legal consciousness: it can create patterns that influence expectations about law, but also the practice.

Literature, by its very nature, has the ability to influence consciousness and thereby influence the legal consciousness and understanding of law in society. Not only in addressees, but also in legal professionals. By cultivating the perception of values, portraying the legal environment, but also by analysing everyday life, it changes the approach to everyday situations.

35 See the judgement of the Supreme Court of 18 February 2003, File Ref. 4 Tz 91/2002, ECLI:CZ:NS:2003:4.TZ.91.2002.1.

36 S. Halliday, M. Bronwen, *I Fought the Law and the Law Won? Legal Consciousness and the Critical Imagination*, "Current Legal Problems" 2013, vol. 66, no. 1, p. 4.

37 S.S. Silbey, *After Legal Consciousness*, "Annual Review of Law and Social Science" 2005, vol. 1, p. 334.

No matter that it portrays fictional worlds. Literature has the ability to develop civil participation by emphasizing the image of law or by reflecting on values. It supports imagination and allows value schemes to be applied to cases previously unsolved.

Its role is not only refining and participatory, but also educational. In sample subjects it can highlight the opportunity to ask for help. It uses narratives to legitimize value elements in law (or, on the contrary, to delegitimize them). This enables the penetration of the values accepted by the legal system into wider social strata and the acceptance (or, on the contrary, rejection) of the concept of law created by legal authorities. It is therefore evident that the indifference mentioned in the title is not desirable. Although literature is a marginal source affecting the constitutional (legal) consciousness, this does not mean that it is right to reject it.

Bibliography

Baudrillard, J., *Simulacra and Simulation*, The University of Michigan Press, Ann Arbor, 1994.

Binder, G., Weisberg, R., *Literary Criticism of Law*, Princeton University Press, Princeton, 2000.

Cornell, D., *From the Lighthouse: The Promise of Redemption and the Possibility of Legal Interpretation*, "Cardozo Law Review" 1990, no. 11.

Cover, R., *Foreword: Nomos and Narrative*, "Harvard Law Review" 1983, vol. 97, no. 4.

Eco, U., *Teorie sémiotiky*, Argo, Praha, 2009.

Gaakeer, J., *The Future of Literary-Legal Jurisprudence: Mere Theory or Just Practice?*, "Law and Humanities" 2011, vol. 5, no. 1.

Greenawalt, K., *Law and Objectivity*, Oxford University Press, New York, 1992.

Halliday, S., Bronwen, M., *I Fought the Law and the Law Won? Legal Consciousness and the Critical Imagination*, "Current Legal Problems" 2013, vol. 66, no. 1.

Havel, V., *Speech presented on 8 May 1993*, http://old.hrad.cz/president/Havel/speeches/1993/0805.html

Hirsch, E.D. jr., *The Politics of Theories of Interpretation*, "Critical Inquiry" 1982, vol. 9, no. 1.

Kosař, D., Vyhnánek, L., *Ústavní identita České republiky*, "Právník" 2018, vol. 157, no. 10.

Levinson, S., *Law as Literature*, "Texas Law Review" 1982, vol. 60, no. 3.

Mańko, R., *W stronę krytycznej filozofii orzekania: Polityczność, etyka, legitymizacja*, Uniwersytet Łódzki, Łódź 2018.

Mannheim, K., *Ideology and Utopia: An Introduction to the Sociology of Knowledge*, Routledge & Kegan Paul, London, 1966.

Masaryk, T.G., *Česká otázka. Snahy a tužby národního obrození*, Pokrok, Praha, 1908.

Preissová, G., *Gazdina roba: drama o třech jednáních*, F. Šimáček, Praha, 1890.

Preissová, G., *Obrázky bez rámů*, J. Otto, Praha, 1896.

Šejvl, M., *Kritika Legal Origins Thesis a pojem právní kultury*, "Právník" 2013, vol. 152, no. 5.

Šejvl, M., *Spravedlnost se dělá v posteli*, http://teorieprava.blogspot.com/2008/11/spravedlnost-se-dl-v-posteli_1543.html

Šejvl, M., *Vyobcovaní a vlkodlaci v právu a v mýtech*, http://leblog.cz/?q=node/292

Silbey, S.S., *After Legal Consciousness*, "Annual Review of Law and Social Science" 2005, vol. 1.

Škop, M., *Law and Literatura – a Meaningful Connection*, "Filozofia Publiczna i Edukacja Demokratyczna" 2015, vol. 4, no. 1.

Škop, M., Smejkalová, T., Štěpáníková, M., *Právo a literatura – brněnská spojení*, "Právník" 2019, no. 1, vol. 158.

Štěpáníková, M., *List of 50 Legal Literary Fictions in Czechoslovakia*, [in:] M. Štěpáníková, M., Malaník, T. Smejkalová, M. Škop, *Argumentation 2019*, Munipress, Brno, 2019.

Ward, I., *Law, Literature and History*, "Law and Critique" 2021, 10.1080/1535685X.2021.1872953.

White, J.B., *Law as Language: Reading Law and Reading Literature*, "Texas Law Review" 1982, vol. 60, no. 3.

White, J.B., *When Words Lose Their Meaning*, University of Chicago Press, Chicago–London, 1985.

Wigmore, J.H., *A List of Legal Novels*, "Illinois Law Review" 1908, vol. 2, no. 9.

Young, K.M., Billings, K.R., *Legal Consciousness and Cultural Capital*, "Law and Society Review" 2020, vol. 54, no. 1.

Zeidler, K., *Prawo i literatura. Garść uwag spóźnionych*, [in:] J. Kamień, J. Zajadło, K. Zeidler, *Prawo i literatura*, Wydawnictwo Uniwersytetu Gdańskiego, Gdańsk, 2019.

Part II

Anna Chmielarz-Grochal[2]

The Limits to Constitutional Amendments and the Question of Constitutional Identity and Citizens' Consciousness (the Polish case)[1]

Abstract

The issue of limits to constitutional amendments in the context of constitutional identity and citizens' consciousness is vitally important. Put briefly, it may be reduced to the basic question about the role and value of a constitution itself in a multilevel (multicentric) legal order or even – in a broader sense – in a contemporary democratic state of law. This question concerns the permissible scope of constitutional amendments and their limits. It is also linked to the concept of the constitutional identity and the level of citizens' constitutional consciousness – both in knowledge and in national identity aspects the constitution's legitimacy has, in fact, a twofold legal and social nature.

The Constitution of the Republic of Poland in Article 235 covers formal limits to its amendments, but it does not provide an eternity clause (as in the cases of France, Germany, Italy or Czechia). Nevertheless, this does not mean that it provides no substantial limits at all. It is possible to identify certain "relatively perpetual and unchangeable" constitutional provisions that allow limits to be determined for the permissible scope of amendments (Chapters I, II, XII). In its very Preamble – which may serve as *sui generis* ground for the fundamental rights of state and Nation – principles are described as "the unshakeable foundation of the Republic of Poland." Similarly, Article 30 of the Constitution makes use of such wording as the "inherent

1 This article is a result of the research project no. 2017/27/L/HS5/03245, "Constitutional Consciousness as a Remedy for the Crisis of Discourse and Democracy Deficit in the European Union", financed by the National Science Center (dec. no. DEC-2017/27/L/HS5/03245).

2 Anna Chmielarz-Grochal – assistant professor at the Faculty of Law and Administration of University of Lodz (Poland) and a specialist on European law in the Judicial Decisions Bureau of the Supreme Administrative Court. She is the author of numerous publications on constitutional law and the judicial review of administration, as well as publications on the system and institutions of the French Republic.

and inalienable dignity of the person" that is of an "inviolable" nature. On the whole, substantial limits to constitutional amendments can be derived from "the constitutional identity." This is determined by the provisions containing primary and general principles of the Constitution as well as the provisions concerning individual rights. The socially and politically motivated changes to the system of powers as well as to constitutional matters and legitimacy may be explained by reference to constitutional identity, since it is related not solely to the "constitution in a book", but also to the "constitution in action" and its political and social context. The European case-law, including the rulings of Polish Constitutional Tribunal, tends to confirm that constitutional identity is a concept providing a certain content which is based on the axiological system of principles and values arising from the very "heart" of the constitution.

Moreover, the constitution not only plays a key legal role within society, but also fulfills integrative and educational functions. If the society is aware of this role and these functions (in other words: if it reaches a high level of constitutional consciousness) it tends to identify itself – as a community – with constitutional rights and values. The citizens' attitudes towards constitutional rights and values is linked, as a result, to a national identity, viewed as a legal, axiological, historical and cultural community. Its importance is even greater, because of the constituent power which belongs to the nation as a sovereign power. The high level of constitutional consciousness – based on informed choices and knowledge – may serve as an additional source of the limits to the constitutional amendment process and as a source of self-restraint for politicians, preventing rash political decisions on such matters. For that reason, proper legal education (including the educational role of courts and their case-law) is of particular and great significance.

Keywords: constitutional amendments, constituent power, constituted power, limits to constitutional amendments, limits to the sovereign's will, constitutional identity, constitutional consciousness

1. General remarks

There is really no dispute nowadays about the need for particular legal protection of constitutional stability due to the system of values provided, since a sustainable constitution is one of the fundamental values in a contemporary democratic state of law.[3] A stable constitution serves as a

3 T. Ginsburg, *Constitutional Endurance*, [in:] T. Ginsburg, R. Dixon (eds.) *Comparative Constitutional Law*, Edward Elgar, Cheltenham–Northampton, 2011, pp. 112–125; Z. Elkins, T. Ginsburg, J. Melton, *The Endurance of National Constitutions*, Cambridge University Press, Cambridge, 2009, pp. 2, 122–146.

guarantee of the legal certainty and stability of the entire state. However, this is not a value of an absolute nature. In general the legal system has ceased to be viewed as unchangeable concept.[4] The constitution as the basic law for such a system shall meet ongoing social changes (a living constitution).[5] An opportunity to amend the constitution shall, paradoxically, serve – in practice – to stabilize a certain paradigm of exercising state powers. Simultaneously, all the necessary changes should comply with the rules and limits arising from such a superior legal act itself, since it is provided as a source for all norms, principles and values and, in consequence, it determines the quality and significance of such changes. The system of constitutional values, arising from European humanistic ideas concerning social life, is the main reason for the specific legal protection of constitutional sustainability and also a tool preventing the constitution from rash changes. Both formal and substantive provisions, including eternal clauses, serve as limits for amending the constitution. At the same time, we cannot exclude the option of derogating the constitution and replacing it with an utterly new basic law. In any case, however, the citizens' (direct or indirect) participation in the amendment procedure is unavoidable in a democratic state of law. According to Jürgen Habermas "legally speaking there is no rule of law without democracy."[6] Modern constitutional law is based on the discursive approach[7] and, as a result, it has been analysed mostly from the "civic dialogue" perspective.[8]

---

4 M. Zamboni, *Law and Politics. A Dilemma for Contemporary Legal Theory*, Springer, Berlin–Heidelberg, 2008, p. 27.

5 D.A. Strauss, *The Living Constitution*, Oxford University Press, Oxford, 2010; A. Coan, *Living Constitutional Theory*, "Duke Law Journal Online" 2017, vol. 66, pp. 99–115; A. Kavanagh, *The Idea of a Living Constitution*, "Canadian Journal of Law and Jurisprudence" 2003, vol. XVI, no. 1, pp. 55–89.

6 J. Habermas, *Uwzględniając Innego. Studia do teorii politycznej* (trans. A. Romaniuk), Wydawnictwo Naukowe PWN, Warszawa, 2009, p. 215.

7 J. Habermas, *Faktyczność i obowiązywanie. Teoria dyskursu wobec zagadnień prawa i demokratycznego państwa prawnego* (trans. A. Romaniuk, R. Marszałek), Wydawnictwo Naukowe Scholar, Warszawa, 2005, p. 146.

8 M. La Torre, *Constitutionalism and Legal Reasoning*, Springer, Dordrecht, 2007, pp. 36, 77.

The issue of constitutional amendment is a matter of a great importance for constitutional science, yet it is a challenge to balance the constitutionalization principle with the democracy principle. In other words, the balance between the constitution as a superior legal act covering the basic state issues and a constitution in the sense of a basic law for a democratic community. The provisions on amendment are arguably the most important rules in any constitution, for they condition the operation of all other provisions. Thus, the special procedure for introducing any constitutional amendments and for determining the limits for their permissible scope should be created with respect to the democratic legitimacy principle, which is a basic factor facilitating the sustainability of the constitution. It is already an established modern legal tradition that constitutional acts themselves stipulate such procedures as well the limits for introducing the changes. Also, citizens' participation in the amendment procedure has become a well-established and common standard. It usually takes the form of a posteriori mechanisms of (dis)approval of the amendments after they have been passed by a certain representative body (a parliament). The usual legal form of citizens' participation is a referendum held in order to express the confirmation or rejection of the amendments.[9]

The paper covers the question of the limits to constitutional amendments in a democratic state and this is examined in the twofold context of constitutional identity of the state and the constitutional consciousness of the people (citizens). The main thesis presents two arguments: firstly – that constitutional consciousness based on respect and due regard to the values fundamental for the identity of the state and nation should ensure both the reasonability of constitutional changes and the possibility of civic debate and citizens' participation in the entire process; secondly – that constitutional identity based on the axiological system of principles and values arising from the very "heart" of the constitution limits the permissible scope of such amendments. In general, the essay is an attempt to address the question of the limits to constitutional law that is an expression of the sovereign's will, although without an unchangeable nature. The inclusion

9 Further reading: R. Albert, *Constitutional Amendments: Making, Breaking, and Changing Constitutions*, Oxford University Press, New York, 2019.

agenda, which means bringing people to participate in the amendment process, also raises questions regarding the forms and limits for such participation. A reference point for such consideration is the procedure provided by the present Polish Constitution of 2nd April 1997.[10]

2. Constitutional consciousness

The notion "constitutional consciousness" has not been defined in legal science. It operates rather within the area of sociology. However, it became recognizable in public discourse. It is also verbalized de lege lata in the constitutions of certain states, such as – perhaps surprisingly – Ghana,[11] Uganda[12] and Zimbabwe,[13] as well as in de lege ferenda provisions of the

10 Published in: *Dziennik Ustaw* No. 78, item 483, https://www.sejm.gov.pl/prawo/konst/angielski/kon1.htm (accessed: 15.03.2022).

11 Chapter Nineteen: National Commission for Civic Education. Article 233: "The functions of the Commission shall be – (a) to create and sustain within the society the awareness of the principles and objectives of this Constitution as the fundamental law of the people of Ghana; (b) to educate and encourage the public to defend this Constitution at all times, against all forms of abuse and violation; (c) to formulate for the consideration of Government, from time to time, programmes at the national, regional and district levels aimed at realising the objectives of this Constitution […]", https://www.constituteproject.org/constitution/Ghana_1996?lang=en (accessed: 15.03.2022).

12 Chapter 1 – The Constitution. Article 4: "The State shall promote public awareness of this Constitution by (a) translating it into Ugandan languages and disseminating it as widely as possible; and (b) providing for the teaching of the Constitution in all educational institutions and armed forces training institutions and regularly transmitting and publishing programmes through the media generally", https://www.statehouse.go.ug/government/constitution (accessed: 15.03.2022).

13 Chapter I: Founding Provisions. Section 7: "The State must promote public awareness of this Constitution, in particular by (a) translating it into all officially recognised languages and disseminating it as widely as possible; (b) requiring this Constitution to be taught in schools and as part of the curricula for the training of members of the security services, the Civil Service and members and employees of public institutions; and (c) encouraging all persons and organisations, including civic organisations, to disseminate awareness and knowledge of this Constitution throughout society", https://www.veritaszim.net/node/4750 (accessed: 15.03.2022).

draft amendments to the constitution (Iceland[14]). This notion refers to the constitution as such (constitutional awareness) as well as to the area of individual rights (human rights awareness).

According to the dictionary definition, "consciousness" has at least three meanings: (1) "awareness or perception of something"; (2) "common – for some certain group – views, beliefs and goals"; and (3) "the state of being aware of and responsive to oneself and one's surroundings."[15]

Constitutional consciousness at first glance seems to be linked to the text of the constitution (the legal knowledge). However, this is a misinterpretation, since it is rather an awareness and understanding of the meaning and impact of the constitution for the individual, society and the state. Constitutional consciousness is the level (and advancement) of citizens' consciousness about the role of the constitution, particularly in the area of human rights protection, as well as the duties and burdens to the Common Good. That is the basis for constitutional identity. In a democratic state, such an identity is an essential basis for providing the citizens or – more broadly – the entire society the room for self-determination in the sense of national identity and, consequently, constitutional identity.

The constitutional consciousness building process is possible only if three conditions are fulfilled. The first consciousness-developing factor is the binding force of the constitution (in its legal, factual and axiological level). This condition is fulfilled, if a constitution: (a) has been enacted (passed) and published; (b) has been used and applied in the decisional process; and (c) has been viewed as a source of values for citizens as the addressee of legislation.

14 Proposal for Article 24: Education. "All shall by law have the right to a general education according to their ability. All subject to compulsory education shall be offered such education without charge. Education shall be adjusted to the general ability of each individual and be in line with critical awareness of human rights, democratic rights and duties", https://www.constituteproject.org/constitution/Iceland_2011D?lang=en (accessed: 15.03.2022).This constitutional amendment was approved in 2011 in a referendum, but rejected by parliament in 2013.

15 https://www.oxfordlearnersdictionaries.com/definition/english/consciousness (accessed: 15.03.2022).

The second consciousness-developing factor is the actual nature of the constitution. This is when a discrepancy between facts and law does not exist or is possibly insignificant. We can talk about the actual nature of the constitution when the constitutional provisions are amplified by the legislator and by the authorities (especially the courts) as the basis of its decisions and judgements.

The last consciousness-developing factor is the representative nature of the constitution. When the constitution reflects the common characteristics of the society, the people may identify themselves with the basic law. Internalization of the basic law is possible in the legislative and amending process as well as in the decisional process. For example, this can happen when the courts refer in their ruling to constitutional provisions in a manner that enhances citizens' trust in the constitution. Possible attempts to amend the constitution with the participation of citizens can be an empirical example of how the representative nature of the constitution should be taken and implemented.

Given that the content of the constitution results from citizens' dialogue, the participants to such dialogue ought to base their arguments on certain knowledge and an understanding of the basic-value-system which is fundamental and invulnerable in a democratic state of law. The values encompass the issues of the system and organization of the state as well as "individual – state" liaisons, the role of the individual in exercising the powers and other ideas basic to social life. Consequently, the constitution is not only a basic law, but also a tool motivating reflection on the state institution and system, to conduct a public debate on such matters and, eventually, to introduce new concepts and changes.[16] A society that is aware of the role of the constitution as well as the rights and values protected within is society is one that is able to identify itself with such rights and values. The citizens' approach to these constitutional rights determines, in turn, national identity as an affiliation to a community of principles and values arising from history, tradition and culture. An adequate and high level of

16 Further reading: K.M. Cern, *Jak rozumieć rolę konstytucji we współczesnym społeczeństwie demokratycznym?*, "Studia Prawno-Ekonomiczne" 2016, vol. CI, pp. 23–39; J. Habermas, *Constitutional Democracy. A Paradoxical Union of Contradictory Principles?*, "Political Theory" 2001 vol. 29, no. 6, pp. 766–781.

constitutional consciousness, also covering an awareness of democracy's failings and threats, may become an additional "democracy guard" and serve as a source of the limitation for authorities, preventing rash decisions and changes.

3. Limits to Polish Constitution amendments

The Polish Constitution (Chapter XII, article 235) provides the formal limits to constitutional amendment process.[17] The first limit is the requirement of a majority. A bill to amend the Constitution shall be adopted by the Sejm (the lower house of the Polish parliament) by a majority of at least two-thirds of the votes in the presence of at least half of the statutory number of deputies, and by the Senate (the upper house) by an absolute majority of votes in the presence of at least half of the statutory number of senators. It is important that amendments to the Constitution shall be

17 Article 235: "(1) A bill to amend the Constitution may be submitted by the following: at least one-fifth of the statutory number of Deputies; the Senate; or the President of the Republic. (2) Amendments to the Constitution shall be made by means of a statute adopted by the Sejm and, thereafter, adopted in the same wording by the Senate within a period of 60 days. (3) The first reading of a bill to amend the Constitution may take place no sooner than 30 days after the submission of the bill to the Sejm. (4) A bill to amend the Constitution shall be adopted by the Sejm by a majority of at least two-thirds of votes in the presence of at least half of the statutory number of Deputies, and by the Senate by an absolute majority of votes in the presence of at least half of the statutory number of Senators. (5) The adoption by the Sejm of a bill amending the provisions of Chapters I, II or XII of the Constitution shall take place no sooner than 60 days after the first reading of the bill. (6) If a bill to amend the Constitution relates to the provisions Chapters I, II or XII, the subjects specified in para. 1 above may require, within 45 days of the adoption of the bill by the Senate, the holding of a confirmatory referendum. Such subjects shall make application in the matter to the Marshal of the Sejm, who shall order the holding of a referendum within 60 days of the day of receipt of the application. The amendment to the Constitution shall be deemed accepted if the majority of those voting express support for such amendment. (7) After conclusion of the procedures specified in para 4 and 6 above, the Marshal of the Sejm shall submit the adopted statute to the President of the Republic for signature. The President of the Republic shall sign the statute within 21 days of its submission and order its promulgation in the Journal of Laws of the Republic of Poland (*Dziennik Ustaw*)".

made by means of a statute adopted by the Sejm and, thereafter, adopted in the same wording by the Senate (it is the same draft text in both legislative chambers). Secondly, the Constitution specifies the terms as well. For example, the Senate adopts constitutional amendments within a period of 60 days (paragraph 2), the first reading of a bill to amend the Constitution may take place no sooner than 30 days after the submission of the bill to the Sejm (paragraph 3), the adoption by the Sejm of a bill amending the provisions of Chapters I, II or XII of the Constitution shall take place no sooner than 60 days after the first reading of the bill (paragraph 4). Furthermore, the Constitution stipulates a special procedure for amending Chapters I, II and XII. They concern, respectively, the state system, the freedoms, rights and obligations of persons and citizens, and amending the Constitution. If a bill to amend the Constitution relates to the provisions in Chapters I, II or XII, Deputies (at least one-fifth of their statutory number), the Senate or the President of the Republic may require, within 45 days of the adoption of the bill by the Senate, the holding of a confirmatory vote (a referendum). Such subjects shall make application in the matter to the Marshal of the Sejm (the parliament speaker), who shall order the holding of a referendum within 60 days from the day of receipt of the application. The amendment to the Constitution shall be deemed accepted if the majority of those voting express support for such amendment (paragraph 5).[18]

However, the Polish Constitution has not provided any explicit restrictions on the possibility of changing its content (substantive limits to constitutional amendment). Certain European countries (such as France, Germany, Italy and Czechia) provided clear rules of limitation for the permissible scope of constitutional amendments – namely the eternity clauses. In other words, an eternity clause in the constitution or basic law of a particular state is a clause intended to ensure that the law or constitution cannot be changed by amendment. The Constitution of the Republic of

18 The Polish Constitution has been modified twice as yet. The first amendment adopted on 8th Sept. 2006 concerned Article 55 in the context of European arrest warrant (EAW). The confirmatory referendum has not been held at that time. The second amendment adopted on 7th May 2009 concerned Article 99 (right to stand for election to Sejm and Senate).

Poland does not provide such clause ("unchangeable provisions"). Nevertheless, this does not mean that it provides no limits at all. It is possible to point out certain "relatively perpetual and unchangeable" provisions that allow the limits for the permissible scope of amendments to be determined.

It should be noted that the Preamble to the Polish Constitution in fine states: "We call upon all those who will apply this Constitution for the good of the Third Republic to do so paying respect to the inherent dignity of the person, his or her right to freedom, the obligation of solidarity with others, and respect for these principles as the unshakeable foundation of the Republic of Poland." These abovementioned principles are the unshakeable foundation of the Republic of Poland. In such manner the preamble implies that the individual rights and freedoms are mandatory part of the constitutional matter. Moreover, according to Article 30 of the Polish Constitution, "the inherent and inalienable dignity of the person shall constitute a source of freedoms and rights of persons and citizens. It shall be inviolable. The respect and protection thereof shall be the obligation of public authorities." These constitutional statements – "unshakeable" principles and "inalienable" human dignity – directly suggest limited possibilities of changing them (either changing their content or repealing them).

Moreover, substantive limits to constitutional amendments can be derived from "the constitutional identity." In other words, it can be considered that the constitutional identity defines the limits of possible changes to the constitution. It functions as a kind of a check on the intentions to revise the constitution.[19] It means, that any possible constitutional amendments must be assesses from the perspective of maintaining the identity of the constitution.[20]

19 Further reading: M. Granat, *Constitutional Identity and its Functions*, "Przegląd Prawa Konstytucyjnego" 2022, vol. 2, pp. 77–84.

20 M. Granat, K. Granat, *The Constitution of Poland: A Contextual Analysis*, Hart Publishing, Oxford–London–New York–New Delhi–Sydney, 2022, pp. 239–240.

4. Constitutional identity and substantive limits to constitutional amendments

Constitutional identity is a term used in the theory of law, the dogmatics of constitutional law, and in judicial decisions, especially constitutional courts.[21] This identity may be regarded in a twofold sense: as a distinguishing otherness (selfhood) or as a unifying community (sameness).[22] The first meaning (selfhood) is based on the assumption of particular characteristics and peculiarities that distinguish the particular state from the others. The second meaning of this notion (sameness) also covers qualitative identity (of the same nature and characteristics). According to Paul Ricoeur,[23] selfhood implies otherness to such an extent that selfhood and otherness cannot be separated. On the other hand – sameness may denote a numerical identity, such as unity (opposed to plurality) and/or an uninterrupted continuity or a lack of variation and diversity.

The essential function of constitutional identity is to distinguish oneself from others. In liberal democratic states, identity based on respect for democracy, the rule of law, and fundamental rights protection serves not

---

21 Further reading: M. Ziółkowski, *Mozaika tożsamości konstytucyjnych*, [in:] A. Wróbel, M. Ziółkowski (eds.) *Tożsamość konstytucyjna w wybranych państwach członkowskich Unii Europejskiej*, Wolters Kluwer, Warszawa, 2021, pp. 11–45 and cited works; M. Ziółkowski, *Tożsamość konstytucyjna jako wzorzec i kryterium kontroli w postępowaniu przed Trybunałem Konstytucyjnym (uwagi na marginesie wyroków K 32/09 i P 7/20)*, [in:] M. Florczak-Wątor, M. Krzemiński (eds.), *Interdyscyplinarny wymiar tożsamości konstytucyjnej*, Wydawnictwo Księgarnia Akademicka, Kraków, 2022, pp. 108–118 and cited works.

22 Further reading: P. Ricoeur, Oneself as Another, University of Chicago Press, Chicago–London, 1990; M. Rosenfeld (ed.), *Constitutionalism, Identity, Difference and Legitimacy. Theoretical Perspectives*, Duke University Press, Durham, 1994; *Idem*, *The Identity of the Constitutional Subject: Selfhood, Culture and Community*, Routledge, London–New York, 2010; G.J. Jacobsohn, *Constitutional Identity*, Harvard University Press, Harvard, 2010; A.S. Arnaiz, C.A. Llivina (eds.), *National Constitutional Identity and European Integration*, Intersentia Ltd, Cambridge, 2013. See also: Ch. Calliess, G. van der Schyff (eds.), *Constitutional Identity in a Europe of Multilevel Constitutionalism*, Cambridge University Press, Cambridge, 2019.

23 P. Ricoeur, *Oneself...*, pp. 2–3, 29, 32, 36–37.

so much in order to distinguish oneself from others, as it does to relate to others and conceptualize one's individuality through a shared or collective identity. Further, regarding the migration of constitutional ideas (constitutional borrowing), identity gains its reflexive and communicative dimension. It benefits from the reciprocal influence of (legal) cultures – and then it may serve the cooperation with other actors, in a unifying or convergent manner.[24] Constitutional identity may develop simultaneously in three dimensions as individual, relational, and collective selves, which remain in constant interaction.[25]

With regard to Polish constitutional identity – in the selfhood sense – there are no constitutional provisions covering such matter, which to some extent makes the entire issue complicated and speculative. Such speculations lead to the thesis that one of the major characteristics, Poland's unique characteristic that distinguishes it from the other states is – unlike in France with its *laïcité* – its Christian heritage (understood in a local manner). The notion of "Christian heritage" is mentioned three times in the Preamble to the Constitution. According to the Constitution, the Roman-Catholic Church has a privileged position (underpinned by the Concordat with the Vatican, the common custom of accommodating religious beliefs and traditions in public life as well as lack of religious neutrality in public sphere). Article 53 provides a broad catalogue of the components of "freedom of religion", excluding diversity of religious movements within Christianity (it does not include "freedom of creed").

---

24 V. Perju, *Constitutional Transplants, Borrowing, and Migrations*, [in:] M. Rosenfeld, A. Sajó (eds.), *Oxford Handbook of Comparative Constitutional Law*, Oxford University Press, Oxford, 2012, pp. 1304–1327; S. Choudhury (ed.), *The Migration of Constitutional Ideas*, Cambridge University Press, Cambridge, 2006, *passim*; W. Osiatyński, *Paradoxes of Constitutional Borrowing*, "International Journal of Constitutional Law" 2003, vol. 1, pp. 244–268.

25 Further reading: A. Śledzińska-Simon, *Koncepcja tożsamości konstytucyjnej: wymiar indywidualny, relatywny oraz zbiorowy*, "Przegląd Prawa i Administracji" 2016, vol. CVII, pp. 335–357, DOI: 10.19195/0137-1134.107.18; A. Śledzińska-Simon, *Constitutional identity in 3D: A model of individual, relational, and collective self and its application in Poland*, "International Journal of Constitutional Law" 2015, vol. 13, no. 1, pp. 124–155, https://doi.org/10.1093/icon/mov007 (accessed: 15.03.2022).

In the sameness-sense Polish constitutional identity is based on the universal constitutional principles common to the European Union member states.[26]

In the context of limits to constitutional amendments it is assumed that constitutional identity is linked to the fact of the pure existence of the constitution, as well as to its content and the substance which the identity operates within. In other words, constitutional identity arises from the constitutional act, although is not synonymous with the constitution itself. On one hand constitutional identity covers fundamental principles and values – the "heart" (core) of the constitution that shall remain constant and unaltered.[27] On the other hand, it results from a constitutional culture – the basis and a reason behind a certain legal order.[28] According to Michel Rosenfeld, references to constitutional identity may explain the manner in which power is exercised as well as the content of the constitution and any changes that are made to it.[29] On the whole, the socially and politically motivated changes to the system of powers, as well as to the constitutional matters and legitimacy, may be explained by reference to constitutional identity, since it is related not solely to the "constitution

---

26 Further reading: A. Śledzińska-Simon, M. Ziółkowski, *Constitutional Identity of Poland: Is the Emperor Putting on the Old Clothes of Sovereignty?*, [in:] Ch. Calliess, G. van der Schyff (eds.), *Constitutional Identity in a Europe of Multilevel Constitutionalism*, Cambridge University Press, Cambridge, 2019, p. 243 and subsequent pages. See also: K. Wójtowicz, *Constitutional courts and European Union Law*, E-Wydawnictwo, Prawnicza i Ekonomiczna Biblioteka Cyfrowa, Wydział Prawa, Administracji i Ekonomii Uniwersytetu Wrocławskiego, Wrocław, 2014, pp. 145–157.

27 G.J. Jacobsohn, *Constitutional Values and Principles*, [in:] M. Rosenfeld, A. Sajó (eds.), *The Oxford Handbook of Comparative Constitutional Law*, Oxford University Press, Oxford, 2012, pp. 777–791.

28 Further reading: R. Hauser, M. Zirk-Sadowski, B. Wojciechowski (eds.), *The Common European Constitutional Culture: Its Sources, Limits and Identity*, Peter Lang Publishing, Frankfurt am Main, 2016. See also: F. Mayer, *L'identité constitutionnelle dans la jurisprudence constitutionnelle allemande*, [in:] L. Burgorgue-Larsen (ed.) *L'identité constitutionnelle saisie par les juges en Europe*, Editions Pedone, 2011, pp. 63–88.

29 M. Rosenfeld, *The Identity...*, p. 5.

in a book", but also to the "constitution in action" and its political and social context.

The concept of constitutional identity has appeared in the jurisprudence of constitutional courts. Here three main areas of its application may be distinguished: (a) references in decisions concerning the legitimacy of constitutional amendments; (b) references in decisions concerning the legitimacy of constitutional migration and engaging in judicial dialogue; and (c) references in decisions concerning integration within a supra- or international organization.[30]

Polish legal practice addressed such a notion and provided an explanation in the case K 32/09 (Constitutional Tribunal's judgment of 24 November 2010),[31] concerning conformity of the Lisbon Treaty with the Polish Constitution. This notion was examined by the Tribunal as an element of the state as a sovereign entity. According to the Tribunal, certain competences and powers of state authorities may not be conferred pursuant to Article 90 of the Constitution ("integration clause"), as they manifest the constitutional identity and thus reflect the values the Constitution is based on. In other words, according to the concept of constitutional identity, the competence to confer (delegate) powers excludes key-matters, "the very heart", i.e. all the issues that are fundamental to the basis of the state's political system. The Tribunal indicated that a complete prohibition of conferral covers the following matters: decisions specifying the fundamental principles of the Constitution, decisions concerning the rights of the individual, which determine the identity of the state, including, in particular: the protection of the inviolable dignity of the person and their constitutional freedoms, the principle of the sovereign state, the principle of democracy and democratic governance, the principle of social justice, the principle of subsidiarity, the rule of law principle, as well as the requirement to ensure the proper implementation of constitutional values and the prohibition on conferring the power to amend the Constitution and the

---

30 A. Śledzińska-Simon, *Constitutional identity in 3D...*, pp. 128–129 and cited works.

31 OTK ZU/A/49.

competence to determine powers.[32] In the case P 7/20 (the judgment of 14 July 2021)[33] the Constitutional Tribunal used constitutional identity as a criterion for reviewing the compatibility of the EU act with the constitutional principle of conferred powers (*ultra vires* review) and, moreover, the Polish judiciary (the system of courts and rules for the appointment of judges) was recognised as an element of constitutional identity.[34] Thus, in the Constitutional Tribunal's jurisprudence the expression "constitutional identity" has emerged in a normative context other than that of constitutional changes.

However, the doctrine of constitutional law points to the legitimacy of a broader reading of constitutional identity as the limit not so much on the transfer of competence as of the limit on the amendment of the constitution – the implied prohibition of its amendment.[35] The expression "constitutional identity" is either used as a name for constitutional norms with a specific function (i.e. setting the boundaries of constitutional change) or is identified with only some unchangeable norms.[36] In the context of constitutional amendments, constitutional identity can be recognized as a source of "unchangeable" or "relatively perpetual and unchangeable" clauses. It is applied internally and aimed at the protection of the constitutional order against abrupt changes that might pose a threat to its very existence.[37]

---

32 See also: K. Wojtyczek, *Przekazywanie kompetencji państwa organizacjom międzynarodowym*, Wydawnictwo Uniwersytetu Jagiellońskiego, Kraków, 2007, p. 284 and subsequent pages.

33 OTK ZU/9A/108.

34 Further reading: M. Ziółkowski, *Tożsamość konstytucyjna...*, pp. 103–133 and cited works.

35 See: M. Granat, *Rozumienie zmiany Konstytucji RP a tożsamość konstytucyjna*, [in:] R. Chruściak (ed.), *Problemy zmiany konstytucji*, Wydawnictwo Sejmowe, Warszawa, 2017, pp. 255–282.

36 Further reading: M. Polzin, *Constitutional Identity, Unconstitutional Amendments and the Idea of Constituent Power: The Development of the Doctrine of Constitutional Identity in German Constitutional Law*, "International Journal of Constitutional Law" 2016, vol. 14, pp. 415–426.

37 A. Śledzińska-Simon, Constitutional identity in 3D..., pp. 129–131 and cited works; K. Gözler, *Judicial Review of Constitutional Amendments. A Comparative Study*, Ekin Press, Bursa, 2008.

From this point of view, constitutional identity appears changeable, but still resistant to its own destruction.[38]

Accordingly, there are two main issues worth raising: firstly – the question of the proper and lawful change of the constitutional provisions regarding constitutional identity; secondly – a question concerning the possibility of exceeding the substantive limits of constitutional amendments by adopting an entirely new constitutional act. In the latter case it is also linked to the question concerning the limits of constitutional power.[39]

5. Constitutional power and the scope of constitutional amendments

The nature and role of constitutional power have been widely analysed, in particular by Joseph Emmanuel Sieyès, who distinguished between "pouvoir constituant" and "pouvoir constitué." According to Sieyès' theory, the constituent power belongs to the nation, and it could not be subjected to any – even formal – limits (restrictions).[40] In the 20th century this concept was examined from two different approaches: by Hans Kelsen[41] and by Carl Schmitt.[42] It also remains a hot issue in contemporary constitutional

38 G.J. Jacobsohn, *Constitutional Identity...*, p. 7.

39 Further reading: Y. Roznai, *Unconstitutional Constitutional Amendments. The Limits of Amendment Powers*, Oxford University Press, Oxford, 2017; M.-F. Rigaux, *La theorie des limites materielles a l'exercice de la fonction constituante*, Larcier, Bruxelles, 1985.

40 E.J. Sieyès *Czym jest stan trzeci? Esej o przywilejach* (trans. M. Jarosz), Wydawnictwo Sejmowe, Warszawa, 2016. See also: M. Loughlin, *The Concept of Constituent Power*, "European Journal of Political Theory" 2014, vol. 13, no. 2, pp. 218–237.

41 H. Kelsen, *Foundations of Democracy*, "Ethics" 1955, vol. 66, pp. 1–101; H. Kelsen, *O istocie i wartości demokracji* (trans. F. Turynowa), Księgarnia Powszechna, Warszawa, 1936.

42 C. Schmitt, *Legality and Legitimacy* (trans. J. Seitzer), Duke University Press, Durham, 2004; C. Schmitt, *Constitutional Theory* (trans. J. Seitzer), Duke University Press, Durham, 2008; C. Schmitt, *Nauka o konstytucji* (trans. M. Kurkowska, R. Marszałek), Fundacja Świętego Mikołaja, Redakcja "Teologii Politycznej" 2013, Warszawa.

science.[43]

Nowadays, in democratic states the conception of the nature of the power authorized to amend the current constitution is not exactly clear. Firstly, there must be a clear distinction between the competence to adopt a new constitution and the competence to introduce the amendments, wherein it is the constituent power, from whom the original text of the constitution comes, that is of primary nature. The authority to amend the constitution does not include the authority to enact a new one. It is presumed that the primary constituent power belongs directly to the nation or to the constitutional assembly arising from its selection (constituents). In respect to the authority to amend the binding constitution, there is a distinction between secondary constituent power (*pouvoir constituant derivé*) and constituted power (*pouvoir constitué*; *pouvoir de révision*). Secondly, the constituent power is a sovereign authority and it is bound by procedural restrictions. However, the constituted power is not a sovereign power and is able to act only within formal and substantial limits.[44]

---

43 Further reading *inter alia*: Y. Roznai, *Amendment Power, Constituent Power, and Popular Sovereignty. Linking Unamendability and Amendment Procedures*, [in:] R. Albert, X. Contiades, A. Fotiado (eds.), *The Foundations and Traditions of Constitutional Amendment*, Hart Publishing, Oxford–Portland, Oregon, 2017, pp. 23–49; Y. Roznai, *Towards A Theory of Constitutional Unamendability. On the Nature and Scope of the Constitutional Amendment Powers*, "Jus Politicum" 2017, no. 18, http://juspoliticum.com/article/Towards-A-Theory-of-Constitutional-Unamendability-On-the-Nature-and-Scope-of-the-Constitutio nal-Amendment-Powers-1183.html (accessed: 15.03.2022); J. Colón-Ríos, *Constituent Power and the Law*, Oxford University Press, Oxford–New York, 2020; J. Colón-Ríos, *The Legitimacy of the Juridical: Constituent Power, Democracy, and the Limits of Constitutional Reform*, "Osgoode Hall Law Journal" 2010, vol. 48, pp. 199–245 and cited works. See also: M. Tushnet, *Peasants with pitchforks, and toilers with Twitter: Constitutional revolutions and the constituent power*, "International Journal of Constitutional Law" 2015, vol. 13, pp. 639–654; J. Komárek, ***Constitutional revolutions and the constituent power: A reply to Mark Tushnet***, "International Journal of Constitutional Law" 2015, vol. 13, pp. 1054–1058; M. Tushnet, *Constitutional revolutions and the constituent power: A rejoinder to Jan Komárek*, "International Journal of Constitutional Law" 2015, vol. 13, pp. 1059–1062.

44 See in particular: G. Burdeau, *Traité de science politique*, vol. 4, *Le statut du pouvoir dans l'État*, Librairie Générale de Droit et de Jurisprudence, R. Pichon et R. Durand-Auzias, Paris, 1969, pp. 181–191, 203–245; O. Duhamel, I.

Moreover, the constituent power engages as an active participant of constitutional discourse which induces a search for new principles, ensuring a balance between the constituent and constituted powers in constitutional democracies. This issue has also been examined in Polish legal science with reference to constituent power limitations (however, neither in Polish legal theory nor in constitutional science is there a clear concept of constitutional identity).[45] According to Krzysztof J. Kaleta, the formal rigidity – which is acknowledged to be a feature defining the written (formal) constitution – is not the sole limit to the constituent power. The axiological arguments expressed in constitutional discourse concerning limitations on the constituent power are derived from both the idea of democracy (by referring to the nature and function of the constituent power) and the principle of constitutionalism (by searching for an internal hierarchy of constitutional norms, or by referring to supra-constitutional principles that express the substance of the rule of law). The dichotomy between the primary and secondary constituent powers adopted in legal science allows us to distinguish discourses concerning two different forms of constitutional amendment. The legislative activity of the secondary constituent power that makes changes within a legal system is subject to double evaluation: from the perspective of legality and legitimacy. However, the issue of the legitimacy of the primary constituent power that changes the legal system is a domain of general argumentative discourse within which juridical arguments lose their dominant position, giving way to a broad spectrum of arguments of a moral, political, and praxeological nature.[46]

Mény, *Dictionnaire constitutionnel*, Paris, 1992, pp. 777–778; X. Magnon, *Quelques maux encore à propos des lois de révision constitutionnelle: limites, contrôlé, efficacité, caractère opératoire et existence. En homage au doyen Louis Favoreu*, "Revue française de droit constitutionnel" 2004, vol. 3, no. 59, pp. 597; K. Kubuj, *Zmiana Konstytucji V Republiki Francuskiej. Przedmiot, tryb, kontrola*, Dom Wydawniczy ELIPSA, Warszawa, 2018, pp. 43–50, 290–291 and cited works.

45 K.J. Kaleta, *Władza konstytuująca jako przedmiot badań nauk prawnych*, "Filozofia Publiczna i Edukacja Demokratyczna" 2018, vol. 7, no. 1, pp. 40–64 and cited works.

46 K.J. Kaleta, *Ograniczenia władzy ustrojodawczej w demokracji konstytucyjnej*, "Państwo i Prawo" 2018, no. 12, pp. 3–18 and cited works.

With respect to the Polish Constitution of 1997, it can be stated that Article 235 (Chapter XII: Amending the Constitution) is the basic regulation for constitutional amendments. There is no doubt that this article concerns modifications of the Constitution, but it is not clear whether these regulations could be used in order to repeal the Constitution and adopt a new one. This issue is difficult to resolve in normative and doctrinal terms.[47]

According to Article 235 of the Constitution, the Sejm and the Senate – as the constituted power – are entitled to amend the Constitution with respect to formal and substantive limitations. Therefore Chapters I, II, XII could not be amended by parliament alone, which gives such provisions a "relatively unchangeable" status. On the other hand, there is no reference to Article 90 (conferring the competence of the sovereign state), or to the Preamble to the Constitution.

The secondary constituent power belongs to parliament as well as to the nation. It is subordinated to the primary constituent power, which means that significant changes require the mandatory participation of the sovereign on the grounds of the binding Constitution. Moreover, it refers to the amendments covering matters of constitutional identity, i.e. Chapters I, II, XII, Article 90 and the Preamble. The secondary constituent power is bound by the procedural (formal) limits of Article 235. In this case replacing the Constitution with a new legal act is inadmissible.

The primary constituent power refers to the constitutional matter in its entirety. The Polish Constitution does not specify the appropriate procedure for adopting a new constitution. Moreover, there is no limits to this constituent power. It is actually a matter of limiting the will of the nation as sovereign. In such case, there is real threat to the principles of certainty and predictability that the legal system is based on. However, Ryszard Piotrowski claims that the principle of the democratic state of law is always binding for the primary constituent power, since the significance of such a rule is comparable to the rules of physics.[48] The consistency of the

---

47 J. Galster, D. Lis-Staranowicz, *Doktryna zastępowalności konstytucji. Rationae materiae wobec rationae temporis*, "Państwo i Prawo" 2016, no. 10, pp. 23–40 and cited works.

48 R. Piotrowski, *Konstytucja i granice władzy suwerena*, [in:] J. Jaskiernia, K. Spryszak (eds.), *Dwadzieścia lat obowiązywania Konstytucji RP. Polska myśl*

concept of the nation's sovereign will with the rule of law depends on political axiology and the acceptance of a fundamental axiom according to which the rule of law has a superior status in the process of exercising sovereignty – i.e. the will of the nation is carried out under the rule of law. This proves that the concepts of "sovereignty" and "law" are strongly related. Democratic law entails a legal guarantee to exercise sovereignty, while it itself is constituted by a sovereign entity of the state power.[49]

In the context of the representative nature of the Constitution, the permissible scope and gravity of constitutional amendments are determined and limited by the sovereign body entitled to interfere with the content of this act constitution.[50] Generally, the most obvious legal forms of civic participation in the exercise of sovereign power are: a) social dialogue (consultations), b) citizens' initiative, and c) a referendum. The Polish Constitution provides for neither consultations or dialogue nor citizens' legislative initiative covering the constitutional amendment. This is inconsistent with Article 118 paragraph 2, which states: "The right to introduce legislation shall also belong to a group of at least 100,000 citizens having the right to vote in elections to the Sejm." Moreover, Polish citizens had such chance during the constitutionalisation process in 1997. Therefore such inconsistency should be pointed out.

The referendum provided for in Article 235 paragraph 6 (confirmatory referendum) is optional. It depends on political factors and it can be held solely in the case of amending Chapters I, II and XII. Moreover, a relevant application may be submitted solely by the following: at least one-fifth of the statutory number of Deputies, the Senate or the President of the Republic. Polish citizens do not have such competence.

In the end it is necessary to consider whether the nation may initiate constitutional amendments pursuant to Article 125. According to such

---

konstytucyjna a międzynarodowe standardy demokratyczne, Wydawnictwo Adam Marszałek, Toruń, 2017, p. 702.

49 M. Kruk, *Przyszłość konstytucji a konstytucja przyszłości*, [in:] B. Hołyst (ed.), *Przyszłość prawa. Księga pamiątkowa XX-lecia Wydziału Prawa i Administracji*, Uczelnia Łazarskiego, Warszawa, 2017, p. 159–160.

50 J. Galster, D. Lis-Staranowicz, *Konstytucja a suweren*, "Państwo i Prawo" 2019, no. 6, pp. 5–27 and cited works.

provisions, a nationwide referendum may be held in respect of matters of particular importance to the state. The right to order a nationwide referendum is vested in: a) the Sejm at its own initiative, b) the Sejm at the initiative of the Senate or the Council of Minister, c) the President of the Republic with the consent of the Senate, and d) the Sejm at the initiative of the group of 500,000 citizens. In the latter case, it should be noted that the citizens' application is not binding, which seems paradoxical, since it is the most obvious example of the "people's will" to challenge the system.[51]

6. Final remarks

Constitutional amendments are a natural component of the evolution of constitutional systems in modern states. Simultaneously, in a democratic state of law there is a strong need for a constitution of a lasting character and with clear legitimacy arising from social support. Such durability does not result from the text itself, but from the lasting character of the system and from the rights and freedoms that are guaranteed by it. The factors playing a crucial role are: the existence and protection of the constitutional identity of the state and the constitutional consciousness of citizens. Moreover, the constitutional consciousness of citizens results from constitutional identity. It is pointless to examine constitutional consciousness alone, without taking into account constitutional identity, which is sourced from the constitution itself as a basic state law.

Constitutional identity – in either the *selfhood* or *sameness* aspect – determines the core, scope and limits of contemporary constitutional law. In the context of constitutional amendments such identity serves as an expression of the very "heart" of the constitution and its non-derogable part. The principles and values recognized as the core of the constitution by the primary constituent power require particular protection from rash changes that may cause a threat to the fundamental order. Therefore, such principles and values serve as the substantive limits for the constitutional changes, which has been illustrated by the case-law of constitutional courts. At the same time, the constitutional identity – which should not only be regarded in individual terms – serves as a community-integrating factor.

51 Further reading: M. Kruk, *Przyszłość konstytucji...*, p. 145 and subsequent pages.

Such a community of law and values is based on observance of democratic principles, the rule of law and fundamental individual rights. According to Peter Häberle,[52] it is the constitutional community in its broad sense (as the public authorities, other bodies that apply the constitution, as well as citizens and their sub-communities) that, in fact, attributes the significance and the identity to the constitution. On the whole, constitutional identity presents a particularly important concept, acting as a barrier that protects the constitution from careless changes. Moreover, the recognition of the concept of constitutional identity would require that an amendment would result from extensive consultation and debate, while also aiming to develop the core principles of the constitution.[53]

Constitutional consciousness is, in turn, a question of understanding the role of the constitution in a democratic society. The constitution plays not only the main legal role within a democratic state ruled by law, but also maintains integrative and educational functions. The approach to law in general, the legal attitude, and the level of respect towards law determine the level of importance attributed to the constitutional act by the society. If such a society is aware of this role and these functions (in other words: if it reaches a high level of constitutional consciousness) it tends to identify itself – as community – with constitutional rights and values. The citizens' attitude towards the constitutional rights and values is linked, as a result, to national identity, viewed as a legal, axiological, historical and cultural community. The high level of constitutional consciousness – based on informed choices and knowledge – may serve as an additional source of the limits to the constitutional amendment process and source of a self-restraint for politicians, preventing rash political decisions on such

52 P. Häberle, *Die offene Gesellschaft der Verfassungsinterpreten: Ein Beitrag zur pluralistischen und „prozessualen" Verfassungsinterpretation*, "Juristische Zeitung" 1975, vol. 30, no. 10, pp. 297 and subsequent pages – Polish translation: P. Häberle, *Otwarte społeczeństwo interpretatorów konstytucji*, "Samorząd Terytorialny" 1992, no. 10, pp. 41–53. Further reading: M. Kotzur (ed.), *Peter Häberle on Constitutional Theory. Constitution as Culture and the Open Society of Constitutional Interpreters*, Nomos/Hart, Baden-Baden, 2018.

53 In the context of the Polish Constitution and the role of constitutional identity in its change under conditions of constitutional crisis see: M. Granat, K. Granat, *The Constitution of Poland*, pp. 225–241.

matters. A nation that is aware and conscious of the role of the constitution may serve as the most perfect and adequate guarantee of reasonable changes. For that reason, appropriate legal education (including the educational role of the courts and their case-law) is an issue of particular and great importance.[54]

To sum up, it is worth pointing out that constitutional changes require not only the certain "constitutional moment", but – above all else – a proper level of stable democracy that is hardly possible to reach without an adequate and high level of constitutional consciousness. Awareness of the need for constitutional change is not a given fact, but a gradual process based on civic education. Such education is of particular relevance, since the concept of the constitution arises from the legal culture, and the concept of law as such shall also conform with the constitution in order that citizens may identify themselves with it.[55]

Moreover, there is no doubt that the participation of citizens in the constitutional amending process is a clear expression of democracy and the sovereignty of the nation. However, it does not mean unlimited power to change the binding constitution. The limits of the sovereign's will are determined by the rule of law and the human rights arising from the inherent and inalienable dignity of the person. The two concepts of "the sovereign will of the nation" and "the rule of law" may achieve conformity solely under the *sine qua non* condition that the people's will is exercised within a rule of law framework.

---

54 K.M. Cern, *On the Intrinsic Correlation Between Public Legitimation of Democratic Law and Discursive Competencies of Citizens*, "Filozofia Publiczna i Edukacja Demokratyczna"/"Public Philosophy and Democratic Education" 2014, vol. III, no. 2, pp. 57–68.

55 U. Volkmann, *Elementos de una teoría de la Constitución alemana* (trans. I. Gutiérrez Gutiérrez), Marcial Pons, Madrid, 2019 (and inside: I. Gutiérrez Gutiérrez, *Sobre una teoría de la Constitución española*). See also: R. Fernández-Carvajal, *Nota sobre el Derecho constitucional como nuevo Derecho común*, "Anuario de Derecho constitucional y parlamentario" 1989, no. 1, pp. 37–46.

Bibliography

Albert, R., *Constitutional Amendments: Making, Breaking, and Changing Constitutions*, Oxford University Press, New York, 2019.

Arnaiz, A.S., Llivina, C.A. (eds.), *National Constitutional Identity and European Integration*, Intersentia Ltd, Cambridge, 2013.

Burdeau, G., *Traité de science politique*, vol 4. *Le statut du pouvoir dans l'État*, Librairie Générale de Droit et de Jurisprudence, R. Pichon et R. Durand-Auzias, Paris, 1969.

Calliess, Ch., van der Schyff G. (eds.), *Constitutional Identity in a Europe of Multilevel Constitutionalism*, Cambridge University Press, Cambridge, 2019.

Cern, K.M., *Jak rozumieć rolę konstytucji we współczesnym społeczeństwie demokratycznym?*, "Studia Prawno-Ekonomiczne" 2016, vol. CI.

Cern, K.M., *On the Intrinsic Correlation Between Public Legitimation of Democratic Law and Discursive Competencies of Citizens*, "Filozofia Publiczna i Edukacja Demokratyczna"/"Public Philosophy and Democratic Education" 2014, vol. III, no. 2.

Choudhury, S. (ed.), *The Migration of Constitutional Ideas*, Cambridge University Press, Cambridge, 2006.

Coan, A., *Living Constitutional Theory*, "Duke Law Journal Online" 2017, vol. 66.

Colón-Ríos, J., *Constituent Power and the Law*, Oxford University Press, Oxford–New York, 2020.

Colón-Ríos, J., *The Legitimacy of the Juridical: Constituent Power, Democracy, and the Limits of Constitutional Reform*, "Osgoode Hall Law Journal" 2010, vol. 48.

Duhamel, O., Mény, I., *Dictionnaire constitutionnel*, Paris, 1992.

Elkins, Z., Ginsburg, T., Melton, J., *The Endurance of National Constitutions*, Cambridge University Press, Cambridge, 2009.

Fernández-Carvajal, R., *Nota sobre el Derecho constitucional como nuevo Derecho común*, "Anuario de Derecho constitucional y parlamentario" 1989, no. 1.

Galster, J., Lis-Staranowicz, D., *Doktryna zastępowalności konstytucji. Rationae materiae wobec rationae temporis*, "Państwo i Prawo" 2016, no. 10.

Galster, J., Lis-Staranowicz D., *Konstytucja a suweren*, "Państwo i Prawo" 2019, no. 6.

Ginsburg, T., *Constitutional Endurance*, [in:] T. Ginsburg, R. Dixon (eds.), *Comparative Constitutional Law*, Edward Elgar, Cheltenham–Northampton, 2011.

Gözler, K., *Judicial Review of Constitutional Amendments. A Comparative Study*, Ekin Press, Bursa, 2008.

Granat, M., *Constitutional Identity and its Functions*, "Przegląd Prawa Konstytucyjnego" 2022, vol. 2.

Granat, M., *Rozumienie zmiany Konstytucji RP a tożsamość konstytucyjna*, [in:] R. Chruściak (ed.), *Problemy zmiany konstytucji*, Wydawnictwo Sejmowe, Warszawa, 2017.

Granat, M., Granat, K., *The Constitution of Poland: A Contextual Analysis*, Hart Publishing, Oxford–London–New York–New Delhi–Sydney, 2022.

Häberle, P., *Die offene Gesellschaft der Verfassungsinterpreten: Ein Beitrag zur pluralistischen und „prozessualen" Verfassungsinterpretation*, "Juristische Zeitung" 1975, vol. 30, no. 10.

Häberle, P., *Otwarte społeczeństwo interpretatorów konstytucji*, "Samorząd Terytorialny" 1992, no. 10.

Habermas, J., *Constitutional Democracy. A Paradoxical Union of Contradictory Principles?*, "Political Theory" 2001, vol. 29, no. 6.

Habermas, J., *Faktyczność i obowiązywanie. Teoria dyskursu wobec zagadnień prawa i demokratycznego państwa prawnego* (trans. A. Romaniuk, R. Marszałek), Wydawnictwo Naukowe Scholar, Warszawa, 2005.

Habermas, J., *Uwzględniając Innego. Studia do teorii politycznej* (trans. A. Romaniuk), Wydawnictwo Naukowe PWN, Warszawa, 2009.

Hauser, R., Zirk-Sadowski, M., Wojciechowski, B. (eds.), *The Common European Constitutional Culture: Its Sources, Limits and Identity*, Peter Lang Publishing, Frankfurt am Main, 2016.

Jacobsohn, G.J., *Constitutional Identity*, Harvard University Press, Harvard, 2010.

Jacobsohn, G.J., *Constitutional Values and Principles*, [in:] M. Rosenfeld, A. Sajó (eds.), *The Oxford Handbook of Comparative Constitutional Law*, Oxford University Press, Oxford, 2012.

Kaleta, K.J., *Ograniczenia władzy ustrojodawczej w demokracji konstytucyjnej*, "Państwo i Prawo" 2018, no. 12.

Kaleta, K.J., *Władza konstytuująca jako przedmiot badań nauk prawnych*, "Filozofia Publiczna i Edukacja Demokratyczna" 2018, vol. 7, no. 1.

Kavanagh, A., *The Idea of a Living Constitution*, "Canadian Journal of Law and Jurisprudence" 2003, vol. XVI, no. 1.

Kelsen, H., *Foundations of Democracy*, "Ethics" 1955, vol. 66.

Kelsen, H., *O istocie i wartości demokracji* (trans. F. Turynowa), Księgarnia Powszechna, Warszawa, 1936.

Komárek, J., *Constitutional evolutions and the constituent power: A reply to Mark Tushnet*, "International Journal of Constitutional Law" 2015, vol. 13.

Kotzur, M. (ed.), *Peter Häberle on Constitutional Theory. Constitution as Culture and the Open Society of Constitutional Interpreters*, Nomos/Hart, Baden-Baden, 2018.

Kruk, M., *Przyszłość konstytucji a konstytucja przyszłości*, [in:] B. Hołyst (ed.), *Przyszłość prawa. Księga pamiątkowa XX-lecia Wydziału Prawa i Administracji*, Uczelnia Łazarskiego, Warszawa, 2017.

Kubuj, K., *Zmiana Konstytucji V Republiki Francuskiej. Przedmiot, tryb, kontrola*, Dom Wydawniczy ELIPSA, Warszawa, 2018.

La Torre, M., *Constitutionalism and Legal Reasoning*, Springer, Dordrecht, 2007.

Loughlin, M., *The Concept of Constituent Power*, "European Journal of Political Theory" 2014, vol. 13, no. 2.

Magnon, X., *Quelques maux encore à propos des lois de révision constitutionnelle: limites, contrôlé, efficacité, caractère opératoire et existence. En homage au doyen Louis Favoreu*, "Revue française de droit constitutionnel" 2004, vol. 3, no. 59.

Mayer, F., *L'identité constitutionnelle dans la jurisprudence constitutionnelle allemande*, [in:] L. Burgorgue-Larsen (ed.), *L'identité constitutionnelle saisie par les juges en Europe*, Editions Pedone, 2011.

Osiatyński, W., *Paradoxes of Constitutional Borrowing*, "International Journal of Constitutional Law" 2003, vol. 1.

Perju, V., *Constitutional Transplants, Borrowing, and Migrations*, [in:] M. Rosenfeld, A. Sajó (eds.), *Oxford Handbook of Comparative Constitutional Law*, Oxford University Press, Oxford, 2012.

Piotrowski, R., *Konstytucja i granice władzy suwerena*, [in:] J. Jaskiernia, K. Spryszak (eds.), *Dwadzieścia lat obowiązywania Konstytucji RP. Polska myśl konstytucyjna a międzynarodowe standardy demokratyczne*, Wydawnictwo Adam Marszałek, Toruń, 2017.

Polzin, M., *Constitutional Identity, Unconstitutional Amendments and the Idea of Constituent Power: The Development of the Doctrine of Constitutional Identity in German Constitutional Law*, "International Journal of Constitutional Law" 2016, vol. 14.

Ricoeur, P., *Oneself as Another*, University of Chicago Press, Chicago–London, 1990.

Rigaux, M.-F., *La theorie des limites materielles a l'exercice de la fonction constituante*, Larcier, Bruxelles, 1985.

Rosenfeld, M., *The Identity of the Constitutional Subject: Selfhood, Culture and Community*, Routledge, London–New York, 2010.

Rosenfeld, M. (ed.), *Constitutionalism, Identity, Difference and Legitimacy. Theoretical Perspectives*, Duke University Press, Durham, 1994.

Roznai, Y., *Amendment Power, Constituent Power, and Popular Sovereignty. Linking Unamendability and Amendment Procedures*, [in:] R. Albert, X. Contiades, A. Fotiado (eds.), *The Foundations and Traditions of Constitutional Amendment*, Hart Publishing, Oxford–Portland, Oregon, 2017.

Roznai, Y., *Towards A Theory of Constitutional Unamendability. On the Nature and Scope of the Constitutional Amendment Powers*, "Jus Politicum" 2017, no. 18.

Roznai, Y., *Unconstitutional Constitutional Amendments. The Limits of Amendment Powers*, Oxford University Press, Oxford, 2017.

Schmitt, C., *Constitutional Theory* (trans. J. Seitzer), Duke University Press, Durham, 2008.

Schmitt, C., *Legality and Legitimacy* (trans. J. Seitzer), Duke University Press, Durham, 2004.

Schmitt, C., *Nauka o konstytucji* (trans. M. Kurkowska, R. Marszałek), Fundacja Świętego Mikołaja, Redakcja "Teologii Politycznej", Warszawa, 2013.

Sieyès, E.J., *Czym jest stan trzeci? Esej o przywilejach* (trans. M. Jarosz), Wydawnictwo Sejmowe, Warszawa, 2016.

Strauss, D.A., *The Living Constitution*, Oxford University Press, Oxford, 2010.

Śledzińska-Simon, A., *Constitutional identity in 3D: A model of individual, relational, and collective self and its application in Poland*, "International Journal of Constitutional Law" 2015, vol. 13, no. 1.

Śledzińska-Simon, A., *Koncepcja tożsamości konstytucyjnej: wymiar indywidualny, relatywny oraz zbiorowy*, "Przegląd Prawa i Administracji" 2016, vol. CVII.

Śledzińska-Simon, A., Ziółkowski M., *Constitutional Identity of Poland: Is the Emperor Putting on the Old Clothes of Sovereignty?*, [in:] Ch. Calliess, G. van der Schyff (eds.), *Constitutional Identity in a Europe of Multilevel Constitutionalism*, Cambridge University Press, Cambridge, 2019.

Tushnet, M., *Constitutional revolutions and the constituent power: A rejoinder to Jan Komárek*, "International Journal of Constitutional Law" 2015, vol. 13.

Tushnet, M., *Peasants with pitchforks, and toilers with Twitter: Constitutional revolutions and the constituent power*, "International Journal of Constitutional Law" 2015, vol. 13.

Volkmann, U., *Elementos de una teoría de la Constitución alemana* (trans. I. Gutiérrez Gutiérrez), Marcial Pons, Madrid, 2019.

Wojtyczek, K., *Przekazywanie kompetencji państwa organizacjom międzynarodowym*, Wydawnictwo Uniwersytetu Jagiellońskiego, Kraków, 2007.

Wójtowicz, K., *Constitutional courts and European Union Law*, E-Wydawnictwo, Prawnicza i Ekonomiczna Biblioteka Cyfrowa, Wydział Prawa, Administracji i Ekonomii Uniwersytetu Wrocławskiego, Wrocław, 2014.

Zamboni, M., *Law and Politics. A Dilemma for Contemporary Legal Theory*, Springer, Berlin–Heidelberg, 2008.

Ziółkowski, M., *Mozaika tożsamości konstytucyjnych*, [in:] A. Wróbel, M. Ziółkowski (eds.), *Tożsamość konstytucyjna w wybranych państwach członkowskich Unii Europejskiej*, Wolters Kluwer, Warszawa, 2021.

Ziółkowski, M., *Tożsamość konstytucyjna jako wzorzec i kryterium kontroli w postępowaniu przed Trybunałem Konstytucyjnym (uwagi na marginesie wyroków K 32/09 i P 7/20)*, [in:] M. Florczak-Wątor, M. Krzemiński (eds.), *Interdyscyplinarny wymiar tożsamości konstytucyjnej*, Wydawnictwo Księgarnia Akademicka, Kraków, 2022.

Marcin Górski[2]

"Tempering Steel" – on Shaping the Standard of Interpretation of the Convention as Exemplified by the Legal Recognition of Same-Sex Relationships[1]

Abstract

The case-law of the European Court of Human Rights concerning the interpretation of Article 8 of the Convention in the context of the right to private life of homosexual persons, and then also the right to private and family life of same-sex couples, has undergone a profound evolution over the last fifty years. The Court, initially – in principle – accepting even the penalization of physical intercourse of homosexual persons, gradually extended protection to the sphere of their intimate life, and then slowly but consistently built a standard of interpretation recognizing the construction of the European consensus on the positive obligation of States Party to ensure the possibility of formalizing same-sex relationships. The judgment *Fedotova and others v. Russia* (the operative part and all the main conclusions of which were recently upheld by the Grand Chamber in its judgment of January 23, 2023) is a *finalité* of this evolution to date, and at the same time the opening of a new stage thereof: new disputes will probably focus on the alleged incompatibility of national legislations with the requirement of normative "adequacy" (required by Article 8 ECHR as interpreted in *Fedotova*), and then probably also on challenging the margin of appreciation of States regarding Article 12 of the Convention. The purpose of this paper is not to present the standard of interpretation of Article 8 ECHR in the context of the issue of formalization of same-sex relationships,

---

1 This text was first published in the Polish language version in "Państwo i Prawo", 2022, vol. 12.

2 . Marcin Górski – professor at the University of Łódź (Department of European Constitutional Law, Faculty of Law and Administration), Dr. Habil. Iuris; member of the Migration Law Research Centre, Polish Academy of Science; visiting professor of the Chandigarh University, India; co-convener of the Research Panel of Freedom of Expression of the International Association of Constitutional Law; attorney; head of the Legal Department of the City of Lodz Local Government.

but rather to illustrate the technology of building this standard. Analysing these mechanisms makes it possible to predict more precisely the future developments of ECtHR case-law.

Keywords: right to privacy, ECtHR, interpretation, same-sex couples, legal recognition, judicial policy

In June 2010, the European Court of Human Rights issued a groundbreaking judgment for the issue of formalizing same-sex relationships[3] in *Schalk and Kopf v. Austria*.[4] After 11 years, the ECtHR "completed" the position presented at that time, issuing in July 2021 the judgment in *Fedotova and others v. Russia*,[5] which was also a groundbreaking, although for different reasons. The significance of the first of these judgments consisted firstly in "re-anchoring" the legal protection of a union of two persons of the same-sex within Art. 8 of the Convention, thus the right to privacy to the protection of family life,[6] and secondly in emphasizing that a European (interpretative) consensus[7] is being formed regarding the legal recognition of same-sex relationships. The groundbreaking nature of the second judgment lies in the clear indication that this consensus has already

---

3 The notion of "legal recognition" will be referred to in this text also as "formalization" due to the essence of the position of the ECtHR, which implies the need to provide a legal framework for the social phenomenon of same-sex relationships.

4 ECtHR judgment of 24 June 2010, *Schalk and Kopf* v. *Austria*, application no. 30141/04.

5 ECtHR judgment of 13 July 2021, *Fedotova and others* v. *Russia*, applications no. 40792/10, 30538/14 and 43439/14. The Russian Federation, acting pursuant to Article 43 of the Convention, requested that the case be referred to the Grand Chamber, which was done on November 22, 2021.

6 Cf. the earlier position of the ECtHR in this case, refusing to treat same-sex unions as "families" within the meaning of Art. 8 of the Convention, in the decision of the European Commission of Human Rights of 3 May 1983 in the case of *X and Y* v. *United Kingdom*, application no. 9369/81.

7 See broadly on the method of establishing an interpretative consensus by the ECHR in Ch. Djeffal, *Consensus, Stasis, Evolution: Reconstructing Argumentative Patterns in Evolutive ECHR Jurisprudence* [in:] P. Kapotas, V. P. Tzevelekos, *Building Consensus on European Consensus. Judicial Interpretation on Human Rights in Europe and Beyond*, Cambridge, 2019, pp. 71–95.

formed, resulting in the obligation to introduce regulations concerning the formalization of same-sex relationships, which also falls on states that clearly opposed its formation. This issue is an interesting illustration of the formation of an interpretative consensus, and the case-law of the Court concerning the issues discussed here shows the logic guiding Strasbourg decisions and the way (technology) of building the standard of interpretation of the Convention. The latest judgment of the ECtHR on this issue also raises questions about the way in which the Convention standard is going to be implemented by states that reject the obligation resulting from the *Fedotova* judgment, such as Poland or Russia.

Currently 46 countries are parties to the ECHR. Among them, 15 countries haev introduced marital equality (understood narrowly as the possibility of two adults of the same-sex marrying, regardless of some differences in the rights related to entering into such marriage), and 19 countries have introduced partnerships (or their equivalents) for same-sex couples, but in 7 countries they operate alongside the possibility of entering into same-sex marriages. Thus, in total, in 27 States of the Convention, i.e. the majority of parties, it is now possible to obtain legal recognition of a same-sex relationship.

Let us emphasize at this point that this paper does not focus on assessing the accuracy of the emerging standard of interpretation of Article 8 of the Convention. Neither does it refer to the arguments of the Parties to the ECHR asserting that when concluding the Convention or acceding to it, they did not include such obligations within their consent, or that enabling 5-10% of citizens to live in a dignified manner in the most personal and sensitive sphere would lead to significant social unrest, from which it follows (with a certain amount of exaggeration) that we need to wait another 100 years for societies to become ready for this "revolution." This paper focuses solely on showing the very dynamics and logic of shaping the new standard of interpretation of the Convention, i.e. presenting a certain "technology" of the ECtHR's case-law that preserves the nature of the Convention as a "living instrument",[8] without discussing the standard

8 For the record, let us only recall that the term "living instrument" to describe the ECHR was employed for the first time by the Court in the judgment of 25 April 1978, *Tyrer* v. *United Kingdom*, application no. 5856/72, paragraph 31.

itself (whether it is right or not). Certain processes, including social processes and, consequently, changes in the understanding of law, take place despite the emotions that accompany them naturally, and it seems pointless to resist them.

1. "How steel was tempered"[9] – on shaping the standard of interpretation of Article 8 of the Convention regarding same-sex relationships

The approach of the ECHR organs to homosexuality has undergone a significant evolution: from rulings accepting the differentiation of the age of consent and the criminalization of sexual contacts between men,[10] through the approval *in principio* of the permissibility of criminalizing "sodomy" and "a certain degree of control over homosexual behaviour",[11] and the disqualification of the same-sex relationship as forms of exercising the right to family life,[12] to a gradual change of position, expressed in the refusal to recognize social prejudices against homosexuals as a legitimate reason for interference in private life and equating them with racism.[13] Earlier Strasbourg decisions concerning the complaints of homosexual persons about their treatment by states may, from contemporary perspective, amaze us with the wording used and the acceptance of some statements concerning

9 The quote is taken from the title of the novel *Как закалялась сталь* by Nikolai Ostrovsky, the avant-gardist of socialist realism.

10 See e.g. the decision of the Commission on inadmissibility of September 30, 1975, X v. *Germany*, application no. 5935/72.

11 ECtHR (full Court) of 22 October 1981, *Dudgeon* v. *United Kingdom*, application no. 7525/76, paragraphs 49 and 62 (finding violation of Article 8 of the ECHR by imposing a criminal penalty on the applicant for sexual contact with a man). Subsequently, the language of the Court's reasoning was significantly "smoothened" – if compared to the above quotations – in the judgment of the (full Court) of the ECtHR of October 26, 1988, *Norris* v. *Ireland*, application no. 8 of the Convention, but this time as a consisting of the very application of the provisions penalizing homosexual sexual contacts.

12 Commission decision on inadmissibility of 3 May 1983, *X. and Y.* v. *United Kingdom*, application no. 9369/81.

13 ECtHR judgment of 27 September 1999, *Smith and Grady* v. *United Kingdom*, applications no. 33985/96 and 33986/96, para. 97.

these persons, which we now generally consider to be obviously erroneous. But they were, for their time, as brave as they could be. Another problem concerning the social functioning of homosexual persons that the Court is faced with today is the issue of the legal recognition of their life as couples. This problem, however, could not have been properly addressed in the Court's reflection, were it not for the gradual evolution of the case-law.

In the practice so far, the Court has repeatedly referred to the issue of the legal obligation under Article 8 of the Convention to formalize same-sex unions. The rulings of the Court follow a logical sequence, devoid of any randomness – their "construction" and relations between them are thoroughly elaborated and fully intentional.

Initially, the Court found the complaints alleging a violation of the Convention for the failure to legally recognize same-sex relationships inadmissible. It did so in two decisions in cases against the United Kingdom (Courten[14] of 2008 and M.W.[15] of 2009), Interestingly enough, the Court examined the Courten complaint, lodged in 2006, alleging only a violation of Article 14 of the ECHR in conjunction with Article 1 of Protocol No. 1 to the Convention before the complaint of M.W., lodged much earlier, already in 2002, and also alleging a violation of Article 14 in conjunction with Article 8 of the Convention. In both cases, the Court "waited" for the enactment of the British Civil Partnership Act (which took place in December 2005). Having "reversed the order" of examining the complaints, the Court found itself in a much more comfortable position, because in the case of M.W., which had been received earlier, but was examined after Courten, it could rely on the latter decision. This was important because the Courten case did not refer directly to the lack of formalization of same-sex relationships, but to the consequences of such failure in the form of the alleged discrimination in access to tax advantages, i.e. it fell within Article 1 of Protocol No. 1 to the Convention, and not in Article 8 ECHR. The Court "equated" the two cases in a legal assessment – although they concerned different aspects: the Courten case related to property issues,

14 ECtHR decision on inadmissibility of 4.11.2008, *Courten* v. *United Kingdom*, application no. 4479/06.

15 The decision of the ECtHR on inadmissibility of June 23, 2009, *M.W.* v. *United Kingdom*, application no. 11313/02.

and the case of M.W. directly to the question of the right to have the relationship legally recognized. The ECtHR found that since the United Kingdom had resolved the problem at the national level by adopting the Civil Partnership Act (in M.W. the Court added that it did so by contributing to the creation of the European interpretative consensus), it could not be reproached for failing to do so sooner. Moreover, the Courten decision was preceded by the judgment in Burden v. United Kingdom[16] concerning the legality of differential treatment for the purposes of inheritance tax between applicants (living together, unmarried and childless sisters) and married couples and registered partnerships – in this case, the Court emphasized the difference between the situation of the applicants and couples who are married and "partnerships", but also the legal differences between opposite-sex marriages and same-sex partnerships. By reversing the order in which the complaints were examined, the Court was thus able to deal first with the slightly more "obvious" Courten case, which was directly related to a less controversial and rather trivial tax issues, while having the "groundwork" already laid in the form of the Burden judgment.

These two rulings (Courten and M.W.) prepared the ground for the landmark 2010 Schalk and Kopf judgment, in which the Court referred to both of them, pointing to the formation of a European consensus[17]. Admittedly, in Schalk and Kopf the Court dismissed (by a slim majority

---

16 ECtHR (Grand Chamber) judgment of April 29, 2008, *Burden* v. *United Kingdom*, application no. 13378/05, paragraphs 62–65.

17 The judgment of the ECtHR of 24 June 2010 in the case of Schalk and Kopf, point 105. In the literature, the judgment is commented on, inter alia, in: M. Górski, *Glosa do wyroku ETPC z dnia 24 czerwca 2010 r., 30141/04*, Lex/El. 2010, M. Bamforth, *Families But Not (Yet) Marriages? Same-Sex Partners and the Developing European Convention 'Margin of Appreciation'*, "Child and Family Law Quarterly" 2011, vol. 23, no. 1, pp. 128–143; K. Bem, *Glosa do wyroku ETPC z dnia 24 czerwca 2010 r., 30141/04*, Lex/El. 2010, W. Brzozowski, *Małżeństwo, życie rodzinne, związki osób tej samej płci. Glosa do wyroku ETPC z dnia 24 czerwca 2010 r., 30141/04*, EPS 2011, vol. 4, pp. 42–45; R. Mizerski, *Dostęp par różnopłciowych do związku partnerskiego. Glosa do wyroku ETPC z dnia 26 października 2017 r., 28475/12*, EPS 2018, vol. 8, pp. 43–48.

of 4 votes against 3) the complaint concerning the alleged violation of Article 14 in conjunction with Article 8 of the Convention due to a failure to legally recognize same-sex unions, but did so 6 years after the applicants had lodged a complaint (symptomatically, the application was received in the same year as in the Courten case), after the adoption of the Austrian Civil Partnership Act (it entered into force on 1 January 2010). The Court emphasized, however, that a European consensus on the legal recognition of of same-sex relationships is being formed, although most of the Convention State-Parties do not participate in it (because admittedly the majority of them did not participate in that consensus at that time), and therefore states must exercise the margin of appreciation as to the moment (let us emphasize) in which such formalization will be introduced. The Court made it clear that it would be artificial in the face of the social changes that have taken place to consider that same-sex couples do not enjoy the right to family life, unlike opposite-sex couples.[18] The Court then repeated the position taken in the Courten and M.W. cases that, although not in the avant-garde, Austria had introduced such a formalization (which the Court had kindly decided to await), therefore it could not be blamed for failing to do so earlier.[19] Judges Rozakis, Spielmann and Jebens disagreed with the position of the majority, pointing out the inconsistency in, on the one hand, recognizing same-sex relationship as a form of "family life"[20] within the meaning of Article 8 of the Convention, and on the other hand,

18 The judgment of the ECtHR of 24 June 2010, Schalk and Kopf, paragraphs 93 and 94. Similarly, soon after, in the judgment of the ECtHR of 22.07.2010, *P.B. and J.S.* v. *Austria*, application no. 18984/02, paragraph 30.

19 The judgment of the ECtHR of 24 June 2010 in the case of Schalk and Kopf, para. 106. The margin of appreciation, as presented in the case of Schalk and Kopf, therefore concerned only the timing of the formalization of same-sex relationships, and not whether they were to be formalized. Moreover, it was already noticeable then that the Court saw a shrinkage of this margin as well. See, also more broadly, A. Paprocka, *Budowanie tożsamości europejskiej w orzecznictwie Europejskiego Trybunału Praw Człowieka*, PiP 2014, vol. 12, pp. 32–34.

20 Which constituted a clear departure from the earlier position expressed, for example, in the decision of the ECtHR on inadmissibility of May 10, 2001, *Mata Estevez* v. *Spain*, application no. 56501/00.

failure to draw conclusions from it in the form of a positive obligation on the part of the state, which was the result of the refusal to find a violation of Article 14 in connection with Article 8 ECHR. The judges emphasized that "Today it is widely recognised and also accepted by society that same-sex couples enter into stable relationships. Any absence of a legal framework offering them, at least to a certain extent, the same rights or benefits attached to marriage [...] would need robust justification, especially taking into account the growing trend in Europe to offer some means of qualifying for such rights or benefits."[21] Let us note the sequence of arguments and a certain deliberate narrative strategy employed by the authors of the dissenting opinion. The judges emphasized that the refusal to grant "rights and benefits" would require "solid justification" due to social acceptance not for formalization itself, but for the fact that same-sex couples create stable relationships. Having said this, they added that what matters "especially [...] is the growing trend in Europe." Therefore, even if this trend did not grow, these judges would still, as one should assume, find it unacceptable to leave same-sex relationships in a legal vacuum.[22]

Despite the doubts raised in the dissenting opinion, the Schalk and Kopf judgment constituted a milestone in the jurisprudence on the discussed issue, because it clearly indicated, as was stated in the literature, that the Court was on the verge of deriving a positive obligation of the state to formalize same-sex relationships.[23]

21 ECtHR judgment of 24 June 2010, Schalk and Kopf, point 9 of the joint dissenting opinion of judges Rozakis, Spielmann and Jebens.

22 For the sake of clarity, let us note that the judgment also received the concurring opinion of judges Malinverni and (of course) Kovler, who criticized the attempt (see paragraph 55 of the judgment) to change the way of interpreting Article 12 of the Convention, as well as the reference in the argumentation of the judgment to Article 9 of the Charter of Fundamental Rights as an argument for such a change.

23 Thus, L. Hodson, *A Marriage by Any Other Name? Schalk and Kopf v. Austria*, "Human Rights Law Review" 2011, vol 11, no. 1, p. 176, holding that "the Court indicated that it is poised on the brink of obliging States to provide same-sex relationships with some form of legal recognition".

The Court crossed this line "a moment later" in the judgment Vallianatos and others v. Greece in 2013.[24] The specificity of this case was that Greece introduced the institution of a civil union, but only (somewhat intriguingly) for heterosexual couples. The Court highlighted the emergence of the European consensus on the formalization of same-sex unions, and then noted that Greece did not provide convincing and sufficiently compelling reasons to prevent same-sex couples from formalization through entering into a civil partnership, which justified the finding of a violation of Article 14 in connection with Article 8 ECHR.[25] The judgment was passed with an overwhelming majority of 16 votes to one, and the dissenting opinion of Judge Pinto de Albuquerque focused on the non-exhaustion of domestic remedies.

The next step in forming the standard of interpretation of Art. 8 of the ECHR in relation to the issue of formalizing same-sex relationships was the judgment in Oliari and others v. Italy.[26] The applicants complained of

---

24 ECtHR (Grand Chamber) judgment of 7 November 2013, *Vallianatos and others* v. *Greece*, applications nos. 29381/09 and 32684/09. The Chamber relinquished its jurisdiction in favour of the Grand Chamber pursuant to Article 30 of the Convention and Rule 72 of the Rules of Court. See the comments of G. Puppinck on this judgment, which are sometimes strongly ideologically marked and erroneous (e.g. to the extent that the author uses a completely ideological and unsupported and prima facie illogical argument about the alleged "family disintegration" due to the formalization of the functioning of families based on same-sex relationships), but in some aspects correct (e.g. to the extent that the author foresees the direction of the Court's subsequent rulings in cases of same-sex families) (G. Puppinck, *Wyrok w sprawie Vallianatos przeciwko Grecji w świetle przemian w sposobie pojmowania rodziny i „życia rodzinnego" w orzecznictwie ETPCz*, https://ordoiuris.pl/rodzina-i-malzenstwo/wyrok-w-sprawie-vallianatos-przeciwko-grecji-w-swietle-przemian-w-sposobie (accessed: 17.08.2021).

25 At para 92.

26 Judgment of the ECtHR of July 21, 2015, *Oliari and others* v. *Italy*, applications no. 18766/11 and 36030/11. The ruling was issued as a result of strategic litigation. The ruling was commented on by, among others, A. Paprocka, *Pozytywny obowiązek uregulowania statusu prawnego związków osób tej samej płci. Glosa do wyroku ETPC z dnia 21 lipca 2015 r., 18766/11 i 36030/11*, EPS 2016, vol. 4, pp. 36–41; V.J. Marzano, *Oliari and the European Court of Human Rights: where the Court failed*, "Pace International Law Review" 2017, vol. 29, no. 1, pp. 250–287; S. Ragone, V. Volpe, *An Emerging Right to a "Gay"*

violation of Article 8 and Article 14 in conjunction with Article 8 of the Convention due to a failure to allow for the formalization of same-sex unions (the applicants were 3 couples) through entering into a marriage or civil partnership. The ruling was issued after the adoption of the Italian law on civil unions, but while awaiting its entry into force. The specificity of the litigation in this case consisted in the prior determination by the Italian constitutional court of the need to introduce the institution of civil unions, stemming from the Italian constitution. The Court recalled its earlier judgment in Schalk and Kopf, noting the "rapidly emerging European consensus" regarding the formalization of same-sex relationships, and underlined the approving statements of the Italian judiciary regarding the need for such formalization. The Italian courts (including the constitutional court) quite consistently, starting from 2012, pointed to the legal necessity to regulate the legal situation of same-sex unions – a duty resulting primarily from the Italian constitution itself. Italian local government bodies also decided to register same-sex marriages concluded abroad. The Court also noted that Italian public opinion polls showed generally increasing support for such a formalization. In conclusion, the Court found there had been a violation of Article 8 of the Convention due to the margin of appreciation being exceeded by the Italian authorities (especially the legislature), who failed to introduce in a timely manner the provisions enabling the formalization of same-sex relationships. In this regard, the Court explicitly pointed to the positive obligation of the state violated by Italy which was derived from Article 8 of the Convention and which concerned providing the applicants with a specific legal framework ensuring the recognition and protection of same-sex unions (the Court held

---

Family Life? The Case Oliari v. Italy in a Comparative Perspective, "German Law Journal" 2016, vol. 17, no. 3, pp. 451–485; C.L. Popescu, *L'obligation positive des États de légiférer les partenariats civils entre les personnes de même sexe Commentaire à l'Arrêt de la Cour européenne des Droits de l'Homme – chambre du 21 juillet 2015, Affaire Oliari et autres c. Italie*, "Analele Universității București – Drept Series (AUB)" 2015, vol. 1, pp. 35–44, and also critically: N. Ziyadov, *From Justice to Injustice: Lowering the Threshold of European Consensus in Oliari and Others versus Italy*, "Indiana Journal of Global Legal Studies" 2019, vol. 26, no. 2, pp. 631–672.

that the judiciary had "failed to fulfil their positive obligation to ensure that the applicants have available a specific legal framework providing for the recognition and protection of their same-sex unions"[27]). In this way, the Court set minimum substantive requirements for the provisions formalizing same-sex relationships.

Similar conditions determined the position of the ECtHR taken in the face of the next strategic litigation, namely Orlandi and others v. Italy.[28] With this judgment, the Court also found a violation of Article 8 of the Convention due to the failure to allow for the formalization a same-sex relationship. The applicants were this time six couples who had married in third countries and requested that they be registered in the Italian civil status registers. The complaints related both to the refusal to register a foreign marriage and the impossibility of contracting such a marriage, or – finally – formalizing the relationship in any other way in Italy. Let us note that on June 5, 2016, the Italian law allowing same-sex partnerships entered into force. Despite this, the ECtHR found a violation of Article 8 of the Convention to the extent that, prior to the entry into force of national provisions, same-sex unions could not be formalized in Italy. However, the Court no longer referred to the positions of the Italian judiciary. In a dissenting opinion, judges Pejchal and Wojtyczek called for a declaration on inadmissibility of the applications, inter alia, as the applicants had lost their status as victims of the violation, because after the applications had been lodged, they had been given thc opportunity to formalize their relations within the institution of civil unions.

27 *Ibidem*, Paragraph 185. Judges Mahoney, Tsotsoria and Vehabović criticized this fragment of the Court's arguments in a concurring opinion, postulating that the grounds of the judgment were limited to the fact that, since the Italian judiciary, including the constitutional court, had themselves determined the existence of constitutional protection for same-sex unions, the generalization made in the argument of the majority (consisting in abstracting – in the opinion of the authors of the concurring opinion – from this key element and deriving instead the positive obligation of the state from Article 8 ECHR as regards the introduction of formalization) was inaccurate.

28 ECtHR judgment of December 14, 2017, *Orlandi and others* v. *Italy*, applications no. 26431/12, 26742/12, 44057/12 and 60088/12.

2. "A Hunter's Sketches"[29] – or the technique of building an interpretation standard

The Vallianatos and Oliari and Orlandi cases had a common element in the construction of the legal background, which consisted in the fact that – luckily for the formation of a standard for the interpretation of Article 8 in this respect – the Court had quite obvious "anchor points" in the domestic legislation (in Greece) or the way it had been first interpreted by domestic courts (in Italy).[30] In the case of Greece, it was a fairly visible lack of logic in their legislation already in force, which introduced a legal "alternative to marriage", but limited its accessibility only to opposite-sex couples with no convincing reasons for such a lack of consistency in the national provisions. In Italy the domestic judiciary "handed the ball" to the Court, pointing to a constitutionally determined, albeit fairly general and vague, obligation to protect same-sex couples. In the commentaries to the Oliari judgment, attention was drawn to the uniqueness of Italian cases, consisting in some advance of legislative changes the judicial decisions,[31] but these exceptional circumstances seemed to be only an additional argument and not the critical reason for finding a violation of the Convention. It was not without reason that the Court, in its Oliari ruling, first referred to the already established standard of interpretation of Article 8 ECHR (at paragraph 177), and only then and "in addition" to the continuing – not only in Europe but also worldwide – trend of formalizing same-sex relationships (paragraph 178), and lastly to the prevailing position of both Italian society and domestic courts (paras 179–181).

---

29 The title of a series of satirical stories by Ivan Turgenev describing the habits of Russians in the mid-nineteenth century.

30 This was rightly pointed out by V.J. Marzano, *Oliari and the European Court of Human Rights*, p. 281.

31 See e.g. P. Johnson, *Ground-breaking judgment of the European Court of Human Rights in Oliari and Others v Italy: same-sex couples in Italy must have access to civil unions/registered partnerships*, http://echrso.blogspot.com/2015/07/ground-breaking-judgment-of-european.html, R. Grzeszczak, M. Gniadzik, *The Right of European Union Citizens and Their Family Members to Move Freely within the Territory of the Member States (In the Light of the Judgment of the European Court of Human Rights in Oliari v. Italy)*, "Polish Review of International and European Law" 2015, vol. 4, no. 1, pp. 81–82.

Judges presenting dissenting and concurring opinions on each of these cases tried to restrain the shaping of a new standard of interpretation of Article 8 ECHR which consisted in deriving from that provision a positive obligation on the part of the state to formalize same-sex relationships. By doing so, they pointed to the failure to exhaust national remedies and the abuse – in their opinion – of the competence of a "European Constitutional Court" by the ECtHR "functioning as a *positive legislator*" (Judge Pinto de Albuquerque in the Vallianatos case), the necessity of "narrow" adjudication by the ECtHR i.e. reasoning strictly within the legal circumstances of a specific case and thus refraining from generalized conclusions about the existence of a positive obligation on the part of the state (judges Mahoney, Tsotsoria and Vehabović in the Oliari case), or the loss of the applicants' victim status (judges Pejchal and Wojtyczek in the Orlandi case).

The authors of the dissenting or concurring opinions, however, seemed to be defeated by the inevitable logic of legal (or more precisely: interpretative) developments that led the Court to its ruling given in the Fedotova case and which appeared – already at the time of passing the Vallianatos, Oliari or Orlandi decisions – quite transparent. This process consisted in the gradual construction of a new standard of interpretation of Article 8 ECHR (and by the way, but more slowly, also of Article 12 ECHR) of the Convention. The Court began by declaring as inadmissible complaints alleging non-formalization of same-sex relationships, thus wisely examining first the relatively minor Courten case (the difference in treatment of a widowed partner in inheritance taxes), then refused to find a violation of Article 8 of the Convention in the Schalk and Kopf case, but – as seems quite clear from the Court's reasoning – solely because of the prior adoption of the law introducing civil partnerships in Austria. Next, the ECtHR examined, this time agreeing with the applicants' pleas, Greek and Italian cases, where the logic of its rulings was rather difficult to challenge if one takes into consideration some, let us say, inharmonicity of the legal *status quo* in both states. Having developed the "foundations" in this way, that is, having shaped the standard of interpretation of Article 8 of the Convention consisting in deriving an explicit positive obligation of states to formalize same-sex relationships, and after waiting until the majority of members of the Council of Europe introduced in one form or another national legislation allowing for the legal recognition of same-sex unions, the Court was prepared to safely resolve the first case on this subject against the state which was a constant opponent of (or perhaps "an objector" to) the shaping of the new standard, i.e. the Russian Fedotova case.

3. "Marriage"[32] – or the *finalité* of the development of the standard of interpretation of Article 8 ECHR regarding same-sex relationships

The judgment in the Fedotova case[33] was issued following the examination of applications brought by three same-sex couples (all residing outside Russia, which is indeed sad and symptomatic) accusing Russia of violating Article 8 ECHR and Article 14 in conjunction with Article 8 of the Convention by failing to discharge the positive obligation to introduce provisions enabling the formalization of their relationships. The Russian case, concerning four complaints filed in 2010, 2016 and 2017, and all communicated in 2018, was examined before a similar Polish case (i.e. concerning the same alleged violation and also being a strategic litigation) of 15 applications filed in 2012, 2014, 2016, 2017 and 2018, and all communicated simultaneously in 2020. The judgment was passed unanimously as regards the violation of Article 8 (and therefore the Russian judge D. Dedov, otherwise known for his homophobic statements,[34] also voted in favour of the ruling).

---

32 The title of the play by Nikolai Gogol from 1836, describing Agafia Tikhonovna's struggle with the challenge of marriage perceived not so much in its romantic dimension, but rather in its socio-prestigious dimension. Her groom-to-be, Ivan Kuzmich Podkolesin, unfortunately escapes before the wedding. This is a risk which (of course, metaphorically) is also faced by the ECtHR, as there is a danger of non-compliance with its rulings, as well as the lack of reception of the standard for the interpretation of Article 8 of the Convention by those States-Parties of the Council of Europe which, due to their social and/or political conditions, have not yet decided to formalize same-sex relationships.

33 ECtHR judgment of July 13, 2021, *Fedotova and others* v. *Russia*...

34 See the dissenting opinion of judge Dedov to the judgment of the ECtHR of June 20, 2017, *Bayev and others* v. *Russia*, applications nos. 67667/09, 44092/12 and 56717/12, criticized – rightly – as scandalously homophobic by L. Lavrysen in *Bayev and Others v. Russia: on Judge Dedov's outrageously homophobic dissent*,

The applicants in the Fedotova case had filed notifications with the domestic authorities of their intention to marry (Russian: *заявление о вступление в брак*) but they were rejected due to the lack of a sex difference between the notifiers. All the refusals were unsuccessfully challenged by the applicants before the domestic courts, which, *inter alia*, stressed the irreconcilability of same-sex marriages with the national and religious tradition, the danger allegedly posed by their conclusion to motherhood and minors, as well as the "prohibition on promoting homosexuality" enshrined in Russian legislation. The Russian courts also pointed out that the Convention does not impose an obligation to introduce same-sex marriages. It should be noted that according to the Russian constitution (Article 72 § 1 g1), federal and regional authorities co-exercise the power to protect "marriage as a relationship between a man and a woman",[35] and according to the results of public opinion polls referred to by the Court, as many as 80% of Russians were against the introduction of same-sex marriages (marriage equality) in 2015. The Court also noted that the Russian constitutional court unambiguously ruled out the admissibility of formalizing same-sex relationships in its 2006 ruling. In other words, unlike in the previous Greek and Italian cases, there was neither a positive attitude in the views of Russian society in this respect, nor any useful points of reference supporting the legal recognition of same-sex relationships in the domestic case-law (which existed for example in Italy, and which were cited in the reasoning of the Court in the Oliari and Orlandi cases).

The Court, referring to the previous authorities (including the Oliari judgment), emphasized at the outset the positive obligation of a state resulting from Article 8 of the Convention and concerning the establishment of a legal framework enabling the effective exercise of the rights

source: https://strasbourgobservers.com/2017/07/13/bayev-and-others-v-russia-on-judge-dedovs-outrageously-homophobic-dissent/ (accessed: 4.04.2022).

35 In Russian: *Всовместном ведении Российской Федерации исубъектов Российской Федерации находятся […] защита семьи, материнства, отцовства идетства; защита института брака как союза мужчины иженщины; создание условий для достойного воспитания детей всемье, атакже для осуществления совершеннолетними детьми обязанности заботиться ородителях.* The provision emphasizing the opposite-sex nature of marriage was added by an amendment that entered into force on July 4, 2020.

arising from this provision, and also noted that although states enjoy a certain margin of appreciation in deciding on the implementation of their positive obligations under Article 8 ECHR, that margin of appreciation is narrowed when it comes to the protection of a particularly important aspect of the functioning or identity of an individual. The Court also noted, referring to its judgments of Schalk and Kopf, Vallianatos and Oliari, that same-sex couples are in a remarkably similar situation to opposite-sex couples in terms of the need for formal recognition and protection of their relationships. The Court also pointed out that the decision on the implementation of the positive obligation of a state under Article 8 of the Convention should be made taking into account a fair balancing of the competing interests of the applicant and of the society as a whole, while taking into consideration the circumstances justifying the interference with the right to privacy and family life as described in the limitation clause (Article 8 § 2 ECHR). Let us note that the structure (or more precisely: the sequence) of the arguments resembles the reasoning of the authors of the already mentioned dissenting opinion in Schalk and Kopf (judges Rozakis, Spielmann and Jebens).

Referring these general observations to the circumstances of the case at hand, the ECtHR held that although Article 8 of the Convention does not impose on states an obligation to formally recognize same-sex unions, it nevertheless implies an obligation to maintain a fair balance between the competing interests of same-sex couples and society as a whole. At the same time, however, it noted that its role was to establish whether Russia had failed in its obligation to ensure the applicants' right to respect for their private and family life, in particular by providing a legal framework in domestic law that would allow their relationship to be recognized and protected. The Court noted in this regard that applicants who are legally permitted to live together are deprived of a number of advantages, such as support for couples purchasing housing, the right to visit each other in hospitals etc., which creates a discrepancy between social reality and the law, thus failing to protect the basic needs of same-sex couples and resulting in serious day-to-day difficulties for these couples.

The ECtHR also considered the issue of negative social attitudes in Russia towards same-sex couples, clearly stating that such attitudes can only be taken into account when extending the Convention guarantees and not for limiting access to rights and freedoms protected by the ECHR. The Court also emphasized that while the protection of "traditional marriage" is a significant factor, it cannot see any threats to such a marriage created by the same-sex couples simply being allowed to formalize their relationships. Also, the argument concerning the alleged danger to minors that would result from "promoting homosexuality" was not accepted by the Court, for reasons already explained in the Bayev and others v. Russia case.[36] In sum, the Court did not find any overriding interests of society which could be balanced against the applicants' right to respect for their private and family life. Taking this into account, the ECtHR found a violation of Article 8 of the Convention, stressing that although states have a margin of appreciation in choosing the most appropriate form of formalization of same-sex relationships, taking into account social and cultural contexts, these limits were exceeded in the material case because Russia failed to provide any regulation capable of protecting the applicants' relationships as same-sex couples. The Court emphasized that allowing the applicants to formally confirm their relationships in a way other than by entering into marriage would not conflict with the "traditional understanding of marriage" prevailing in Russia, nor would it be contrary to the views of the majority of Russian society invoked by the government, as these oppose same-sex marriages and not any other form of legal confirmation that might be introduced.

The reactions of Russian politicians to the Fedotova ruling were not difficult to predict: they point to the alleged incompatibility of the obligation to formalize same-sex unions stemming from Article 8 ECHR, as confirmed by the judgment in the Fedotova case, with the Russian constitution. At the same time some Russian legal scholars presented the opposite view, failing to see such a contradiction.[37] Bearing in mind the 2015 Russian law on amendments to the federal constitutional law on the Constitutional

36 ECtHR judgment of June 20, 2017, *Bayev and others* v. *Russia*...

37 See https://www.advgazeta.ru/novosti/espch-priznanie-odnopolykh-soyuzov-ne-v-forme-braka-ne-protivorechit-traditsionnomu-ponimaniyu-braka/ and the statement of the Russian constitutionalist prof. Olga Kryazhakova.

Court of the Russian Federation,[38] which empowered that court to adjudicate on the legality of enforcement of an international court's ruling under the Russian constitution.[39] it seems hard to assume that the judgment of the ECtHR in the Fedotova case could be enforced. Further events and the termination of the membership of the Russian Federation in the Council of Europe, as well as Russia's withdrawal from the Conventions, although formally not precluding adjudication on applications concerning events that took place previously,[40] may in practice make the continuation of the proceedings, let alone the execution of the Court's judgments, at least problematic.[41]

4. "Tomorrow morning"[42] – or how can events go on? (instead of conclusions)

Summarizing the developments of the Court's case-law to date concerning the development of the standard of interpretation of Article 8 of the Convention regarding the right to legal recognition of same-sex unions, one can make the following observations.

First, the Court confirmed the obligation of States Parties to balance the competing interests of individuals and society as a whole in the context of

---

38 Федеральный закон от 14 декабря 2015 г. N 7-ФКЗ о внесении изменений в Федеральный конституционный закон "О Конституционном Суде Российской Федерации".

39 The Constitutional Court of the Russian Federation first declared the ruling of the ECtHR in Russia unenforceable in its judgment of April 19, 2016, concerning the judgment of the ECtHR of July 4, 2013, *Anchugov and Gladkov v. Russia*, applications nos. 11157/04 and 15162/05. See information on the judgment of the Constitutional Court of the Russian Federation: http://www.ksrf.ru/ru/News/Pages/ViewItem.aspx?ParamId=3281.

40 See point 2 of the resolution of the ECtHR of March 22, 2022 on the consequences of termination of the membership of the Russian Federation in the Council of Europe in the light of Article 58 of the European Convention on Human Rights.

41 Cf. the remarks of L. Garlicki (in:) L. Garlicki, P. Hofmański, A. Wróbel (ed.), *Konwencja o Ochronie Praw Człowieka i Podstawowych Wolności. Komentarz do artykułów 19–59 oraz Protokołów dodatkowych. Tom II. Komentarz*, Warsaw, 2010, in item 7 on Article 58 ECHR.

42 The title of the book by Lev Nikolaevich Urvantsov.

the issue of formalization of same-sex relationships.[43] The interest of the public must be defined, concrete and real, because blank statements similar to those made by the Russian Government in the Fedotova case do not constitute a proper counterbalance to the quite self-evident interest of the applicant same-sex couples.

Secondly, this does not automatically mean, as matters stand in respect of the development of interpretation of the Convention, the existence of the right to marry for same-sex couples, which does prevent this position from changing in the future provided that there is a European consensus in favour of granting this right.[44]

Third, Article 8 of the Convention provides implicitly[45] for an obligation to provide same-sex unions with measures to protect tchem,[46] which are a form of exercising their right to both private and family life,[47] by providing a specific legislative framework for their legal recognition and protection.[48]

Fourth, the state's margin of appreciation does not concern the decision to grant protection through formalization as such, but only regards what legal form this protection is to take exactly, and in doing so states must carefully balance the interests of same-sex couples and society as a whole.[49]

Fifth, the prevailing views expressed by the majority of society should be taken into account in dynamizing the scope of the guarantees provided

---

43 ECtHR judgment, *Fedotova...*, paragraph 49.

44 ECtHR judgment in Schalk and Kopf, paragraph 61, in which the Court held that "it cannot be said that Article 12 is inapplicable to the applicants' complaint. However, as matters stand, the question whether or not to allow same-sex marriage is left to regulation by the national law of the Contracting State". The position assuming the future derivation of the right to marital equality from Article 12 of the Convention, when the "European consensus" in this respect is fully formed, is presented by S. Ragone, V. Volpe, *An Emerging Right to a "Gay" Family Life?*, "German Law Journal", vol. 17, no. 3/2016, pp. 451–486, p. 485.

45 ECtHR judgment, *Fedotova...*, paragraph 49.

46 ECtHR judgment, *Orlandi...*, paragraph 210.

47 ECtHR judgment, *Schalk and Kopf...*, paragraphs 94 and 95.

48 ECtHR judgment, *Oliari...*, paragraph 185.

49 ECtHR judgment, *Fedotova...*, paragraph 56.

by the Convention[50] but they are not sufficient to justify the refusal to allow individuals to exercise their right to respect for private and family life.[51]

Sixth, the positions of the domestic courts pointing to the need to formalize same-sex relationships are relevant,[52] but only to the extent that they would serve to justify the dynamization of the scope of the Convention guarantees.

And seventh, it should be noted that a European consensus has emerged regarding the obligation of states to ensure – in a form that takes into account the above-mentioned balancing of competing interests – the possibility of legal recognition of a same-sex relationship. Thus, at present, states no longer enjoy the margin of appreciation to decide when to introduce such a possibility, contrary to the situation a decade ago.[53]

The judgment in the Fedotova case is of a paramount importance for the development of the interpretation of the Convention and for the appraisal of similar cases pending before the ECtHR, not only those concerning Poland, but also those concerning applications against Romania[54] (and possibly also other states in the future). According to this ruling, the failure to identify convincing reasons against the introduction of the legal recognition of same-sex relationships, and neither an ideological interpretation of the constitution that has little juridical relevance,[55] nor the social views

50 ECtHR judgment, *Oliari…*, paragraphs 179 and 181.

51 ECtHR judgment, *Fedotova…*, paragraph 52.

52 ECtHR judgment, *Oliari…*, paragraph 180.

53 Cf. the decisions of the ECtHR in the Courten case (in which the Court held that "States must also enjoy a margin of appreciation in the timing of the introduction of legislative changes") and the M.W. case (with the passage explaining that "by acting as they did and when they did, the United Kingdom authorities remained within their margin of appreciation").

54 The cases of *S.K.K. and A.C.G. and 14 other applicants* v. *Romania*, application no. 5926/20, communicated on March 30, 2020, and *Buhuceanu and Ciobotar and 24 other applicants* v. *Romania*, application no. 20081/19, communicated on January 16, 2020.

55 See critical remarks on this kind of arguments made in the Polish debate in: E. Łętowska, J. Woleński, *Instytucjonalizacja związków partnerskich a Konstytucja RP z 1997 r.*, PiP 2013, no. 6, pp. 15–40, as well as in J. Pawliczak, *Zarejestrowany związek partnerski a małżeństwo*, Warsaw, 2014.

that view the formalization with reluctance (especially if they show some incoherence resulting from different social attitudes towards, on one hand, the concept of marital equality and, on the other hand, extending specific rights in consequence of the formalization of same-sex relationships), or finally the critical standpoints of the domestic judiciary towards the formalization, cannot be considered as convincing reasons, and thus must lead to the finding of a violation of Article 8 ECHR due to refusing to provide for the formalization of same-sex relationships. Another characteristic issue is addressed in the (apparently well-thought-out) decision of the Court to decide the Russian case before the Polish one. For if there are – and in all likelihood will be – problems with Russia's implementation of the Fedotova judgment (especially in view of the recent tragic developments and the termination of Russia's membership in the CoE) it will be understandable for the European public opinion, and not as a manifestation of a genuine problem with the execution of this particular judgment but rather as a manifestation of Russia's general and systemic resistance to discharging obligations under Article 46 ECHR. Against this background, the foreseeable difficulties that a possible judgment of the ECtHR that finds a violation of Article 8 ECHR may encounter in similar Polish cases will be perceived by the European public opinion as a problem related to this specific issue, i.e. the issue of formalization of same-sex relationships. This, in turn, is likely to change the perspective of the problem of execution, and in particular determine a different perception of the problem in the context of the political mechanism of enforcement of judgments.

Both the logic manifested by the set of successive rulings of the ECtHR and consideration of the European legal context, which is one of the factors determining the evolving understanding of the Convention, allow one to assume that the next step of the Court is likely to be to derive the right to marital equality from Article 12 of the Convention (applied alone or in conjunction with the prohibition of discrimination under Article 14 ECHR). The Court had in a way already announced this likelihood first in Schalk and Kopf holding that "as matters stand, the question whether or not to allow same-sex marriage is left to regulation by the national law of the Contracting State",[56] then reiterated it carefully in the Hämäläinen judgment (which did not directly concern the right to legal recognition of same-sex unions, but rather the issue of "forcing" the spouse after a sexual transition to convert the previously concluded marriage into a registered partnership under the pain of refusing to legally recognize the effects of the transition[57]), and then verbally strengthened the reservation that this state of affairs is temporary only in Oliari[58] and Orlandi.[59] Interestingly, although neither in the Oliari nor in Fedotova cases was any complaint raised concerning the violation of Article 12 of the Convention, the Court addressed this issue in the first of these cases and remained silent on it in the second one. This was – again – logical because the ECtHR had to approach the issue in reference to Russia with greater "sensitivity" and shape the argumentation so as to make the execution of its ruling in Russia at least potentially possible, and at the same time it had to take into account the different (Italy v. Russia) constitutional realities even if in its opinion this difference was purely ostensible. It also seems very likely that in Fedotova we were in fact dealing with the preparation of a possible later line of argumentation in favour of a decision on marital equality based on Article 12 of the Convention. In the Fedotova case the Court noted, inter alia, that "the protection of *traditional marriage* stipulated by the amendments to the Russian Constitution in 2020 [...] is in principle weighty and legitimate interest, which may have positive effect in strengthening family unions. The Court, however, cannot discern any risks

56 ECtHR judgment, *Schalk and Kopf...*, paragraph 61.

57 Judgment of the ECtHR (Grand Chamber) of July 16, 2014, *Hämäläinen* v. *Finland*, application no. 37359/09, para. 96.

58 ECtHR judgment, *Oliari...*, paragraph 191, where the ECtHR held that "as matters stood (at the time only six out of forty-seven CoE member States allowed same-sex marriage), the question whether or not to allow same-sex marriage was left to regulation by the national law of the Contracting State. The Court felt it must not rush to substitute its own judgment in place of that of the national authorities."

59 ECtHR judgment, Orlandi, paragraph 192, where the Court emphasized that "States are still free, under Article 12 of the Convention as well as under Article 14 taken in conjunction with Article 8, to restrict access to marriage to different-sex couples".

for traditional marriage which the formal acknowledgment of same-sex unions may involve, since it does not prevent different-sex couples from entering marriage, or enjoying the benefits which the marriage gives."[60] It is not difficult to imagine a reference to this passage of reasoning, e.g. in the possible future judgment in the Szypuła and others v. Poland case[61] where one of the questions posed to the parties related directly to whether, by preventing the conclusion of homosexual marriages, the right to conclude marriage as guaranteed by Article 12 of the Convention was violated by Poland. Moreover, it is also not difficult to imagine the Court's reference to the passage – otherwise considered a regressive interpretation in this respect[62] – in the Oliari judgment where the Court in turn referred, while symptomatically using the past tense, to the observations made in the judgments of Schalk and Kopf and Hämäläinen in relation to Article 12 of the ECHR, and concluded that "despite the gradual evolution of States on the matter (today there are eleven CoE states that have recognised same-sex marriage) the findings reached in the cases mentioned above remain pertinent."[63] The *clou* of the Court's future argument concerning Article 12 of the Convention and marital equality may come down not so much to the assessment of the very advancement of this evolution (which is only a measure of the trend[64]), but rather to confronting it with the arguments (embedded in – accurate or not – interpretation of national constitutional provisions) already directly disqualified in the fragment of the Fedotova

60 ECtHR judgment, *Fedotova...*, paragraph 54.

61 The cases of *Szypuła* v. *Poland* and *Urbanik and Rodriguez* v. *Poland*, applications nos. 78030/14 and 23669/16, communicated to the government on June 20, 2020.

62 Thus: P. Johnson, *Ground-breaking judgment of the European Court of Human Rights in Oliari and Others v Italy*; http://echrso.blogspot.com/2015/07/ground-breaking-judgment-of-european.html (accessed: 5.04.2022).

63 ECtHR judgment, *Oliari...*, paragraph 192.

64 Although it should be noted that this trend is remarkable and includes also the recognition by the Austrian constitutional court (let us emphasize – without any reference to Article 12 of the Convention) that the restriction of the subjective right to marry to opposite-sex couples is inconsistent with the Austrian Basic Law (see the judgment of the Austrian Verfassungsgerichtshof of December 4, 2017, reference number G 258-259 / 2017-9, point 1).

judgment quoted above. Taking into account the logic of the previous judgments and their sequence that make up the title ("tempering steel") for this essay, such a scenario should be considered likely. Therefore, one might expect in a future judgment (e.g. in Polish cases) argumentation to be constructed that is similar to that used by the Court in the Oliari case in relation to Article 8 of the Convention, the sequence of which was as follows: reference to the standard (in this case – to the judgment passed in the Fedotova case), and only then (as an auxiliary argument) to noting a trend that would be assessed as increasing (with reference to the judgment of Oliari).

The history of laying the narrative "bricks" of the standard of interpretation of Article 8 of the Convention, discussed here, is only one of a series of such stories in the Court's case-law. Another famous example is the issue of the admissibility of differentiating the treatment of children born in and out of wedlock in reference to the scope of the guarantees under Article 8 of the Convention or Article 1 of Protocol No. 1 to the ECHR.[65] Analysing this process and describing a specific "technology" of shaping the interpretative standard developed by the Court allows one not only to forecast in a fairly reliable manner (because it is based on establishing a certain logic in a series of judgments concerning the same legal problem) the future direction of changes in the interpretative position of the Court (of course with the reservation that this direction is influenced by various factors, ranging from changes in the law in the States Parties to the ECHR, through changes in social attitudes, to the interpretative approaches of lawyers taking the office of judges of the Court), but also to adapt domestic law in advance of the standard of interpretation that is likely to develop in in the near future, and thus – to somehow pre-empt the Court and "knock out" arguments that could be employed when appraising an application against a given state. And although J. Pawliczak commented

65 See the judgments of the ECtHR: of February 1, 2000, *Mazurek* v. *France*, application no. 34406/97 (with a clever, although risky reference in paragraph 49 to the judgment of the ECtHR of 28 May 1985 passed in the case of *Abdulaziz, Cabales and Balkandali* v. *United Kingdom*, applications no. 9214/80, 9473/81 and 9474/81), and then of February 13, 2004, *Pla and Puncernau* v. *Andorra*, application no. 69498/01.

on the significance of the Strasbourg jurisprudence for the issue discussed here quite cautiously, writing that so far it has not had a breakthrough significance for the opening of marriage for same-sex couples,[66] it seems that while expecting a possible judgment of the ECHR finding a violation by Poland (just as in the Russian case) of Article 8 of the Convention, it would be right to consider adopting such national provisions that would give Poland a chance to claim that it has completed this formalization "in some form" and therefore even if it lost in Strasbourg (as Italy did in the Oliari case), the state could claim that the judgment had already been executed by general measures because the provisions expected by the Court had been adopted before the judgment was delivered. At the level of the political enforcement mechanism provided for by Article 46 of the Convention, such a line of argumentation could prove sufficient. Of course, one should be aware that to that end it would be necessary to respect the state's interest in maintaining credibility in the face of international obligations, but this is a political requirement that Poland does not currently seem to be meeting.

66 J. Pawliczak, *Drogi do równości małżeńskiej (w 30 lat od instytucjonalizacji związków partnerskich)*, PiP 2020 r., no. 4, p. 12. A slightly more moderate approach was presented by O.M. Piaskowska and P.F. Piesiewicz, who argued hat "the lack of any institution in the domestic order to protect same-sex relationships is a violation of Art. 8 of the ECHR" and "the state cannot ignore the situation where the legislation does not provide for any form of protection of same-sex unions" (O.M. Piaskowska, P.F. Piesiewicz, *Prawo do zawarcia związku jednopłciowego jako wyraz poszanowania prawa do ochrony życia prywatnego i rodzinnego*, EPS 2018, no. 5, p. 15).

Bibliography

Bamforth, M., *Families But Not (Yet) Marriages? Same-Sex Partners and the Developing European Convention 'Margin of Appreciation'*, "Child and Family Law Quarterly 2011", vol. 23, no. 1.

Bem, K., *Glosa do wyroku ETPC z dnia 24 czerwca 2010 r., 30141/04*, Lex/El.

Brzozowski, W. *Małżeństwo, życie rodzinne, związki osób tej samej płci. Glosa do wyroku ETPC z dnia 24 czerwca 2010 r., 30141/04*, EPS 2011, vol. 4.

Djeffal, Ch., *Consensus, Stasis, Evolution: Reconstructing Argumentative Patterns in Evolutive ECHR Jurisprudence*, [in:] P. Kapotas, V.P. Tzevelekos, *Building Consensus on European Consensus. Judicial Interpretation on Human Rights in Europe and Beyond*, Cambridge, 2019.

Garlicki, L., [in:] L. Garlicki, P. Hofmański, A. Wróbel (ed.), *Konwencja o Ochronie Praw Człowieka i Podstawowych Wolności. Komentarz do artykułów 19–59 oraz Protokołów dodatkowych. Tom II. Komentarz*, Warsaw, 2010.

Górski, M., *Glosa do wyroku ETPC z dnia 24 czerwca 2010 r., 30141/04*, Lex/El. 2010.

Grzeszczak, R., Gniadzik, M., *The Right of European Union Citizens and Their Family Members to Move Freely within the Territory of the Member States (In the Light of the Judgment of the European Court of Human Rights in Oliari v. Italy)*, "Polish Review of International and European Law" 2015, vol. 4, no. 1.

Hodson, L., *A Marriage by Any Other Name? Schalk and Kopf v Austria*, "Human Rights Law Review" 2011, vol 11, no. 1

Johnson, P., *Ground-breaking judgment of the European Court of Human Rights in Oliari and Others v Italy: same-sex couples in Italy must have access to civil unions/registered partnerships*, http://echrso.blogspot.com/2015/07/ground-breaking-judgment-of-european.html

Łętowska, E., Woleński, J., *Instytucjonalizacja związków partnerskich a Konstytucja RP z 1997 r.*, PiP 2013, no. 6.

Marzano, V.J., *Oliari and the European Court of Human Rights: where the Court failed*, "Pace International Law Review" 2017, vol. 29, no. 1.

Mizerski, R., *Dostęp par różnopłciowych do związku partnerskiego. Glosa do wyroku ETPC z dnia 26 października 2017 r., 28475/12*, EPS 2018, vol. 8.

Paprocka, A., *Budowanie tożsamości europejskiej w orzecznictwie Europejskiego Trybunału Praw Człowieka*, PiP 2014, vol. 12

Paprocka, A., *Pozytywny obowiązek uregulowania statusu prawnego związków osób tej samej płci. Glosa do wyroku ETPC z dnia 21 lipca 2015 r., 18766/11 i 36030/11*, EPS 2016, vol. 4.

Pawliczak, J., *Drogi do równości małżeńskiej (w 30 lat od instytucjonalizacji związków partnerskich)*, PiP 2020, no. 4.

Pawliczak, J., *Zarejestrowany związek partnerski a małżeństwo*, Oficyna Wolters Kluwer Polska, Warsaw, 2014.

Piaskowska, O.M., Piesiewicz, P.F., *Prawo do zawarcia związku jednopłciowego jako wyraz poszanowania prawa do ochrony życia prywatnego i rodzinnego*, EPS 2018, no. 5.

Popescu, C.L., *L'obligation positive des États de légiférer les partenariats civils entre les personnes de même sexe Commentaire à l'Arrêt de la Cour européenne des Droits de l'Homme – chambre du 21 juillet 2015, Affaire Oliari et autres c. Italie*, "Analele Universității București – Drept Series (AUB)" 2015, vol. 1.

Puppinck, G., *Wyrok w sprawie Vallianatos przeciwko Grecji w świetle przemian w sposobie pojmowania rodziny i „życia rodzinnego" w orzecznictwie ETPCz*, https://ordoiuris.pl/rodzina-i-malzenstwo/wyrok-w-sprawie-vallianatos-przeciwko-grecji-w-swietle-przemian-w-sposobie

Ragone, S., Volpe, V., *An Emerging Right to a "Gay" Family Life?*, "German Law Journal", vol. 17, no. 3/2016.

Ziyadov, N., *From Justice to Injustice: Lowering the Threshold of European Consensus in Oliari and Others versus Italy*, "Indiana Journal of Global Legal Studies" 2019, vol. 26, no. 2.

Vygantė Milašiūtė[2]

Freedom of the Rule of Law-Promoting Expression of Prosecutors under European Law[1]

Abstract
The paper examines what protection of the freedom of expression is guaranteed under European law to prosecutors when they exercise this freedom in their professional capacity to promote the rule of law.

Starting with the ECtHR judgment in *Kövesi v. Romania*, the investigation focuses on the issue of whether freedom of expression is protected as a human right when a person is expressing views on behalf of a state institution. The relevant ECtHR's freedom of expression case-law is examined in the light of the ECtHR's conception of the rule of law. The importance of also being also bound by EU law and notably its rule of law provisions is also examined. Furthermore, the importance

---

1 The research was conducted within the scope of the project "Constitutional Consciousness as a Remedy for the Crisis of Discourse and Democracy Deficit in the European Union", Lietuvos mokslo taryba. Narodowe Centrum Nauki. DAINA – Polish-Lithuanian Funding Initiative, contract no. S-LL-19-4 / LSS-220000-1395, 10 August 2018.

2 Vygantė Milašiūtė is an associate professor at the Faculty of Law, Vilnius University, and a policy analyst at the Government Strategic Analysis Centre in Lithuania. She holds a lawyer's qualification (Vilnius University, Faculty of Law, 1999), a Master's degree in International Law (Lund University, Raoul Wallenberg Institute of Human Rights and Humanitarian Law, 1999), and a PhD in law (Vilnius University, 2007). She was a civil servant at the Ministry of Justice in Lithuania and has experience of cooperation with the UN, the Council of Europe, and EU institutions, *inter alia* in the capacity of a substitute member of the Venice Commission, a delegate and a chairperson at the EU Council Working Party on Fundamental Rights (FREMP), and a national liaison officer at the EU Agency for Fundamental Rights. Her main research interests include European human rights law and anti-discrimination law. She is the Action Vice Chair of the Global Digital Human Rights Network funded by COST (EU).

of the link between the independence of the prosecutor and her freedom of expression is addressed.

The paper confirms that freedom of expression of judges and prosecutors is a rule of law issue both under the ECHR and EU law. When judges or prosecutors exercise their freedom of expression specifically to promote the rule of law, their freedom of expression should attract an even higher level of protection. Under the ECHR, the freedom of expression of prosecutors needs to be protected at least to the extent which is necessary to ensure their judicial independence. In the EU law context, prosecutors are not necessarily seen as independent of the executive in a manner analogous to judges. However, for those Member States where prosecutors enjoy such independence it is possible to argue that judicial independence protected by the EU law strengthens the protection of the freedom of expression of prosecutors.

The study contributes to the field studying judicial independence in the light of the rule of law. It focuses on a less explored issue of the independence of prosecutors and connects the ECHR and the EU law perspectives.

Keywords: judicial independence, prosecutors, freedom of expression, rule of law

Do the aims of rule of law promotion matter for the level of protection of expression? – Rule of law under the European Convention on Human Rights and EU law – Protection of the freedom of expression under the Convention – The link between judicial independence and the freedom of expression under the Convention – Prosecutors as judicial authorities under EU law – Rule of law aims heighten the level of protection of expression of prosecutors

1. Introduction

This paper addresses the question of what protection of the freedom of expression is guaranteed under European law to prosecutors when they exercise this freedom in their professional capacity in order to promote the rule of law but suffer negative consequences as a result. The starting point is the European Court of Human Rights judgment in the case *Kövesi v. Romania*,[3] in which the freedom of expression of a prosecutor who expressed her critical opinion on legislative reform – which was likely to have an impact on the judiciary and its independence – was protected, stressing

3 ECtHR, 5 May 2020, No. 3594/19, *Kövesi* v. *Romania*.

the importance of judicial independence. The issue of whether freedom of expression is protected as a human right when a person is expressing views on behalf of a state institution and, consequently, on behalf of the state itself is investigated. The relevant freedom of expression case-law of the Court is examined in the light of the conception of the rule of law as developed by the Court. In addition, the question of the importance of the fact that the state in question is also bound by European Union law and notably its provisions aimed at safeguarding the value of the rule of law is examined. The importance of the link between the independence of the prosecutor and her freedom of protection is addressed. The ultimate question is this: do the aims of rule of law promotion matter for the scope and level of protection of expression by prosecutors in EU Member States, and if so, how?

2. The European Court of Human Rigths case *Kövesi* v. *Romania*

In the recent case *Kövesi v. Romania*, the Court found a violation of the freedom of expression (Article 10 of the European Convention on Human Rights) where an anti-corruption prosecutor (chief of the national anti-corruption prosecutor's office) had been dismissed for criticising legislative reform in the area of corruption which could have an impact on the judiciary and its independence. There was no way for her to bring a claim in court against her dismissal, as such proceedings would only have been able to examine the formal aspects of the presidential decree for her removal, and not her substantive argument that she had been incorrectly removed for criticising the legislative changes in corruption law. The Court found that her right to freedom of expression had been violated because she had been dismissed for those criticisms which she had made in the exercise of her duties on a matter of great public interest. Her premature removal had defeated the very purpose of maintaining judicial independence and must have had a chilling effect on her and other prosecutors and judges taking part in public debate on legislative reforms affecting the judiciary and judicial independence.

The above case showed, *inter alia*, the difference between the views of the Government of Romania and those of the Court on how rule of law aims should be served in this context. Romania argued that the removal of the prosecutor had been aimed at protecting the rule of law. In his report which indicated the reasons for the applicant's removal from her position, the Minister of Justice specifically noted that the chief prosecutor exercised her role in a discretionary manner, turning the anti-corruption activities and the whole anti-corruption prosecutor's office away from their constitutional and legal role, which was intolerable in a State of the rule of law.[4] The Court took the opposite view. It considered that no evidence had been brought to show that the removal of the chief prosecutor served the aim of protecting the rule of law or any other legitimate aim.[5] The applicant expressed her views on and criticisms of legislative reforms affecting the judiciary, which concerned issues related to the functioning and reform of the judicial system and the prosecutor's competence to investigate corruption offences, all of which are questions of public interest. Her statements did not go beyond criticism from a strictly professional perspective. The applicant's position and statements, which clearly fell within the context of a debate on matters of great public interest, called for a high degree of protection for her freedom of expression and for strict scrutiny of any interference, with a correspondingly narrow margin of appreciation being afforded to the authorities of the respondent State.[6]

3. The rule of law under the Convention and EU law

As we have seen in *Kövesi* case, the notion of the rule of law can be used to support opposing views regarding the need for restrictions of the freedom of expression. It could be asked whether the multi-faceted nature of the rule of law and the resulting variety of views on its meaning can explain some of the difficulty in ensuring the rule of law in practice. It is well known that a variety of views exists at the level of the philosophical accounts of the idea of the rule of law, which leads sceptics "to move from apparent disagreement and conflict about its meaning to the conclusion that it is meaningless", while at the same time this encourages proponents

4 *Ibidem*, § 32.
5 *Ibidem*, § 196.
6 *Ibidem*, § 207.

of the rule of law to assert the existence of one concept behind the different conceptions.[7] It is from this latter perspective that the approach of the European Convention on Human Rights and the EU to the rule of law is addressed below.

3.1. *Convention*

At the outset, it is worth recalling that the Convention is established within the auspices of and operates on the basis of values of the Council of Europe as reflected in various Council of Europe instruments.

Under the Statute of the Council of Europe,[8] every member of the Council of Europe must accept the principles of the rule of law and of the enjoyment by all persons within its jurisdiction of human rights and fundamental freedoms (Article 3). Members of the Council of Europe shall collaborate sincerely and effectively in the realisation of the aim of the Council, which is to achieve a greater unity between its members for the purpose of safeguarding and realising the ideals and principles which are their common heritage and facilitating their economic and social progress (Article 1). This shows that there is a strong link between the commitment to the rule of law and the protection of human rights. The rule of law is a necessary precondition for the protection of human rights. It enables protection of human rights in a formal manner[9] by prohibiting arbitrariness in the application of law. In the context of the Convention it is evident that arbitrariness would amount to a negation of the rule of law.[10] The rule of law may also contain, if a broad conception is adopted, certain substantive elements that create conditions for preventing human rights violations or rectifying them.[11] The rule of law conception relied on by the Court does

7 W. Lucy, *Access to Justice and the Rule of Law*, "*Oxford Journal of Legal Studies*" 2020, vol. 40, no. 2, p. 385.
8 Statute of the Council of Europe.
9 B. Tamanaha, *On the Rule of Law: History, Politics, Theory*, Cambridge University Press, Cambridge, 2004, pp. 91–101.
10 ECtHR 21 June 2016, No. 5809/08, *Al-Dulimi and Montana Management Inc. v. Switzerland*, § 145.
11 B. Tamanaha, *On the Rule of Law...*, pp. 102–113.

indeed contain such substantive elements.[12] As early as in 1975, in its first case where the rule of law was discussed as an element of the Convention, namely *Golder v. the United Kingdom*, the Court held that in civil matters one can scarcely conceive of the rule of law without there being a possibility of having access to the courts.[13]

Among those substantive elements covered by the rule of law as interpreted by the Court, experts identify, for example, the themes of (i) the separation of powers, (ii) the role of the judiciary, (iii) impunity, (iv) a tribunal established by law, and (v) sufficiently accessible and foreseeable law.[14] These themes embrace requirements related to the functioning of democratic society and the quality of law, with the functioning of the judicial branch of power featuring very prominently. Notably, the Court has produced rich case-law on the independence of judges[15] and has ruled on the importance of the separation of powers in the process of selecting and appointing judges.[16] In *Guðmundur Andri Ástráðsson* v *Iceland* the Grand Chamber of the Court clarified that in this process, a certain interaction between the three branches of government is necessary, but only to the extent that the respective powers do not unduly encroach upon one another's functions and competences.[17] In this connection, it is essential to

12 R. Spano, *The rule of law as the lodestar of the European Convention on Human Rights: The Strasbourg Court and the independence of the judiciary*,"European Law Journal" 2021, https://doi.org/10.1111/eulj.12377, pp. 7–12.

13 ECtHR 21 February 1975, No. 4451/70, *Golder* v. *the United Kingdom*, § 34.

14 J. Polakiewicz, *The Rule of Law – Dynamics and Limits of a Common European Value*. Presentation to the Scientific-Consultative Council on International Legal Issues of the Ministry of Foreign Affairs of Belarus, 20 September 2019, https://www.coe.int/en/web/dlapil/-/the-rule-of-law-dynamics-and-limits-of-a-common-european-value (accessed: 31.03.2021).

15 A. Nußberger, *Rule of Law in Europe Demands and Challenges for the European Judiciary*, [in:] P. Craig *et al.* (eds.), *Rule of Law in Europe Perspectives from Practitioners and Academics*, European Judicial Training Network 2019, https://www.ejtn.eu/News/Rule-of-Law-in-Europe--Perspectives-from-Practitioners-and-Academics1/ (accessed: 31.03.2021), pp. 81–82.

16 J. Polakiewicz, *The Rule of Law*...; ECtHR 12 March 2019, No. 26374/18, Guðmundur Andri Ástráðsson, § 122.

17 ECtHR 1 December 2020, No. 26374/18, *Guðmundur Andri Ástráðsson* v. *Iceland*, § 215.

ensure that appointees are free from influence or pressure when carrying out their adjudicatory role.[18] Moreover, the Court has held that the principle of the rule of law encompasses not only the principle of separation of powers and the independence and legitimacy of the judiciary, but also other principles, such as those of legal certainty and of the irremovability of judges, which can come into competition with each other,[19] but which can be reconciled by applying the tests developed by the Court, notably in the context where legal certainty and the irremovability of judges were apparently in competition.[20]

Even those researchers who hold that the core elements of the rule of law under the Convention are formal admit that the Court does refer to the rule of law in relation to substantive values and that rule of law safeguards are instrumental to achieving the substantive aims of the Convention.[21]

One substantive requirement of the rule of law is to resist (i.e. prevent and sanction) corruption. Within the Council of Europe, corruption has been identified as a threat for the rule of law by the Venice Commission in its Rule of Law checklist,[22] which has been formally endorsed by the Committee of Ministers, the Congress of Local and Regional Authorities, and the Parliamentary Assembly of the Council of Europe.[23] The specialised Council of Europe expert body GRECO (Group of States against Corruption) also emphasises the close link between the rule of law and the fight against corruption. As corruption leads to arbitrariness and the abuse of powers, it undermines the very foundations of the rule of law.[24]

---

18 *Ibidem*, § 207.

19 *Ibidem*, § 237–239.

20 *Ibidem*, § 243–252.

21 G. Lautenbach, *The Concept of the Rule of Law and the European Court of Human Rights*, Oxford University Press, Oxford, 2013, pp. 214–215.

22 Venice Commission, Rule of Law Checklist, 18 March 2016, CDL-AD(2016)007-e, § 114.

23 J. Polakiewicz, *The Rule of Law…*; Parliamentary Assembly of the Council of Europe, Venice Commission's Rule of Law Checklist, 11 October 2017, Resolution 2187 (2017).

24 J. Polakiewicz, *The Rule of Law…*

3.2. *EU law*

In its first annual report on the rule of law situation in the EU, the Commission of the EU provides the following description of the rule of law:

> The rule of law is enshrined in Article 2 of the Treaty on European Union as one of the common values for all Member States. Under the rule of law, all public powers always act within the constraints set out by law, in accordance with the values of democracy and fundamental rights, and under the control of independent and impartial courts. The rule of law includes principles such as legality, implying a transparent, accountable, democratic and pluralistic process for enacting laws; legal certainty; prohibiting the arbitrary exercise of executive power; effective judicial protection by independent and impartial courts, effective judicial review including respect for fundamental rights; separation of powers; and equality before the law. These principles have been recognised by the European Court of Justice and the European Court of Human Rights. In addition, the Council of Europe has developed standards and issued opinions and recommendations which provide well-established guidance to promote and uphold the rule of law.[25]

It is worth mentioning that the link between the Council of Europe, including the Convention on Human Rights, and the EU standards of the rule of law is noted in the Commission rule of law report as being also evident from the Court of Justice case-law.

The first report focused on four main pillars: the justice system, the anti-corruption framework, media pluralism, and other institutional checks and balances.[26] This shows that the EU's conception of the rule of law contains the same essential elements for our research as we have seen under the Convention, i.e. effective and independent judiciary as well as an anti-corruption element.

The report specifically identified the importance of the European Court of Human Rights *Kövesi v. Romania* case for the rule of law in the EU. The report noted frequent political attacks (e.g. disciplinary measures) and media campaigns against judges and prosecutors in EU Member States, and highlighted their chilling effect and negative impact on public trust in the judiciary, which affect its independence. In a number of cases,

---

25 European Commission, 2020 Rule of Law Report. The rule of law situation in the European Union, 30 September 2020, COM/2020/580 final, p. 1.

26 *Ibidem*, p. 4.

the attacks have targetted judges and prosecutors who are taking public positions to denounce developments which could damage the judiciary as a whole. In *Kövesi v. Romania* the Court "reaffirmed the freedom of expression for prosecutors and judges to participate in public debates on legislative reforms affecting the judiciary, and more generally on issues concerning the independence of the judiciary."[27]

It follows from this brief overview of rule of law conceptions developed under the Convention and EU law that the freedom of expression of judges and prosecutors is a rule of law issue and, as such, it is of fundamental importance for the functioning of democratic society. It seems to be a plausible assumption that when judges or prosecutors exercise their freedom of expression specifically to promote the rule of law (identify corrupt practices, dangerous legislative initiatives, etc.) their freedom of expression is even more important and should receive an even higher level of protection. We shall now see whether we can find specific evidence of such a higher level of protection in the Strasbourg Court and the Luxembourg Court case-law.

4. Protection of the freedom of expression under the Convention

This section looks into the issue of the protection of professional expression of prosecutors under Article 10 of the Convention. This analysis is also relevant for the sphere of application of EU law because the EU Charter for Fundamental Rights contains a freedom of expression guarantee analogous to that of Article 10 of the Convention. Official explanations of the Charter make it clear that the meaning and scope of this right are the same as those guaranteed by the Convention.[28]

4.1. *Specifics of different categories of information*

The freedom of expression is generally understood as involving the communication of ideas, opinions, convictions, beliefs, and information. On

---

27 *Ibidem*, p. 11.

28 Explanations relating to the Charter of Fundamental Rights, *OJ C 303, 14.12.2007*, p. 21.

the one hand, it is of internal value to an individual, as it involves the external communication of an individual's *forum internum*, and it is then connected to values such as personal autonomy and human dignity. On the other hand, the freedom of expression has consequentialist and epistemic value and is valuable to democracy because political participation, criticism of government, media freedom and the act of voting are aspects of the freedom of expression.[29] Some freedom of speech theories focus on the speaker, while others are chiefly concerned with the effect of the speech on society. International adjudicators apply a more consequentialist approach to freedom of expression,[30] but without adhering to one particular theory of freedom of expression. In *Handyside v. the United Kingdom*, the Court established that "Freedom of expression constitutes one of the essential foundations of [a democratic] society, one of the basic conditions for its progress and for the development of every man."[31] In cases following *Handyside*, the Court replaced the term "the development of every man" with "each individual's self-fulfilment."[32] This shows that when interpreting the freedom of expression the Court seeks to protect both individual and collective interests, while being silent on the underlying theory. The questions of how the collective interest is identified and how its importance is assessed are decisive, but it is worth noting that the very recognition of the importance of collective interests along with individual rights suggests that expression that serves collective interests has better chances of being protected by the Court than expression that does not serve any such aims.

Gunatilleke explains that many jurisdictions, including that of the Court, apply the proportionality test when evaluating the permissibility of the limitations on the freedom of expression. The proportionality test has been criticised at a normative level for failing to adequately recognise the special value of the freedom of expression, as the test expects a court

29 G. Gunatilleke, *Justifying Limitations on the Freedom of Expression*, "Human Rights Review" 2021, vol. 22.

30 J. Oster, *Media Freedom as a Fundamental Right*, Cambridge University Press, Cambridge, UK, 2015, p. 28.

31 ECtHR 7 December 1976, No. 5493/72, *Handyside* v. *the United Kingdom*, § 49.

32 J. Oster, *Media Freedom...*, p. 18–19.

to weigh rights such as the freedom of expression with collective interests such as national security, public order, health, or morals. Such weighing arguably places the freedom of expression on the same normative plane as these collective interests, thereby undermining its peremptory value. The Court can encounter such normative problems in practice, as Article 10 § 2 the Convention explicitly permits states to limit the freedom of expression on the grounds of collective interests, and broad governmental discretion in limiting this freedom is permissible. Such discretion has raised concerns among scholars with respect to how well proportionality meets normative priorities such as the rule of law or legal predictability. The incommensurability of the individual interest and the collective interest make the balancing task impossible and in practice often leads to decisions in favour of the state, respecting its margin of appreciation. States define their collective interests by relying on majoritarian conceptions and often justify limitations on individual expressions that go against the views of the majority.[33] While defining the collective interest often falls within the margin of appreciation of the state, some collective interests are nevertheless sufficiently well defined as international standards, and in that case the Court should rely on those definitions. Such would be the case of the rule of law. It follows that where individual expression serves the interests of the rule of law the protection of such expression should be heightened under the Convention.

4.2. *Specifics of expression serving rule of law-promoting aims*

An important factual circumstance of the *Kövesi* case was that it was a case of an anti-corruption prosecutor expressing her professional opinion and thus exercising her professional duties. This raises a broader question of whether critical professional opinions expressed by state officials should attract a higher level of protection of their freedom of expression when this expression serves the aims of the rule of law or whether, on the contrary, their freedom of expressing critical opinions could be limited to ensure the smooth functioning of the state apparatus and thus serve the

33 G. Gunatilleke, *Justifying Limitations...*

aims of the rule of law. In *Kövesi* the Court found in favour of the freedom of expressing critical opinions. Observers note[34] that this judgment is therefore likely to encourage the participation of judges and prosecutors in debates on the independence and modernization of the justice system in Romania. However, the fact that in *Kövesi* the Court nevertheless chose to analyse the necessity of the impugned measure in a democratic society, even though it had found that the legitimate aim of that measure was missing,[35] may indicate that the rule of law aims do not in themselves justify the unlimited expression of opinions. In other words, there is some room for arguing that the freedom of expression of state officials can be limited, at least as regards its manner, in order to show sufficient respect for the rule of law-based state structures, such as the legislature, the executive, and the judiciary. Arguably, the analysis of the necessity in a democratic society of measures restricting the freedom of expression of state officials makes it possible to double-check whether restrictions on the freedom of expression for allegedly being against the rule of law served any identifiable need of the democratic society, even where any legitimate aims could not be identified at an earlier stage of the analysis. Full analysis of the circumstances of the case focusing on the question of such necessity in a democratic society provides an opportunity to look into multiple possible interpretations of the meaning of the rule of law. Where the state invokes the necessity to protect the rule of law as a justification for restrictions on the freedom of expression of the critics of the government who have their

---

34 D. Călin, *The Recent ECtHR Judgment Kövesi v. Romania. Reactions of Romanian Authorities and Implications regarding the Rule of Law*, "Strasbourg Observers", 16 June 2020, https://strasbourgobservers.com/2020/06/16/the-recent-ecthr-judgment-kovesi-v-romania-reactions-of-romanian-authorities-and-implications-regarding-the-rule-of-law/ (accessed: 31.03.2021).

35 *Kövesi* v. *Romania*..., §196: "[...] the Court considers that no evidence has been brought to show that the impugned measure served the aim of protecting the rule of law or any other legitimate aim"; § 199: "In cases where it had concluded that the interference did not pursue a "legitimate aim", the Court found a violation of the Convention without further investigating whether that interference was "necessary in a democratic society" [...]. Nevertheless, in the circumstances of the current case the Court considers it useful to continue its examination and establish also whether the interference was necessary in a democratic society."

version of what is required to safeguard the rule of law in the country concerned, comprehensive analysis of the competing versions is a tool that can be used to reach a better understanding of the rule of law as a value underpinning human rights and in certain cases determining their scope. The requirements of the rule of law may place certain limits on the freedom of expression even where those exercising this freedom are of the view that their expression also serves those needs, or even better serves them.

The latter approach is well in line with the established case-law of the Court to the effect that even though civil servants do not lose their freedom of expression it is in fact limited because of the special function civil servants perform. In *Vogt v. Germany*[36] the Court noted that civil servants qualify for the protection of Article 10 but at the same time admitted that it is legitimate for a State to impose on civil servants, on account of their status, a duty of discretion. In *Guja v. Moldova* it further explained that it is "mindful that employees have a duty of loyalty, reserve and discretion to their employer. This is particularly so in the case of civil servants since the very nature of civil service requires that a civil servant is bound by a duty of loyalty and discretion."[37] Moreover, "in view of the very nature of their position, civil servants often have access to information which the government, for various legitimate reasons, may have an interest in keeping confidential or secret. Therefore, the duty of discretion owed by civil servants will also generally be a strong one."[38]

How this principle of a narrower protection relates to – and whether it is modified by – the specific type of expression, in particular where it is aimed at increasing the respect for the rule of law, notably by highlighting and thus fighting corruption, needs to be further examined.

In *Guja v. Moldova* the Court dealt with a situation where a civil servant (the Head of the Press Department of the Prosecutor General's Office) publicly disclosed internal information (letters alleging corruption of prosecutors) following a call by the President of the Republic to fight corruption and trading in influence. The Court held "that the signalling

36 ECtHR 26 September 1995, No. 17851/91, *Vogt* v. *Germany*, § 52–53.
37 ECtHR 12 February 2008, No. 14277/04, *Guja* v. *Moldova*, § 70.
38 *Ibidem*, § 71.

by a civil servant or an employee in the public sector of illegal conduct or wrongdoing in the workplace should, in certain circumstances, enjoy protection. This may be called for where the employee or civil servant concerned is the only person, or part of a small category of persons, aware of what is happening at work and is thus best placed to act in the public interest by alerting the employer or the public at large." The Court was guided by the statement from the Explanatory Report to the Council of Europe's Civil Law Convention on Corruption that "in practice corruption cases are difficult to detect and investigate and employees or colleagues (whether public or private) of the persons involved are often the first persons who find out or suspect that something is wrong."[39] In the light of the duty of discretion, disclosure should be made in the first place to the person's superior or other competent authority or body. It is only where this is clearly impracticable that the information could, as a last resort, be disclosed to the public. In assessing whether the restriction on freedom of expression was proportionate, therefore, the Court had to take into account whether there was available to the applicant any other effective means of remedying the wrongdoing which he intended to uncover.[40] The first relevant factor in assessing the proportionality of interference with the civil servant's freedom of expression is the public interest involved in the disclosed information. In a democratic system, the acts or omissions of government must be subject to the close scrutiny not only of the legislative and judicial authorities but also of the media and public opinion. The interest which the public may have in particular information can sometimes be so strong as to override even a legally imposed duty of confidence.[41]

4.3. *No office v. private distinction*

For the purposes of examining the freedom of expression of judges and prosecutors it is necessary to examine a preliminary question, i.e. in which situations this freedom is protected as an individual human right, given that judges and prosecutors may also speak in their official capacity and

39 *Ibidem*, § 72.
40 *Ibidem*, § 73.
41 *Ibidem*, § 74.

do so on behalf of the state institution they represent and, consequently, on behalf of the state itself.

The question is pertinent because the jurisdiction of the Court under the Convention specifically excludes disputes between the state and its emanations such as branches of power, state institutions, and municipalities. As Dijkstra notes, it is not self-evident that complaints of judges under Article 10 meet the requirements of Article 34 of the Convention because the judge can be seen both as an individual and as a representative of the State.[42] Where judges express opinions as judges there is a need to draw a line between the situations where the judge speaks on behalf of the judiciary power and where she expresses her individual opinions. Where the judge speaks about a professional matter because she is required to provide her expert opinion on a certain issue, it seems possible that this is expression on behalf of the institution and thus not individual expression. It would then not be protected under Article 10 of the Convention. The Court, however, has taken a different approach.

In *Kövesi* the Court found a violation of the freedom of expression with regard to criticisms the applicant had made in the exercise of her duties as a prosecutor.[43] The same approach had been taken in an earlier Grand Chamber judgment in *Baka v. Hungary*[44] where a violation of Article 10 was found in a situation where a person was dismissed from the position of the President of the Supreme Court after expressing his opinion, which was his statutory task, on parliamentary bills. The distinction between private and public expression was noted by Judge Wojtyczek in a dissenting opinion to the effect that Baka's opinions are to be seen as public speech

---

42 S. Dijkstra, *The Freedom of the Judge to Express his Personal Opinions and Convictions under the ECHR*, "Utrecht Law Review" 2017, vol. 13, no 1, p. 3.

43 *Kövesi* v. *Romania*…, § 204: "[…] the applicant expressed her views on the legislative reforms at issue in her professional capacity as chief prosecutor of the national anticorruption prosecutor's office. The applicant also used her legal power to start investigations into suspicions of corruption crimes committed by members of the Government in connection with highly disputed pieces of legislation and to inform the public about these investigations She also availed herself of the possibility to express her opinion directly in the media or during professional gatherings."

44 ECtHR, 23 June 2016, No. 20261/12, *Baka* v. *Hungary*.

not covered by the Convention. Dijkstra demonstrates that in cases filed by judges the Court does not distinguish between the judge as an individual and as a representative of public authorities. This is so despite the Court case-law regarding other categories of office holders, such as mayors and municipality council members, whose applications regarding actions performed in their official capacity were found inadmissible in the *Demirbaş and Others v. Turkey* case.[45]

It follows that even where judges and prosecutors have a legal obligation to express their expert opinions, the exercise of this duty is protected as an exercise of the right to freedom of expression. There remains a valid question of how the existence of such professional duties affects the level of protection of expression. In particular, if a person's expression derives from her professional obligation to respond to certain facts, does it heighten the level of protection because her professional expression by definition serves the rule of law aims? Is this level heightened in situations where, because of specific circumstances (such as the rule of law crisis in the State concerned), such professional expression particularly serves the rule of law aims? Should critical professional opinions expressed by state officials attract a higher level of protection of their freedom of expression when their expression serves the aims of the rule of law? Or should, on the contrary, their freedom of expressing critical opinions be limited to ensure the smooth functioning of the state apparatus and thus serve the aims of the rule of law? The specificity of the protection of the freedom of expression of judges and prosecutors by the Court needs to be examined more closely.

4.4. *Specifics of judges*

A report by the Venice Commission shows that when assessing whether interference in the right to freedom of expression of a judge corresponds to a "pressing social need" and "was proportionate to the legitimate aim pursued" the Court considers the impugned statement in the light of all the concrete circumstances of the case, including (1) the office held by the

45 ECtHR 9 November 2010 (dec.), No. 1093/98 et al., *Demirbaş and Others* v. *Turkey*.

applicant, (2) the content of the impugned statement, (3) the context in which the statement was made, and (4) the nature and severity of the penalties imposed.[46] Dijkstra holds that factors used by the Court for assessing the margin of appreciation – or the discretion – of the state, in balancing the freedom of expression of judges against a legitimate aim include: (1) the consequences of the exercise of the freedom on the judicial office; (2) the consequences of the interference for the judge; (3) the consequences of the interference for society, in particular chilling effect; (4) the context of a public debate; (5) the motive of the judge; (6) the appropriateness of the expressions; (7) the existence of a fair procedure at the national level.[47] Under any of the above approaches, some of these factors, such as the effect on the judicial office, i.e. on the exercise of the judicial function, point towards narrowing the freedom of expression. Some other factors, for instance the importance of the subject matter of expression for the public debate, indicate the need for a broader protection of this freedom. The tension between the various factors is noticeable in the relevant case-law of the Court.

In *Wille v. Liechtenstein*[48] (which concerned a lecture delivered by a high-ranking judge, which had political implications) the Court considered that the extent of the margin of appreciation in the case of judges who seek the protection afforded by Article 10 of the Convention is related to the capacity of the judge as a civil servant because of their duties and responsibilities. The existence of the latter justifies leaving to the national authorities a "certain margin of appreciation" in striking a balance between the freedom of expression and the public interest. *Pitkevich v. Russia*[49] (which concerned proselytising at the court and expression of religious views by the judge during the court hearing) shows that in the case of judges the national authorities' margin of appreciation is particularly justified because of the "prominent place among State organs" the judiciary occupies

46 Venice Commission. Report on the Freedom of Expression of Judges, 23 June 2015, CDL-AD (2015) 018, § 67.
47 S. Dijkstra, *The Freedom…*, pp. 7–10.
48 ECtHR 28 October 1999, No. 28396/95, *Wille* v. *Liechtenstein*; S. Dijkstra, *The Freedom…*, p. 5.
49 ECtHR 8 February 2001 (dec.), No. 47936/99, *Pitkevich* v. *Russia*.

in a democratic society. In other words, because of their very important functions, members of the judiciary enjoy very little freedom of expression in connection with the performance of those functions. However, in *Baka v. Hungary,* where the mandate of the applicant as the President of the Supreme Court was terminated because he had expressed his views in his official capacity on various legislative reforms affecting the judiciary, the Court applied a different formula regarding the margin of appreciation and considered that the margin had to be "narrow" rather than "certain." This was so because "the applicant's position and statements, which clearly fell within the context of a debate on matters of great public interest, called for a high degree of protection for his freedom of expression and strict scrutiny of any interference."[50] According to Dijkstra,[51] the Court apparently takes the view that the contribution of the judge to an important public debate prevails over the obligations that flow from the (strong) bond between the judge and the public authorities. As regards the permissibility for a judge to participate in a public debate regarding legal reform, the Court had explained in *Previti v. Italy*[52] that this was in line with the judicial functions. In particular, "the fact that, in application of the principles of democracy and pluralism, certain judges or groups of judges may, in their capacity as legal experts, express reservations or criticism regarding the Government's legislative proposals does not undermine the fairness of the judicial proceedings to which these proposals might apply."[53]

Kudeshkina v. Russia[54] shows tension between the Convention requirement to protect the "authority of the judiciary" and the high level of protection of political speech. The Court considered that dismissing a judge from her office for this reason was not permissible where the judge, whose functions had been temporarily suspended for the purpose of running for a seat of a member of the Parliament, voiced public criticism with regard to the conduct of various officials dealing with a large-scale corruption case in which she had been sitting as a judge. The duty of loyalty and discretion

---

50 ECtHR *Baka* v. *Hungary*..., § 171.
51 S. Dijkstra, *The Freedom*..., p. 6.
52 ECtHR 8 December 2009 (dec.), no 45291/06, *Previti* v. *Italy*.
53 *Ibidem*.
54 ECtHR 26 February 2009, No. 29492/05, *Kudeshkina* v. *Russia*, § 93–95.

owed by civil servants, and particularly the judiciary, requires that the dissemination of even accurate information be carried out with moderation and propriety. It was important that her decision to make this information public was based on her personal experience and was taken only after she had been prevented from participating in the trial in her official capacity. Even if the applicant allowed herself a certain degree of exaggeration and generalisation, characteristic of the pre-election agitation, her statements were not entirely devoid of any factual grounds, and therefore were not to be regarded as a gratuitous personal attack but as a fair comment on a matter of great public importance. The Court considered that expression was not excessive even in view of her judicial status. The judgment in *Kudeshkina* contrasts with the case of *Simić v. Bosnia and Herzegovina*[55] in which the Article 10 complaint by a former Constitutional Court judge who was dismissed because of a letter sent to high public officials – and due to a media interview (as well as an unauthorised press conference) in which he discussed the work of the Constitutional Court, accusing it of corruption – was found inadmissible. The Court observed that the dismissal decision had essentially related to his actions damaging the authority of the Constitutional Court and the reputation of a judge.

Most importantly, judges are entitled to speak out in a proportionate way in relation to reforms impacting the judiciary[56] although other views exist.[57] Judges, like all other citizens, are entitled to take part in public

55 ECtHR 15 November 2016 (dec.), No. 75255/10, *Simić* v. *Bosnia and Herzegovina.*

56 ECtHR Judicial Seminar 2018, *The Authority of the Judiciary*. Background document prepared by the Registry, https://www.echr.coe.int/Documents/Seminar_background_paper_2018_ENG.pdf (accessed: 31.03.2021), p. 16; K. Aquilina, *The Independence of the Judiciary in Strasbourg Judicial Disciplinary Case Law: Judges as Applicants and National Judicial Councils as Factotums of Respondent States*, [in:] P. Pinto de Albuquerque, K. Wojtyczek (eds.), *Judicial Power in a Globalized World: Liber Amicorum Vincent de Gaetano*, Springer, Cham, 2019, p. 28: a judge has a right to express views in a professional capacity on the administration of justice and the judiciary.

57 S. Shetreet, *Reflections on Contemporary Issues of Judicial Independence*, [in:] P. Pinto de Albuquerque, K. Wojtyczek, (eds.), *Judicial Power…*, p. 513: carefully shaped restrictions should be put on the ability of judges to take part in

debate, provided that it is consistent with maintaining their independence or impartiality.[58] Even when an issue under debate has political implications as it touches upon issues relating to the separation of powers, this is not in itself sufficient to prevent a judge from making a statement on the matter.[59] As regards the standards applicable to judges of the European Court of Human Rights, judges should exercise their freedom of expression in a manner compatible with the dignity of their office; they should refrain from public statements or remarks that may undermine the authority of the Court or give rise to reasonable doubt as to their impartiality,[60] but participation in public debate, including on legal matters, is generally not excluded.

4.5. *Specifics of prosecutors*

In *Kövesi v. Romania*, which concerned a prosecutor who, in the exercise of her duties, criticised legislative reform which could have an impact on the judiciary and its independence, the Court protected her freedom of expression in order to protect the judiciary and judicial independence. It thus shows a link between the rights of judges and the rights of prosecutors. In the words of the Court, "particular consideration [is] to be given to the nature of the judicial function as an independent branch of State power and to the principle of the independence of prosecutors, which – according to Council of Europe and other international instruments – is a key element for the maintenance of judicial independence."[61] Independence of the prosecution service is among the current challenges to the rule of law in Europe[62] also because it is linked to and is a precondition

---

external activities (including in preparing legislation and academic writings and debates) while in office.

58 Consultative Council of European Judges. Opinion no. 18 (2015), *The position of the judiciary and its relation with the other powers of state in a modern democracy*, 16 October 2015, CCJE (2015) 4, § 42.

59 *Baka* v. *Hungary*..., § 165.

60 European Court of Human Rights. Resolution on Judicial Ethics, 2008, § VI.

61 *Kövesi* v. *Romania*..., § 208.

62 E. Holmøyvik, A. Sanders, *A Stress Test for Europe's Judiciaries*, [in:] E. Hirsch Ballin *et al.* (eds.), *European Yearbook of Constitutional Law 2019*, vol. 1, T.M.C. Asser Press, 2020, p. 296.

for the appropriate work of courts. The Consultative Council of European Prosecutors has noted that without the non-interference of the executive in the prosecution service, certain criminal cases may not reach the courts at all.[63] Additional issues arise when, as is the case in Poland, the Minister of Justice is also made a Prosecutor General.[64] On the one hand, the prosecution service then becomes dependent on the executive. On the other hand, as the Minister of Justice may have a role to play in the process of selecting and appointing judges, the increased role of the person with many accumulated powers may pose a threat to the independence of judges. This has direct negative consequences for the independence of the prosecutorial system from the political sphere, but also for the independence of the judiciary and hence the separation of powers and the rule of law.[65]

Naturally then, specificity of the freedom of expression of judges leads to the question of whether prosecutors should enjoy an analogous scope and level of the protection of their freedom of expression. This question is related to the question of the status of prosecutors more generally. Researchers note that the status of prosecutors differs considerably across Europe. In many civil law jurisdictions, prosecutors are civil servants who have special powers in the application of the law on behalf of the state. In other jurisdictions, however, prosecutors belong to the same body of civil servants as the judges or magistrates. In common law jurisdictions, prosecutors are entirely separate from the judiciary, and they operate much as any other represented party would operate before the courts.[66] The Court has held that "prosecutors are civil servants whose task it is to

63 Consultative Council of European Prosecutors. Opinion No. 9 (2014) on European Norms and Principles Concerning Prosecutors ("Rome Charter"), 17 December 2014, CCPE(2014)4Final.

64 E. Holmøyvik, A. Sanders, *A Stress Test...*, p. 296; Venice Commission. Poland – Opinion on the Act on the Public Prosecutor's office, 11 December 2017, CDL-AD(2017)028.

65 Venice Commission. Poland..., § 115.

66 European Network of Councils for the Judiciary. Independence and Accountability of the Judiciary and of the Prosecution. Performance Indicators 2015. ENCJ Report 2014-2015, https://www.encj.eu/images/stories/pdf/workinggroups/independence/encj_report_independence_accountability_2014_2015_adopted_ga_corr_2016.pdf (accessed: 31.03.2021), p. 76.

contribute to the proper administration of justice. In this respect they form part of the judicial machinery in the broader sense of this term."[67] The Parliamentary Assembly of the Council of Europe takes the view that judges, along with prosecutors and other civil servants, should enjoy certain guarantees, such as against collective dismissals.[68] The Consultative Council of European judges holds that the independent status for prosecutors is a fundamental requirement of the rule of law.[69] At the same time, researchers admit that there are differences in the required independence of judges and prosecutors because the legislature or the executive can legitimately ask the prosecution service to prioritize the prosecution of one type of criminal activity over another. However, judges and prosecutors share the guarantee of their independence as regards decisions in particular cases.[70] The Venice Commission identifies the "internal independence" of prosecutors other than the Prosecutor General, which essentially means non-interference in the exercise of their legislatively mandated activities from the hierarchical superior.[71] To summarise, there are similarities in the status of judges and prosecutors, but because of their different procedural role there are also differences. A shared feature is that neither judges nor prosecutors should in principle suffer negative consequences for performing their statutory activities, as holding otherwise would threaten their independence in particular cases.

---

67 ECtHR 11 March 2003, No. 35640/97, *Lešník* v. *Slovakia*, § 54.

68 Parliamentary Assembly of the Council of Europe. New threats to the rule of law in Council of Europe member states: selected examples, 11 October 2017, Resolution 2188 (2017), § 12.4.

69 Consultative Council of European Judges. Magna Carta of Judges (Fundamental Principles), 17 November 2010, CCJE (2010)3 Final, § 11.

70 European Network of Councils for the Judiciary, *supra* n. 64, p. 77–78.

71 Venice Commission. Report on European Standards as regards the Independence of the Judicial System: Part II -the Prosecution Service, 3 January 2011, CDL-AD(2010)040, § 31.

5. The link between judicial independence and the freedom of expression under the Convention

Bearing in mind the specifics of prosecutors resulting in a narrower scope of independence compared to judges but stressing that to some extent judges and prosecutors enjoy comparable independence, in this section the term judicial independence is understood to embrace both judges and prosecutors. The question addressed in this section is whether freedom of expression is protected as an aspect of judicial independence under the Convention. If it is, then, firstly, this would be an argument to support the idea that there is a judge's or prosecutor's subjective right to judicial independence under Article 6, and if she suffers consequences due to exercising her freedom of expression, she could file a complaint under Article 6 in addition to or instead of under Article 10. Secondly, it would also have implications for EU law, since while there may be doubts as to whether the Court of Justice has the competence to review issues of judicial freedom of expression, it would certainly have this competence if it is embraced by the concept of judicial independence which is essential for safeguarding the rule of law in the EU.

Sicilianos shows[72] that as of now the Court has not recognised the judge's subjective right to independence, but a movement towards such a right in the Convention system can be discerned. The letter of Article 6 § 1 has led the Court to analyse the issue of judicial independence from the perspective of the rights of persons involved in the court proceedings and not from that of a judge's subjective right to have their own independence guaranteed and respected by the State. However, in the case of *Baka*[73] the Court was confronted with the question of judicial independence, as the judge suffered negative consequences for his professional expression. As the applicant relied only on the access to a court as provided under Article 6, the Court also limited its analysis of Article 6 issues to this aspect without addressing the independence element also provided under Article

72 L.A. Sicilianos, *The Subjective Right of Judges to Independence: Some Reflexions on the Interpretation of Article 6, Para. 1 of the ECHR*, [in:] P. Pinto de Albuquerque, K. Wojtyczek (eds.), *Judicial Power...*

73 *Baka* v. *Hungary...*

6. It also examined the case under Article 10. Sicilianos notes, however, that the principle of judicial independence is omnipresent in the judgment. Relying on non-binding texts as well as examples of case-law of the United Nation Human Rights Committee and the Inter-American Court of Human Rights, Sicilianos shows that if applicants are judges, their right to judicial independence can in principle be examined under fair trial provisions (which are analogous to those contained in Article 6 of the Convention). Relying on the *Golder*[74] judgment, which stressed the importance of teleological interpretation of the Convention and the importance of the rule of law, Sicilianos reaches the conclusion that an interpretation of Article 6 § 1 which finds that it protects the judge's subjective right to independence would be perfectly compatible with that provision's object and purpose. For Sicilianos, this right is inherent in Article 6 § 1. For our research, it is important that this interpretation has support. Notably, also the Consultative Council of European Judges has held that legislation limiting judges' freedom of expression in the exercise of their duties **may endanger judicial independence.**[75] If adopted by the Court, this interpretation would result in stronger protection of judicial independence than is currently provided indirectly via the freedom of expression (Article 10 of the Convention) or access to a court (Article 6 of the Convention) avenue. The fact that judicial independence, a right guaranteed by the Convention, is at stake where judges and prosecutors suffer for their professional, rule of law-promoting expression, should necessarily heighten the level of protection of their expression. The importance of what judges and prosecutors have to say on rule of law issues matters for a democratic society and deserves a high degree of protection.

---

74 *Golder* v. *the United Kingdom.*

75 Consultative Council of European Judges. Opinion of the CCJE Bureau following a request by the Romanian Judges Forum Association as regards the situation on the independence of the judiciary in Romania, 25 April 2019, CCJE-BU (2019) 4, § 62–65.

6. Prosecutors as judicial authority under EU law

Under EU law, in certain cases prosecutors can be considered to be a judicial authority. The Court of Justice has found that a "judicial authority" with the competence to issue a European arrest warrant can include the authorities of a Member State which, although not necessarily judges or courts, participate in the administration of criminal justice in that Member State.[76] The Court has further held that such other authorities, where they perform functions of a judicial authority, have to meet the requirements of independence. "That independence requires that there are statutory rules and an institutional framework capable of guaranteeing that the issuing judicial authority is not exposed, when adopting a decision to issue such an arrest warrant, to any risk of being subject, inter alia, to an instruction in a specific case from the executive."[77] As the case-law regarding the Lithuanian Prosecutor General shows, prosecutors in certain EU Member States can and do actually meet these requirements.[78] This means, *inter alia*, means that, at least in some EU Member States, when exercising some of their powers prosecutors enjoy the independence of a judicial authority on the basis of EU law and can rely on EU law in claiming safeguards of their independent status.

It could be asked whether the EU law requirement that a prosecutor should be independent when issuing a European arrest warrant implies that this prosecutor should enjoy the freedom of expression analogous to that of judges generally, or whether those specific freedom of expression guarantees should be limited to situations whose link with the exercise of powers of a judicial authority by the prosecutor can be established. At some risk of oversimplifying, the question can be addressed in the following way.

Prosecutors perform various functions. Some of these functions clearly require them to support a certain interpretation of evidence and one particular version of events to justify indictment and proceeding to trial rather than discontinuing the case.[79] Some other functions may call for a more

---

76 ECJ 27 May 2019, Case C-509/18, *Minister for Justice and Equality* v. *PF*, § 30.
77 *Ibidem*, § 52.
78 *Ibidem*, § 56.
79 ECtHR 10 October 2000, No. 42095/98, *Daktaras* v. *Lithuania*, § 44.

neutral and impartial attitude. Similarly, the required levels of independence of the prosecutor may vary. The case-law of the Court of Justice shows that prosecutors should be independent if and when they are issuing European arrest warrants. However, regarding matters related to a European investigation order, the concepts of "judicial authority" and "issuing authority" include prosecutors regardless of whether they are independent of the executive.[80] For a prosecutor who has powers to issue a European arrest warrant and a European investigation order it can, arguably, mean that when making comments to the public about the need for changes of legal regulation this prosecutor is free to speak about the European arrest warrant but may be required to have the permission of the executive to address the issue of the European investigation order. As these issues may be substantively interlinked, notably in the context of a required legal reform, such a distinction would malfunction. From the perspective of the EU law, there would also be no good reason to lower the level of protection of prosecutors' freedom of expression guaranteed by the Strasbourg Court in *Kövesi.* As we have seen in *Kövesi*, prosecutors generally enjoy their freedom of expression where they can contribute to a public debate on the need for legal reform as legal experts, and this is in no way incompatible with the rule of law. Making the protection of freedom of professional expression dependent on the protection of the independence in exercising a particular function would have the effect of lowering the level of protection of expression. The independence guaranteed to a prosecutor issuing a European arrest warrant would not then protect her

---

80 ECJ 8 December 2020, Case C-584/19, *A and Others* v *Staatsanwaltschaft Wien*: "Article 1(1) and Article 2(c) of Directive 2014/41/EU of the European Parliament and of the Council of 3 April 2014 regarding the European Investigation Order in criminal matters must be interpreted as meaning that the concepts of 'judicial authority' and 'issuing authority', within the meaning of those provisions, include the public prosecutor of a Member State or, more generally, the public prosecutor's office of a Member State, regardless of any relationship of legal subordination that might exist between that public prosecutor or public prosecutor's office and the executive of that Member State and of the exposure of that public prosecutor or public prosecutor's office to the risk of being directly or indirectly subject to orders or individual instructions from the executive when adopting a European investigation order."

against possible restrictions of her freedom to speak about the need for legal reform embracing various legal matters, even though a judge issuing a European arrest warrant would be so protected. The interpretation that a prosecutor who is required to be independent in issuing a European arrest warrant is also independent in exercising her freedom of professional expression, notably in expressing expert opinions related to her broader field of expertise as a prosecutor and a legal expert, seems to be a better interpretation of EU law. It would ensure that irrespective of the choices made by Member States in transposing the European Arrest Warrant Framework Decision, i.e. irrespective of whether the issuing judicial authority is a judge or a prosecutor, the practical experience gained in issuing European arrest warrants can inform public debate on the functioning of the legal system and can thus serve aims connected with the rule of law. It would also ensure that prosecutors in those Member States that grant them the status of a judicial authority in issuing European arrest warrants, such as Lithuania, can be more confident of the high level of protection of their professional expression as, in addition to the Convention, they could also base their freedom of expression claims on EU law.

7. Conclusion

The freedom of expression of judges and prosecutors is a rule of law issue both under the European Convention on Human Rights and EU law. As such, this freedom is of fundamental importance for the functioning of a democratic society in line with the values on which both the Convention and the EU legal system is based. When judges or prosecutors exercise their freedom of expression specifically to promote the rule of law (identify corrupt practices, dangerous legislative initiatives, etc.) their freedom of expression is even more important and should attract an even higher level of protection. Even though the principle of the rule of law encompasses principles that can sometimes compete with one another, the case-law of the Strasbourg Court suggests that the difficulty in identifying the content of the rule of law and expression promoting this value is not insurmountable.

The instrumental approach of the Strasbourg Court towards the freedom of expression and the absence of a distinction between personal and official expression strengthens the protection of the freedom of expression if judges and prosecutors express their ideas regarding the rule of law matters on which they have professional expertise as a result of their statutory functions. As regards prosecutors specifically, the *Kövesi* case shows that professional expression on legal reform affecting rule of law issues and falling into the scope of the prosecutors' competence, namely to investigate corruption offences, enjoys a high degree of protection. This is so because of its connection to judicial independence protected by the Convention, and it is so despite existing limits on civil servants' freedom of expression and specific limits for judicial expression. The freedom of expression of prosecutors needs to be protected at least to the extent which is necessary to ensure their judicial independence.

In the EU law context, prosecutors are not necessarily seen as independent of the executive in a manner analogous to judges. However, for those Member States where prosecutors enjoy such independence, notably in issuing EU-law based European arrest warrants, it is possible to argue that judicial independence protected by the EU law strengthens the protection of the freedom of expression of prosecutors, both in the context where the EU law requires independence from the executive and also beyond that context, in particular in discussing the need for legal reform.

Bibliography

Aquilina, K., *The Independence of the Judiciary in Strasbourg Judicial Disciplinary Case Law: Judges as Applicants and National Judicial Councils as Factotums of Respondent States*, [in:] P. Pinto de Albuquerque, K. Wojtyczek (eds.), *Judicial Power in a Globalized World: Liber Amicorum Vincent de Gaetano*, Springer, Cham, 2019.

Călin, D., *The Recent ECtHR Judgment Kövesi v. Romania. Reactions of Romanian Authorities and Implications Regarding the Rule of Law*, "Strasbourg Observers" 2020, 16 June, https://strasbourgobservers.com/2020/06/16/the-recent-ecthr-judgment-kovesi-v-romania-reactions-of-romanian-authorities-and-implications-regarding-the-rule-of-law/

Dijkstra, S., *The Freedom of the Judge to Express his Personal Opinions and Convictions under the ECHR*, "Utrecht Law Review" 2017, vol. 13, no. 1.

ECtHR Judicial Seminar 2018, *The Authority of the Judiciary*, https://www.echr.coe.int/Documents/Seminar_background_paper_2018_ENG.pdf

European Commission, 2020 Rule of Law Report. The rule of law situation in the European Union, 30 September 2020, COM/2020/580 final.

European Network of Councils for the Judiciary. Independence and Accountability of the Judiciary and of the Prosecution. Performance Indicators 2015. ENCJ Report 2014-2015, https://www.encj.eu/images/stories/pdf/workinggroups/independence/encj_report_independence_accountability_2014_2015_adopted_ga_corr_2016.pdf

Explanations relating to the Charter of Fundamental Rights, *OJ C 303, 14.12.2007*

Gunatilleke, G., *Justifying Limitations on the Freedom of Expression*, "Human Rights Review" 2021, vol. 22.

Holmøyvik, E., Sanders, A., *A Stress Test for Europe's Judiciaries*, [in:] E. Hirsch Ballin et al. (eds.), *European Yearbook of Constitutional Law 2019*, vol. 1, T.M.C. Asser Press, The Hague, 2020.

Lautenbach, G., *The Concept of the Rule of Law and the European Court of Human Rights*, Oxford University Press, Oxford, 2013.

Lucy, W., *Access to Justice and the Rule of Law*, "*Oxford Journal of Legal Studies*" 2020, vol. 40, no. 2.

Nuβberger, A., *Rule of Law in Europe Demands and Challenges for the European Judiciary*, [in:] P. Craig et al. (eds.), *Rule of Law in Europe Perspectives from Practitioners and Academics*, European Judicial Training Network 2019, https://www.ejtn.eu/News/Rule-of-Law-in-Europe--Perspectives-from-Practitioners-and-Academics1/

Oster, J., *Media Freedom as a Fundamental Right*, Cambridge University Press, Cambridge, UK, 2015.

Polakiewicz, J., *The Rule of Law – Dynamics and Limits of a Common European Value*. Presentation to the Scientific-Consultative Council on International Legal Issues of the Ministry of Foreign Affairs of Belarus, 20 September 2019, https://www.coe.int/en/web/dlapil/-/the-rule-of-law-dynamics-and-limits-of-a-common-european-value

Shetreet, S., *Reflections on Contemporary Issues of Judicial Independence*, [in:] P. Pinto de Albuquerque, K. Wojtyczek, (eds.), *Judicial Power in a Globalized World: Liber Amicorum Vincent de Gaetano*, Springer, Cham, 2019.

Sicilianos, L.A., *The Subjective Right of Judges to Independence: Some Reflexions on the Interpretation of Article 6, Para. 1 of the ECHR*, [in:] P. Pinto de Albuquerque, K. Wojtyczek (eds.), *Judicial Power in a Globalized World: Liber Amicorum Vincent de Gaetano*, Springer, Cham, 2019.

Spano, R., *The rule of law as the lodestar of the European Convention on Human Rights: The Strasbourg Court and the independence of the judiciary*, "European Law Journal" 2021, https://doi.org/10.1111/eulj.12377

Tamanaha, B., *On the Rule of Law: History, Politics, Theory*, Cambridge University Press, Cambridge, 2004.

Rasa Ragulskytė-Markovienė[1], Jurgita Paužaitė-Kulvinskienė

Right of Access to Justice in Environmental Matters as One of the Forms of Public Participation in Governance and an Instrument for Upholding the Values of the European Union

Abstract

Environmental protection, as a value of the European Union, is manifested not only as an objective that is to be adopted and implemented in legislation, but also in the joint actions undertaken by all the citizens of the European Union[2]. The article analyses the notion of environmental protection as a value of the European Union,

1 Rasa Ragulskytė-Markovienė, PhD in law, LL.M. (Berlin), professor at the Institute of Public Law of the Law School, Mykolas Romeris University, Lithuania, since 2021 judge of the Supreme Administrative Court of Lithuania, since 2016 court-mediator. She was a judge's assistant at the Constitutional Court of the Republic of Lithuania (2000–2007), and a judge of the Vilnius Regional Administrative Court (2007–2021). She is a member of the European Administrative Judges Association (AEAJ) (since 2016 a member of the board and a vice-president), a member of the Lithuanian Judges Association (LRTA) (since 2021 a member of the board). She is the author or co-author of publications on environmental and territorial planning law, administrative, constitutional and EU law, and on the status of judges.

2 Jurgita Paužaitė-Kulvinskienė, PhD in law, LL.M. (Frankfurt/Main), professor of Administrative Law and Administrative Proceeding Law at the Faculty of Law, Vilnius University, Lithuania, since 2022 a vice-dean for Science at the Faculty of Law, Vilnius University, since 2010 an academic member of the European Administrative Judges Association (AEAJ). She was a director of the Law Institute at the Ministry of Justice of Lithuania (2014–2019), a member of the Ethic Commission for Prosecutors (2012–2016), and a member of the Ethic and Disciplinary Commission for Judges (2016–2020). She is an author or co-author of numerous publications on administrative and administrative procedural law, judicial review, administrative liability, supervision of activities of economic (business) entities, constitutional law, and comparative public law.

the concepts of the public and the public concerned, and the scope of the rights enjoyed by the public in the area of environmental protection[3]. It focuses on public participation in environmental decision-making and on the right to access justice as important guarantees of public participation in public governance. By exercising the right of access to information about the environment, the right to participate in environmental decision-making, and the right of access to a court on environmental matters, the public concerned makes a significant contribution to the implementation of the principles of good governance.

Keywords: environmental protection, EU values, right of access to justice in environmental matters, public participation, public concerned, environmental decision-making, Aarhus Convention, public governance, participatory democracy, principles of good governance

1. Introduction

Exercise of the right to access justice in environmental matters gives rise to more and more questions and challenges both on the national and European Union level. The dramatic increase in environmental disasters and a clearer understanding of their causes make it necessary to revise national and European values and consider their priorities. The values existing in particular times also have a particular content, and are attributed particular importance during a specific period. The recognition of environmental protection as a value of the European Union has been predetermined by the changing attitude of the Member States to the human right to healthy and clean environment and to the consequences of failure to respect this right. Environmental protection, as a value of the European Union, is currently manifested not only as an objective that is to be adopted and implemented in legislation, but also in the joint actions undertaken by all the citizens of the European Union in order to uphold this value.

The article analyses the values of the European Union as well as the notion of environmental protection as a value of the European Union, the concepts of the public and the public concerned, as well as the scope of

3 The research was conducted within the scope of the project "Constitutional Consciousness as a Remedy for the Crisis of Discourse and Democracy Deficit in the European Union", Lietuvos mokslo taryba. Narodowe Centrum Nauki. DAINA – Polish-Lithuanian Funding Initiative, contract no. S-LL-19-4 / LSS-220000-1395, 10 August 2018.

the rights enjoyed by the public in the area of environmental protection. It focuses on public participation in environmental decision-making and on the right to access justice as important guarantees of public participation in public governance. Good public governance, underpinned by public involvement, is a security for ensuring environmental protection as a public interest and value.

2. The Identification of European Union values

2.1. The notion of a value of the European Union

According to Georg Jellinek, all human activities have content, which is the outcome of the pursuit for "something" which is identified as a good (German – *ein Gut*). Jellinek referred to a subjectively accepted good as an interest. In his view, the purpose of a law is the protection of goods and interests.[4]

Values are understood as guiding human perceptions that are somewhat anchored, distinguished by a belief in their correctness, and that have an emotional basis.[5] Values are diverse and quite often mutually antagonistic, going beyond the limits of intended rational purpose, shifting in meaning depending on the context. Values occupy positions between "being" and "being obliged to", between law and morals, between mandatoriness and resistance, between universality and plurality, between a heated emotion and a cold reason and they can alter along with changing situations in society.[6] Values have a guiding and regulatory function to distinguish between good and evil, between correct and wrong.[7] Each legal norm is underpinned by a value, which is fleshed out and transformed by means of

---

4 G. Jellinek, *System der subjektiven oeffentlichen Rechte*, Mohr Siebeck, Tübingen, 1919, pp. 43–44.

5 U. Di Fabio, *Grundrechte als Werteordnung*, "JuristenZeitung" 2004, no. 1, pp. 1–8, p. 3; Ch. Callies, *Europa als Wertegemeinschaft – Integration und Identität durch europäisches Verfassungsrecht?*, "JuristenZeitung" 2004, no. 21, pp. 1033–1045, 1034.

6 U. Di Fabio, *Grundrechte...*, p. 3.

7 *Ibidem*; Ch. Callies, *Europa...*, p. 1034.

them. Values are the guidelines for interpreting a legal norm and the basis of its control; they acquire a particular legitimation function.[8]

Hence, a legal norm is indivisible from a particular value that exists in the relevant society at a particular time; the value has inherent content and defines the relevant context for the interpretation of the legal norm.

European integration, its meaning and substance, have long been the subject of discussion. European integration has itself become a European project. In order to explain the significance of this project, better life visions were used: following two world wars, after the National Socialist period which was distinguished by the prevalence of lawlessness, the idea of the European Community was linked with the establishment of a political world that aimed to bring an end to barbarism and lawlessness. The creation of the common market was understood as a tool that promised welfare. The policy geared towards the common good was expected to ensure a better life for people.[9] The formation, promotion and establishment of values is a political-constitutional response to the question of meaning; they must fill the gaps emerging in modern society, including also the market-oriented union.[10]

Changes in the political situation in Europe (the end of the conflict between the East and the West, the collapse of the Soviet Union) intensified discussions on European identity and the democratisation of the European Union (hereinafter also the EU). The democratisation of the EU was envisaged as arising through the creation of the political identity of Europe based on common values. The community of values (German – *die Wertegemeinschaft*) was the response to the question of what the social construction of the collective entity – the EU – should be.[11]

---

8 Ch. Callies, *Europa...*, p. 1034.

9 M. Nettesheim, *"Gegründet auf Werten...": Das Narrativ der Wertegemeischaft und der Sabktionsmechanismus des Art. 7 EUV*, [in:] C. Franzius, F.C. Mayer, J. Neyer (eds.), *Recht und Politik in der Europäischen Union*, Band 9: *Die Neuerfindung Europas*, Nomos, Baden-Baden, 2019, p. 94.

10 *Ibidem*, p. 96.

11 *Ibidem*.

The aim of the EU is set out in Article 3 of the Treaty on European Union[12]: to promote peace, its values and the well-being of its peoples. Under Article 2 of the EU Treaty, the Union is founded on the following values: respect for human dignity, freedom, democracy, equality, the rule of law and respect for human rights, including the rights of persons belonging to minorities; these values are common to the Member States in a society in which pluralism, non-discrimination, tolerance, justice, solidarity and equality between women and men prevail. The values referred to in Article 2 of the EU Treaty have been, in one form or another, recognised in the Member States; they constitute the basis of the Constitutions of the Member States and express the European constitutional framework of the Union.[13] The EU values are also set out in the conditions (Copenhagen Criteria[14]) to be satisfied by the Member State in order to become a member of the EU. Based on these values, in particular, Europe has become a creation that has enabled the development of higher standards for public authority and civil society by focusing on the implementation of the rule of law principles, guaranteeing the right to join political parties and professional associations, consolidating the principles of democratic governance, and thereby acquiring its attractiveness.[15]

EU values are rooted in the national values established in the Constitutions of the Member States. Therefore, the Constitutions of the Member States play an important integrative role.[16] EU values, despite their links to national values, have autonomous content. In other words, EU values derive from the values of the Member States, however to some extent they have been promoted to Union level in order to ensure the framework of EU values.[17] Hence, the content of EU and national values

12 https://eur-lex.europa.eu/LexUriServ/LexUriServ.do?uri=OJ:C:2008:115:0013:0045:LT:PDF
13 Ch. Callies, *Europa...* p. 1042.
14 https://ec.europa.eu/commission/presscorner/detail/en/DOC_93_3
15 P. Taylor, *The End of European Integration: Anti-Europeanism Examined*, Routledge, London, 2018, p. 136.
16 U. Volkmann, *Vom Ursprung und Ziel der Europäischen Union: Die Perspektive der Rechtswissenschaft*, [in:] G. Kirchhof, H. Kube, R. Schmidt (eds.), *Von Urpsrung und Ziel der Europäischen Union: Elf Perspektiven*, Mohr Siebeck, Tübingen, 2016, p. 66.
17 Ch. Callies, *Europa...*, p. 1042.

undergoes constant interchange, meaning that not only the content of abstractly recognised EU values is supplemented by the content of national values, but, conversely, EU values also shape national values.[18] The awareness of European citizens that "we" are making a union of values is a political-cultural basis for the recognition and promotion of European integration by the community of Member States.[19] The union of values is a prerequisite for common legal and political growth.[20]

On the one hand, values indicate some unity, and on the other hand differences in the interpretation of the values as such, and the resultant outcomes also reveal potential differences in the content of the values.[21] In this light, such values as tolerance, pluralism and democracy are of great importance.[22]

Democracy creates the space of freedom and law underpinned by the power of the nation, which is exercised under the principle of majority established and implemented according to constitutional norms.[23] Democracy means that decision-making is attributed to the *demos* (meaning "people" in Greek), and the *demos* operates through their representatives, i. e. the *demos* hands over the right of governance to their representatives and thereby make their governance legitimate. With the growing discontent of citizens with the politics pursued by their representatives, the search for a solution to this problem began in recent decades, with the view to strengthening the relationship between private individuals and the governing authorities – the link between state-community and state-apparatus.[24] In this light, the concept of advisory democracy has been

---

18 *Ibidem.*

19 H. Joas, Ch. Mandry, *Europa als Werte- und Kulturgemeinschaft*, [in:] G.F. Schuppert, I. Pernice, U. Haltern (eds.), *Europawissenschaft*, Nomos, Baden-Baden, 2005, p. 551.

20 *Ibidem.*

21 *Ibidem*, p. 568.

22 *Ibidem.*

23 *Ibidem*, p. 569.

24 C. Fraenkel-Haeberle, *Participatory Democracy and the Global Approach in Environmental Legislation*, [in:] E.J. Lohse, M. Poto (eds.), *Participatory Rights in the Environmental Decision-Making Process and the Implementation of the Aarhus Convention: a Comparative Perspective*, Duncker & Humblot, Berlin, 2015, Schriften zum Internationalen Recht (205), pp. 34–35.

developed, based on the culture of dialogue and supported by consultations and negotiations before decision-making.[25] The EU is a modern project and its successful implementation is, in principle, only possible if common values are not only named in abstract terms but also if each citizen is allowed to contribute to their formation.[26] Hence, the involvement of citizens in consultations and negotiations on decisions of public relevance is an instrument that can foster public awareness and the recognition of EU values.

2.2. Environmental protection – an European Union value

One of the EU values declared in Article 2 of the EU Treaty is the respect for human rights. In the sphere of environmental protection, human rights are recognised both on the national and international level. These rights were not explicitly established in the 1948 Universal Declaration of Human Rights[27] or the 1950 European Convention for the Protection of Human Rights and Fundamental Freedoms.[28] The environmental movements that started in the 1950s helped identify the damage done to people and communities as a result of environmental degradation. In order to fight the increase in pollution and landscape destruction, a switch was made to the concept of the protection of human rights. The Declaration adopted in the United Nations Conference in 1972[29] established that man has the fundamental right to adequate conditions of life, in an environment of a quality that permits a life of dignity and well-being, and he bears a responsibility to protect and improve the environment for present and future generations (Principle 1). Later, human rights to a healthy and clean environment were elaborated and, with the adoption of the Aarhus Convention[30] in 1998, it

25 *Ibidem*, p. 35.
26 M. Nettesheim, "*Gegründet...*, p. 98.
27 https://www.un.org/en/about-us/universal-declaration-of-human-rights
28 https://www.echr.coe.int/documents/convention_eng.pdf
29 https://www.soas.ac.uk/cedep-demos/000_P514_IEL_K3736-Demo/treaties/media/1972%20Stockholm%201972%20-%20Declaration%20of%20the%20United%20Nations%20Conference%20on%20the%20Human%20Environment%20-%20UNEP.pdf
30 https://unece.org/fileadmin/DAM/env/pp/documents/cep43e.pdf

already embodied very extensive content: right of access to information, right of participation, right of access to justice. The Aarhus Convention was underpinned by a new concept, under which international and national environmental law is balanced with fundamental human rights and freedoms, as well as with the empowerment of associations to represent public interests.[31] To ensure the effective enforcement of environmental law, the involvement of citizens in the process of environmental decision-making was strengthened.[32] Hence, the adoption of the Aarhus Convention was a pivotal outcome of environmental law harmonisation on the international level.

At the outset, the EU-level environmental policy guidelines were set out in environmental action programmes. Already in the first programme of action on the environment adopted in 1973[33] it was established that the protection of the environment is a matter for all and that everybody should be made aware of its importance; the success of an environmental policy presupposes that everybody should protect and improve the environment. Subsequent programmes of environmental action[34] kept developing the concept of environmental protection and construed it as a common good, goal, and value. The content of environmental protection, as an EU value, stems from the provisions of the treaties, in principle. The status of environmental protection, as a key value of the EU, is confirmed

31 C. Fraenkel-Haeberle, *Participatory…*, p. 39.

32 S.R. Laskowski, *Demokratisierung des Umweltrechts*, "Zeitschrift für Umweltrecht" 2010, no. 4, p. 171.

33 Declaration of the Council of the European Communities and of the representatives of the Governments of the Member States meeting in the Council of 22 November 1973 on the programme of action of the European Communities on the environment, https://eur-lex.europa.eu/legal-content/SV/TXT/?uri=CELEX:41973X1220

34 Seven environmental action programmes had been approved by 2020. In 2013, the seventh programme of environmental action was approved. Decision No 1386/2013/EU of the European Parliament and of the Council of 20 November 2013 on a General Union Environment Action Programme to 2020 "Living well, within the limits of our planet" Text with EEA relevance, https://eur-lex.europa.eu/legal-content/EN/TXT/?uri=CELEX:32013D1386. The eighth programme of environmental actions is currently under development. https://ec.europa.eu/environment/strategy/environment-action-programme-2030_en

by the objectives of the EU environmental policy (preserving, protecting and improving the quality of the environment, protecting human health, prudent and rational utilisation of natural resources, promoting measures at the international level to deal with regional or worldwide environmental problems, and in particular to combat climate change) as laid down in Article 191 of the Treaty on the Functioning of the European Union and in its Article 11 requiring environmental protection requirements to be integrated into the definition and implementation of the Union's policies and activities, in particular with a view to promoting sustainable development.

The significance of environmental protection, as an EU value, was strengthened with the EU Charter of Fundamental Rights[35] (hereinafter also the Charter). The Preamble of the Charter states that the peoples of Europe, in creating an ever-closer union among them, are resolved to share a peaceful future based on common values. Under Article 6 of the EU Treaty, the Union recognises the rights, freedoms and principles set out in the Charter; the Charter shall have the same legal value as the Treaties. Hence, individuals have the right of access to a court concerning violations of their right established *expressis verbis* in the Charter (e.g. the right to receive information under Article 11, the right to property under Article 17 of the Charter, etc.). The provision set out in Article 37 of the Charter, namely that a high level of environmental protection and the improvement of the quality of the environment must be integrated into the policies of the Union, and ensured in accordance with the principle of sustainable development, has not been formulated as a right but as a principle[36] to be taken into consideration in the implementation of any measures at the EU level.[37] It is most often argued that the provision established in Article 37

35 https://www.europarl.europa.eu/charter/pdf/text_en.pdf

36 L. Krämer, *Direct Effect and Consistent Interpretation: Strengths and Weakness of the Concepts*, [in:] J.H. Jans, R. Macrory, A.-M. Moreno Molina (eds.), *National courts and EU Environmental Law*, Europa Law Publishing, Groningen, 2013, p. 60.

37 This approach supplements the provision set out in Article 11 of the EU Treaty: "Environmental protection requirements must be integrated into the definition and implementation of the Union's policies and activities, in particular with a view to promoting sustainable development."

of the Charter does not, in itself, form the basis to apply to the court,[38] however, it can be presumed that, in some cases, both the high level of environmental protection and the improvement of environmental quality can constitute the basis to initiate a litigation. In any case, there is no doubt that Article 37 of the Charter fleshes out the content of environmental protection as an EU value, i.e. it is linked to the high level of environmental protection and improvement, as well as ensuring environmental quality.

3. The concepts of the public and the public concerned

Environmental protection, as an EU value, is expressed not only as the aim to adopt EU legal acts and control their implementation on the level of EU institutions, but also as the obligation of all EU citizens to act together in order to uphold this value.

The Treaty on the Functioning of the EU refers to the concepts of the public, civil society, and associations. After the EU citizenship was introduced by the 1992 Maastricht Treaty, citizens of the EU Member States acquired additional rights and obligations. EU citizenship has been useful as an instrument for unifying citizens of the EU Member States and as an instrument for strengthening them as a European society.

In terms of the public, this term primarily refers to the public space that is generated when individuals discuss common issues. The public has three inherent elements: participants (actors), discussion (topics, participants) and a common sphere (newspapers, cafe, radio, television, etc.).[39] The following quality criteria of the public are distinguished: unhindered and free-of-charge accessibility to discussion for all citizens, non-exclusion of any participant from a particular discussion topic, consultative decision-making based exclusively on the best arguments, consensus and solidarity as a discussion goal, and the public authorities not having any influence on the public sphere.[40] The existence of the public is the existential backbone

---

38 L. Krämer, *Direct…*, p. 60.

39 J. Ruiz-Soler, *Gibt es eine europäische Öffentlichkeit? Forschungsstand, Befunde, Ausblicke*, "Aus Politik und Zeitgechichte" 2017, no. 37, p. 35.

40 *Ibidem.*

of any democratic formation because public discussion and information sharing is ensured through the public.[41]

European society is marked by all three of the abovementioned elements transposed to the European level. European society is significant in terms of creating a common space where the European *demos* are in a position to consult and discuss, to reduce the distance between the EU authorities and citizens.[42] Habermas has noted that the deficit of democracy can be eliminated only through the involvement of the European public, in order to reinforce democratic procedures.[43] Hence, the European public[44] consists of citizens who have a common interest in certain topics and matters of European significance related to all citizens of the EU, in one way or another.

The principle of democracy in Europe is fleshed out through different forms of citizen participation. The fundamental rights and freedoms are the binding element through which democratic elements are implemented.[45] Democratic participation in the EU is not confined to the exercise of the right to election; it embraces the rights to consultations, accessibility to information, and procedural rights to make proposals. In its case-law in the area of the protection of human rights and fundamental freedoms as well as democratic participation, the Court of Justice of the European Union (hereinafter also the CJEU) expands the interpretation of the EU citizen, as a member of European society: not only does a citizen of the EU have the participation rights guaranteed by EU law but also as a subject with certain values who, as an active participant in the Member State, influences and changes the scope of fundamental rights and freedoms.[46]

---

41 *Ibidem.*

42 *Ibidem*, p. 36.

43 J. Habermas, *Warum braucht Europa eine Verfassung?*, "Die Zeit" 2001, no. 27, www.zeit.de

44 For more on different theories on the notion of the European society, see J. Ruiz-Soler, *Gibt...*, p. 36.

45 Ch. Callies, *Europa...*, p. 89.

46 *Ibidem*, p. 90. E. g., in Case No. C-60/00 (Carpener), the CJEU recognised the priority of respect for family life; in Case No. C-144/04 (Mangold), the CJEU held that the principle of non-discrimination on account of age should be understood as a general principle of Community law.

On the basis of national and EU rights, subjects acquire particular legal positions, which, according to Jellinek's theory, can be classified as negative (*status negativus)*, positive (*status positivus)* and active (*status activus)* status.[47] *Status negativus* means that the person is in the position to act freely in the pursuit of his/her personal goals; *status positivus* implies the person's right to make use of the power of the state and its authorities for the exercise of his/her rights and set particular requirements for them; *status activus* means that the state recognises particular personal rights in the exercise whereof the person acts for the benefit of the state, i.e. he/she exercises his/her political rights.[48] It is *status activus* that gives rise to the rights of an individual to participate when state authorities make decisions in the democratic process of decision-making.[49] Hence, *status activus* finds expression through a person's interest in having the decisions of relevance for him/her and for the entire society made with his/her knowledge and participation, and in having an impact on the adoption of such decisions. This leads to the public concerned, which acts both in its own right and together with state authorities for the purposes of enforcing particular values. The public concerned within the territory of EU Member States operates for the pursuit of common goals and the values of the EU.

Activities of the public concerned are in particular clearly manifested in the area of environmental protection. The fundamentals for this have been laid down by the abovementioned Aarhus Convention, the provisions of which have been (partly) transposed to the EU law and, accordingly, to the domestic law of its Member States. Under Article 2(5) of the Aarhus Convention, "the public concerned" means the public affected or likely to be affected by, or having an interest in, the environmental decision-making; for the purposes of this definition, non-governmental organizations promoting environmental protection and meeting any requirements under national law shall be deemed to have an interest. This definition of the "public concerned", which has been developed in the case-law of the CJEU for some time, indicates the agreement of all the people to act together on

47 G. Jellinek, *System...*, pp. 86–87; Ch. Callies, *Europa...*, pp. 90–91.
48 G. Jellinek, *System...*, p. 87.
49 Ch. Callies, *Europa...*, p. 91.

the international and EU level, with the aim of ensuring a cleaner and safer environment for human health. Thanks to the Aarhus Convention, the "public concerned" has acquired legal status with new content, which, as already mentioned, finds expression through three essential dimensions – the right of access to information about the environment, the right to participate in decision-making in the area of environmental protection, and the right of access to justice regarding issues of environmental protection.

4. Public participation in environmental decision-making

4.1. The scope of the rights of the public in the area of environmental protection

Participatory democracy is a political, democratic idea that advances public participation in various decision-making forums.[50] Environmental protection is one of the areas where the elements of participatory democracy are most visible. That is predetermined by the content of environmental protection as a value. The aim of the Aarhus Convention is set out in its Article 1 – the protection of the right of every person of present and future generations to live in an environment adequate to his or her health and well-being. Hence, the protection of the environment is, above all, connected with the person's right to live in the environment favourable for his/her health and well-being. The importance of this right drives the common interest of the public to be active in order to ensure such a level of the environment which would guarantee the exercise of this right. Secondly, environmental protection is one of the most important policy areas of every state where the state (public authorities) has an obligation to protect the environment and, through various measures, ensure the human right to live in an environment adequate to health and well-being. In implementing this obligation, the state must involve the public in the process of decision-making concerning the environment. Principle 10 of the Rio Declaration 1992[51] establishes participation in environmental

50 T. Berman, *Public Participation as a Tool for Integrating Local Knowledge into Spatial Planning*, Springer, 2017, p. 22.

51 Rio Declaration on Environment and Development (Rio de Janeiro, 3–14 June 1992); Principle 10 of the Rio Declaration states that environmental issues are

decision-making as one of the key principles of environmental governance, and this principle is developed in the Aarhus Convention.[52] The necessity of public participation in public governance to address environmental issues, as clearly declared in the Rio Declaration, was later rapidly elaborated in other international, EU and national legal acts. The following major arguments reflecting the advantages of public participation in the process of decision-making can be distinguished: (1) participation will increase the legitimacy of the decisions taken and reduce the level of conflict; (2) participation will contribute to the quality of the decision-making because it will give the government the information necessary for decision-making and contribute to the systematic identification of problems and their causes, and to the consideration and assessment of alternative strategic options; and (3) through participation, people will learn of the environmental problems that society faces and change their behaviour.[53] Representatives of the public who actually take part in decision-making, in principle, identify themselves with decision-makers, feel responsible for the decisions made and for their implementation. The rights of public representatives in the area of environmental protection correlate with their obligations and responsibility in ensuring the protection of the environment as a value. This considerably expands the scope of public rights in the area of environmental protection. The public becomes an equal partner of the competent authorities in dealing with the issues of public relevance.

---

best handled with the participation of all concerned citizens at the relevant level. At the national level, each individual shall have appropriate access to information concerning the environment that is held by public authorities, including information on hazardous materials and activities in their communities, and the opportunity to participate in decision-making processes. States shall facilitate and encourage public awareness and participation by making information available.

https://www.un.org/en/development/desa/population/migration/generalassembly/docs/globalcompact/A_CONF.151_26_Vol.I_Declaration.pdf.

52 F. Coenen, *Introduction*, [in:] F.H.J.M. Coenen (ed.), *Public Participation and Better Environmental Decisions: The Promise and Limits of Participatory Processes for the Quality of Environmentally Related Decision-making*, Springer, 2009, p. 8.

53 *Ibidem*, p. 9.

This approach was clearly set out in the Aarhus Convention, which affirms the obligation of every person to protect the environment and improve its conditions for the benefit of present and future generations. This obligation presupposes the person's capacity to be involved in the decision-making of relevance to the environment and thereby contribute to the control of whether the requirements imposed in the area of environmental protection are implemented in a proper manner. The Aarhus Convention distinguishes three fundamental groups of rights, which define the scope of rights of the public in the environmental sphere – the right to have access to information about the environment, the right to participate in decision-making in the area of environmental protection, and the right of access to justice on environmental issues. These rights have been recognised in all Member States, however, the exercise of each of them depends, *inter alia*, on the specifics of national legal regulation. As a result, the scope and content of the rights of the public in the area of environmental protection in different Member States can be different. However, the rather wider range of issues regulated by EU legislation, as well as the case-law of the CJEU on the relevant matters pertaining to public participation in environmental decision-making, gradually lead to the approximation of the scope and content of the rights of the public in the environmental area. Both the Aarhus Convention and its implementing EU and national legal acts have, presumably, been the major factors that predetermined the recognition (legitimation) of the public as a subject who, together with the competent authorities, is responsible for the protection of the environment in all EU Member States, which is expressed through the granting of the abovementioned rights and responsibility in their exercise.

4.2. The right of access to justice as security for the effectiveness of public participation in environmental decision-making

Right of access to justice in the area of environmental protection is, first of all, understood as the right of access to a court that protects the personal right to healthy and clean environment.[54] On the other hand, the

54 For more about the content of the right to healthy and clean environment, see R. Ragulskytė-Markovienė, I. Žvaiždinienė, *Teisės į sveiką ir švarią aplinką*

right of access to justice in the area of environmental protection is understood as the right to defend the public interest in environment protection, i.e. as a collective right. The collective nature of this right is most accurately reflected by the provisions of the Aarhus Convention which introduces the concepts of "the public" and "the public concerned."[55] The Aarhus Convention defines the areas where the right of access to justice can be exercised and indicates its specific limits. That includes the right of access to a court in the event of inadequate provision or failure to provide information about the environment (Article 9(1) of the Aarhus Convention), concerning decisions the procedure of adoption whereof presupposes public participation (Article 9(2) of the Aarhus Convention), concerning acts or omissions by private persons and public authorities which contravene provisions of its national law relating to the environment (Article 9(3) of the Aarhus Convention). As mentioned, the scope of rights enjoyed by the public in the area of environmental protection and, *inter alia*, the possibilities of exercising the right of access to a court depend on the domestic legislative provisions which lay down the conditions for exercising this right. Hence, the effectiveness of public participation in environmental decision-making is measured not only by the range of decision-making where public participation is foreseen, but also by legal remedies and instruments available to it in case it is dissatisfied with the decision made.

---

teoriniai ir praktiniai aspektai [en. *Theoretical and practical issues of the right to a healthy and clean environment*], [in:] V. Valančius *et. al.*(eds.) *Žmogus, teisinė valstybė ir administracinė justicija: mokslo studija, skirta Lietuvos vyriausiojo administracinio teismo dešimtmečiui* [en. *Human Rights, the Rule of Law and Administrative Justice: the study devoted for the 10th anniversary of the Supreme Administrative Court of Lithuania*], Supreme Administrative Court of Lithuania 2012, pp. 412–417.

55 "The public" means one or more natural or legal persons, and, in accordance with national legislation or practice, their associations, organizations or groups (Art. 2 (4) Aarhus Convention); "the public concerned" means the public affected or likely to be affected by, or having an interest in, the environmental decision-making; for the purposes of this definition, non-governmental organizations promoting environmental protection and meeting any requirements under national law shall be deemed to have an interest (Art. 2 (5) Aarhus Convention).

Implementation of the principle of effective remedies is of major relevance for the ensuring of the right of access to courts in the area of the environment. The European Commission noted in its Communication of 21 December 2016[56] that where citizens' rights under EU law are affected at national level, the public have to be granted access to rapid and effective national redress mechanisms; these must comply with the principle of effective judicial protection. The principles of effective judicial remedies are set out in Article 19 of the EU Treaty. It has also been reinforced in Article 47 of the Charter: everyone whose rights and freedoms are violated shall have the right to a remedy, the case shall be disposed of within a reasonable time by an independent and impartial court, the possibility of being advised, defended and represented shall be ensured, and those who lack sufficient resources shall be provided with legal aid. An effective remedy also means that the person has real rather than hypothetical possibility of accessing the court. In terms of the right of members of the public to access the court in challenging the decisions made in the area of environmental protection, much importance is attributed to the provisions of Article 6 of the Aarhus Convention, which define the conditions and limits of public participation as an integral part of the decision-making process. Article 6 of the Aarhus Convention reinforces the rights of the public in the taking of decisions pertaining to proposed activity types listed in Annex I to the Aarhus Convention, as well as concerning proposed activity types not listed in Annex I but capable of having a major impact on the environment. Hence, such a non-finite list of activity types implies a broad discretion granted for the state seeking to implement the obligations under the Aarhus Convention to decide to what extent it will entitle the public to participate in environmental decision-making. That also predetermines the possibilities of exercising the right of access to a court. Participation in decision-making presupposes access to information about intended activities. With such information, the public is engaged in a discussion on environmental issues. This factor alone drives the focus of

56 Communication from the Commission of 21 December 2016 C(2016) 8600 final "EU law. Better results through better application", p. 4, https://ec.europa.eu/transparency/documents-register/detail?ref=C(2016)8600&lang=lt

members of the public on the solution of particularly important environmental issues. Such engagement in itself also develops responsibility for the decision to be taken. Active participation of the public in the taking of decisions important for all increases the quality of the decisions made because the decision-maker becomes accountable to the public and other subjects involved in the decision-making process for the decision made. Ultimately, such participation in decision-making is in direct relationship with the right of access to court. Normally the subjects who participate in a decision-making process and meet the requirements set out in legal acts are allowed to have access to court. This right stems from the Aarhus Convention. Enabling the public to access justice on environmental issues is a guarantee of the effectiveness of public participation in decision-making in the area of environmental protection. Where members of the public are in the position not only to participate in decision-making process by voicing their opinion, making proposals and objections, etc., but can also question the legitimacy and justification of the decisions made, they undoubtedly play the role of guardian of the lawfulness of such decisions. This role of the public is essential in order to ensure the quality of environmental decisions, their conformity to the requirements set out in legal acts, and their recognition. The right of the public to access a court in disputing decisions in the area of environmental protection should be understood not as a privilege but as an important instrument of control over the lawfulness of such decisions, through which the public directly contributes to the promotion of environmental protection as a value and to the enhancement of its significance.

4.3. Public participation in addressing environmental issues – an important guarantee of public participation in public governance

Public governance by states requires participation of the public (citizens). That can be understood as the right of every citizen to participate in decision-making relating to his/her life, informing local communities about what it taking place, providing an opportunity to citizens to control whatever happens around them, and expressing their opinion.[57] Being informed as to what is happening, the opinions formed on the basis of such information, making comments and proposals, as well as consensus building, are the elements through which the public contributes to public governance. Public participation allows local representatives to improve their knowledge of public problems, have an impact on activities of citizens' groups, reduce tensions among stakeholder groups, improve the quality of decision-making, and exercise more effective management and control of activities of public institutions.[58] Public participation in public governance requires the development of a mechanism to create conditions for educating and informing the public and to enable their participation in and influence on governance processes.[59]

Public participation in addressing environmental issues plays a special role in public governance because it relates to ensuring that environmental protection is an issue of public interest and an EU value. As can be seen from the provisions of the Aarhus Convention, public participation in decision-making in environmental matters is understood in the broad sense – not only meaning participation in decisions on specific activities (Article 6), but also participation concerning plans, programmes and policies relating to the environment (Article 7) and participation during the preparation of executive regulations and / or generally applicable legally binding normative instruments (Article 8). Public participation in decision-making on environmental issues most often implies consultations with public representatives. Proposals received during consultations with

57 L. Marcinkevičiūtė, R. Petrauskienė, *Piliečių dalyvavimo viešojo administravimo institucijų valdyme galimybės: Vilniaus ir Jurbarko rajonų savivaldybių pavyzdys* [en. *Possibilities of citizens` participation in management of public administration institutions: cases of Vilnius and Jurbarkas district municipalities*], *Vadybos mokslas ir studijos – kaimo verslų ir jų infrastruktūros plėtrai* [en. *Management theory and studies for rural business and infrastructure development*], mokslo darbai, 2008, vol. 14, no. 3, pp. 102–109, 103.

58 *Ibidem*, p. 108.

59 A. Stasiukynas, *Visuomenės dalyvavimas Lietuvos elektros energetikos sektoriaus valdyme* [en. *Public participation in the governance of the Lithuanian electrical energy sector*], Viešoji politika ir administravimas, 2010, no. 32, pp. 104–119, 112.

the public are only recommendations by nature, they are taken into consideration when making the relevant decision, however, they are not binding (e.g. in the procedure of environmental impact assessment of intended economic activities, the procedure of strategic assessment of the effects of plans and programmes on the environment, the territorial planning procedure). Therefore, public participation in these processes may be viewed as symbolic, not decisive for the content of a decision as such. The right of the public to appeal against such decisions to the court (or pre-litigation dispute resolution bodies), on the other hand, considerably changes the significance of public participation as an integral part of the decision-making procedure. The right enjoyed by the public to access court adds importance to its participation in decision-making on environmental matters. That is a highly important guarantee that secures public participation in public governance. The public being granted the right to access a court, as was mentioned, should not be understood as a privilege. Quite the contrary: it should be understood as an obligation of the public (not only the public authorities) to apply to a court in the case of any doubts concerning the lawfulness of the decisions made in order to pursue the objective of ensuring environmental protection.

Hence, public participation in public governance through decision-making in the area of environmental protection is inseparable from the right of the public to contest such decisions through judicial procedure. The development of the mechanism that enables this particular right to be exercised both on the national and EU level, as well as international levels, is crucial for achieving the effective cooperation and partnership of the state authorities and the public in environmental decision-making. The Communication of the European Commission on Access to Justice in Environmental Matters[60] (hereinafter also the Communication) and the sizeable CJEU case-law it refers to set out the main guidelines on how this mechanism should be developed. This Communication was adopted after the failure of the Council to agree on the proposal made by the European

60 European Commission, Communication from the Commission of 28.4.2017 "Commission Notice on Access to Justice in Environmental Matters", C(2017) 2616 final // https://ec.europa.eu/environment/aarhus/pdf/notice_accesstojustice.pdf

Commission in 2003 for a directive on access to environmental justice,[61] which was withdrawn in 2014. Although there are big gaps in how EU legislation is put into practice in different Member States, as noted in the Communication, the need to improve the mechanism for accessing justice in environmental matters by providing the public with wider and real access to justice is still relevant. Public participation in decision-making in the environmental area is an important precondition for open and transparent public governance. The right of the public to contest such decisions in the case of doubts concerning their lawfulness must be recognised as an integral part of the process of public participation in environmental matters. Public governance in certain areas where environmental decisions are made is inconceivable without participation of the public concerned. In pursuing common goals and implementing the values of the EU, the public concerned plays an important role in ensuring the effectiveness of EU law. Both acting on its own account and together with the public authorities, and exercising the right to have access to information about the environment, the right to participate in environmental decision-making, and the right of access to court on environmental matters, the public concerned contributes considerably to the implementation of the principles of good governance. Good governance requires the public authorities to apply methods to ensure effective provision of quality services, to to ensure compliance with with laws, provisions and standards, to satisfy the needs of citizens, and to meet public expectations concerning honesty, accountability and transparency.[62] Good public governance in the area of environmental protection that involves the public and provides it with the opportunity to participate in decision-making is a prerequisite for ensuring environmental protection as a public interest and value.

---

61 Commission of the European Communities, Proposal for a Directive of the European Parliament and of the Council on access to justice in environmental matters, COM/2003/0624 final - COD 2003/0246//https://eur-lex.europa.eu/legal-content/LT/ALL/?uri=CELEX:52003PC0624

62 R. Petrauskienė, E. Predkelytė, *Gero valdymo principų įgyvendinimą viešosiose institucijose lemiantys veiksniai: teorinis pagrindimas, Visuomenės saugumas ir viešoji tvarka* [en. *Implementation of Good Governance Principles in Public Institutions: Theoretical Aspect, Public Security and Public Order*] 2014, no. 12, pp. 147–160, 154.

5. Conclusions

The EU is based on the values rooted in the national values established in the Constitutions of the Member States. The content of the EU and national values undergoes constant interchange, i.e. the content of EU values is supplemented by the content of national values while EU values keep shaping the national values. The involvement of citizens in the process of making decisions of relevance to the public, in consultations and negotiations, is a means for forming public awareness and identification with EU values.

The content of environmental protection as an EU value is linked with a high level of environmental protection and improvement, as well as concerted attempts to ensure environmental quality. It is expressed not only in the objective to adopt EU legal acts and control their implementation at the level of EU institutions, but also in the obligation of all EU citizens to act together in order to enforce this value. The principle of democracy in Europe is fleshed out through different forms of citizen participation. Environmental protection is one of the areas where the elements of participatory democracy are most visible. The fundamentals for this have been laid down by the Aarhus Convention, the provisions whereof have been (partly) transposed to the EU law and, accordingly, to the domestic law of its Member States. The effectiveness of public participation in environmental decision-making is measured not only by the range of decision-making where public participation is foreseen, but also by legal remedies and instruments available to the public in the event that it is dissatisfied with the decisions made. The right of the public to access justice in contesting decisions in the area of environmental protection should understood not as a privilege but as an important instrument of supervision over the lawfulness of such decisions, though which the public directly contributes to the promotion of environmental protection as a value and to the enhancement of its significance. Public participation also contributes to the improved openness and transparency of public governance. The right of the public to contest such decisions in the case of doubts concerning their lawfulness must be recognised as an integral part of the process of public participation in addressing environmental matters. By exercising the right of access to information about the environment, the right to participate in environmental decision-making, and the right of access to court on environmental matters, the public concerned makes a significant contribution to the implementation of the principles of good governance.

Bibliography

Jellinek, G., *System der subjektiven oeffentlichen Rechte*, Mohr Siebeck, Tübingen, 1919.

Fabio, Di U., *Grundrechte als Werteordnung*, "JuristenZeitung" 2004, no. 1.

Callies, Ch., *Europa als Wertegemeinschaft – Integration und Identität durch europäisches Verfassungsrecht?*, "JuristenZeitung" 2004, no. 21.

Nettesheim, M., *"Gegründet auf Werten...": Das Narrativ der Wertegemeischaft und der Sabktionsmechanismus des Art. 7 EUV*, [in:] C. Franzius, F.C. Mayer, J. Neyer (eds.), *Recht und Politik in der Europäischen Union*, Band 9: *Die Neuerfindung Europas*, Nomos, Baden-Baden, 2019.

Taylor, P., *The End of European Integration: Anti-Europeanism Examined*, Routledge, London, 2018.

Volkmann, U., *Vom Ursprung und Ziel der Europäischen Union: Die Perspektive der Rechtswissenschaft*, [in:] G. Kirchhof, H. Kube, R. Schmidt (eds.), *Von Urpsrung und Ziel der Europäischen Union: Elf Perspektiven*, Mohr Siebeck, Tübingen, 2016.

Joas, H., Mandry, Ch., *Europa als Werte- und Kulturgemeinschaft*, [in:] G.F. Schuppert, I. Pernice, U. Haltern (eds.), *Europawissenschaft*, Nomos, Baden-Baden, 2005.

Fraenkel-Haeberle, C., *Participatory Democracy and the Global Approach in Environmental Legislation*, [in:] E.J. Lohse, M. Poto (eds.), *Participatory Rights in the Environmental Decision-Making Process and the Implementation of the Aarhus Convention: a Comparative Perspective*, Duncker & Humblot, Berlin, 2015, Schriften zum Internationalen Recht (205).

Laskowski, S.R., *Demokratisierung des Umweltrechts*, "Zeitschrift für Umweltrecht" 2010, no. 4.

Krämer, L., *Direct Effect and Consistent Interpretation: Strengths and Weakness of the Concepts*, [in:] J.H. Jans, R. Macrory, A.-M. Moreno Molina (eds.), *National courts and EU Environmental Law*, Europa Law Publishing, Groningen, 2013.

Ruiz-Soler, J., *Gibt es eine europäische Öffentlichkeit? Forschungsstand, Befunde, Ausblicke*, "Aus Politik und Zeitgechichte" 2017, no. 37

Habermas, J., *Warum braucht Europa eine Verfassung?*, "Die Zeit" 2001, no. 27, www.zeit.de

Berman, T., *Public Participation as a Tool for Integrating Local Knowledge into Spatial Planning*, Springer, 2017.

Coenen, F.H.J.M., *Intruduction*, [in:] F.H.J.M. Coenen (ed.), *Public Participation and Better Environmental Decisions: The Promise and Limits of Participatory Processes for the Quality of Environmentally Related Decision-making*, Springer, Dordrecht, 2009, p. 8.

Ragulskytė-Markovienė, R., Žvaiždinienė, I., *Teisės į sveiką ir švarią aplinką teoriniai ir praktiniai aspektai* [en. *Theoretical and practical issues of the right to a healthy and clean environment*], [in:] V. Valančius *et. al.* (eds.) *Žmogus, teisinė valstybė ir administracinė justicija: mokslo studija, skirta Lietuvos vyriausiojo administracinio teismo dešimtmečiui* [en. *Human Rights, the Rule of Law and Administrative Justice: the study devoted for the 10th anniversary of the Supreme Administrative Court of Lithuania*], Supreme Administrative Court of Lithuania, 2012.

Marcinkevičiūtė, L., Petrauskienė, R., *Piliečių dalyvavimo viešojo administravimo institucijų valdyme galimybės: Vilniaus ir Jurbarko rajonų savivaldybių pavyzdys* [en. *Possibilities of citizens` participation in management of public administration institutions: cases of Vilnius and Jurbarkas district municipalities*], *Vadybos mokslas ir studijos – kaimo verslų ir jų infrastruktūros plėtrai* [en. *Management theory and studies for rural business and infrastructure development*]: mokslo darbai, 2008, vol. 14, no. 3.

Stasiukynas, A., *Visuomenės dalyvavimas Lietuvos elektros energetikos sektoriaus valdyme* [en. *Public participation in the governance of the Lithuanian electrical energy sector*], Viešoji politika ir administravimas, 2010, no. 32.

Petrauskienė, R., Predkelytė, E., *Gero valdymo principų įgyvendinimą viešosiose institucijose lemiantys veiksniai: teorinis pagrindimas, Visuomenės saugumas ir viešoji tvarka* [en. *Implementation of Good Governance Principles in Public Institutions: Theoretical Aspect, Public Security and Public Order*] 2014, no. 12.

Jarosław Sułkowski[2]

Participatory Budgeting as a Tool for Increasing Constitutional Awareness[1]

Abstract
Nowadays, in view of the crisis of democracy, the concept of deliberative (discursive) democracy, in which communication plays a fundamental role, is gaining a growing number of supporters. The process of deliberation occurring between citizens and the authorities requires that citizens be involved in public life, and this is what, in turn, fosters the development of democracy.

There are numerous mechanisms for participation in the management of public affairs, the classification of which depends on the degree of civic participation. One of these mechanisms is a participatory budget.

The growing interest in this type of budgeting is the result of numerous social and political processes. It should be viewed in a broader perspective – as an effect of globalization; and in a narrower perspective – as evidence of citizens' interest in local politics and as a result of widespread disaffection with national politics. However, the reception of a participatory budget should not be limited to getting certain groups of community members interested in proposing municipal projects worthy of funding. A participatory budget should not be a plebiscite but an instrument of democratic deliberation, and it only makes sense if the procedures are properly introduced, taking into account the basic conditions that ensure the proper functioning of a mechanism leading to real social change, rather than simply calling any procedure a participatory budget.

Keywords: participatory budgeting, local democracy, pure democracy, deliberation

---

1 This paper is a result of the research project no. 2017/27/L/HS5/03245, "Constitutional Consciousness as a Remedy for the Crisis of Discourse and Democracy Deficit in the European Union", financed by the National Science Center (dec. no. DEC-2017/27/L/HS5/03245).

2 Jarosław Sułkowski – doctor of law, assistant professor at the Department of Administrative Procedure at the Faculty of Law and Administration of the University of Lodz; graduate of Iberian studies; Legal Counsel. In 2008–2017, an employee of the Office of the Constitutional Tribunal; author of publications in the field of constitutional law and human rights.

1. As a political system, democracy clearly presupposes that citizens should be involved in the in the decision-making processes of the modern constitutional state – this amounts to a truism. Joint decision-making takes diverse forms and plays a role in many of the state's functioning procedures, whether electoral or legislative. The legal effects of collaborative civic decision-making also vary: a decision taken by members of a particular community often – though not always – binds the public authorities.

Participation in the democratic decision-making process should require some knowledge of the issue that the decision concerns. Of equal – or perhaps greater – importance is some awareness of the key role that public participation can play in the consolidation of democratic mechanisms. The direct involvement of citizens provides the greatest legitimacy to the decisions taken and, more importantly, should create a sense of community among the decision-makers, since they have shared responsibility for the decisions taken and can together hold the public authorities accountable for their actions. By definition, citizen participation strengthens the bonds between members and representatives of a local or state community. The creation of procedures that encourage public participation, and which facilitate involvement in the management of public affairs, is therefore crucial.

The importance of participatory mechanisms is growing in the face of the changes taking place in modern states, particularly the threat of abusive constitutionalism as described by David Landau,[3] which consists of a turn from liberal democracy to the democratic establishment of authoritarian governments. The effects of this abusiveness are extremely harmful but difficult to counteract. One possible response is to foster mature discourse on the topic of the political community, a pertinent example of which is the civic discourse associated with the concept of the nation as a civic community, a community of free and equal citizens, irrespective of individual characteristics.[4]

---

3 D. Landau, *Abusive Constitutionalism*, "UC Davis Law Review" 2013, no. 1, pp. 189–260.

4 G. Skąpska, *Znieważający konstytucjonalizm i konstytucjonalizm znieważony. Refleksja socjologiczna na temat kryzysu liberalno-demokratycznego konstytucjonalizmu w Europie postkomunistycznej*, "Filozofia Publiczna i Edukacja Demokratyczna" 2018, no. 1, p. 298.

2. Nowadays, in view of the aforementioned crisis of democracy, the concept of deliberative (discursive) democracy, in which communication plays a fundamental role, is gaining a growing number of supporters. Considered the founder of deliberative democracy, the German philosopher Jürgen Habermas draws attention to the key role of communication in the law-making process. In his view, in modern societies law is only able to perform the function of stabilising expectations pertaining to behaviour if it retains an intrinsic connection to the socially integrative power of communicative action.[5] The process of deliberation between citizens and the authorities requires that citizens be involved in public life, and this is what, in turn, fosters the development of democracy.

The theory of deliberative democracy draws on political ideals and the participatory politics of civic self-government.[6] According to deliberative democracy, the relationship between the rule of law and the sovereignty of the people should be based on discussion and negotiation that leads to compromise. This aligns with the concept of civil society, which also underlies the Constitution of the Republic of Poland. Furthermore, deliberative democracy can be realised if citizens are aware of the rights guaranteed to them at the constitutional and statutory level, as well as of the need for and legitimacy of political and socio-economic changes.

Deliberative politics, based on the mutual exchange of claims, can manifest itself in practice when civil society actors (individuals or groups) identify specific social problems, undertake to work on them, and then – once the issues have been properly publicised in the public sphere – become able to influence the political system. An important role in the identification of social problems is played by the level of awareness of civil society actors,

5 J. Habermas, *Faktyczność i obowiązywanie. Teoria dyskursu wobec zagadnień prawa i demokratycznego państwa prawnego*, (trans. A. Romaniuk, R. Marszałek), Wydawnictwo Naukowe Scholar, Warszawa 2005, especially p. 100.

6 P.W. Juchacz, *Deliberacja – demokracja – partycypacja. Szkice z teorii demokracji ateńskiej i współczesnej*, Poznań, 2006, p. 28.

and this is linked to the way they perceive contemporary social and political processes.[7]

3. Habermasian deliberation may prove useful in efforts to combat disregard for the constitution. This is because members of the community will be more inclined to defend a system whose functioning they consciously co-create. One form of "deliberating" public affairs is to involve citizens in the process of participatory public governance. This basically means that citizens are involved in activities that are ultimately aimed at a particular decision being taken (e.g. by the local authorities). One of the prerequisites for implementing such participation is the broad cooperation of local government representatives with the local community, including the use of specific tools that enable such cooperation and collaboration. It is therefore a question of cooperation between the public body and the local people, as well as the activation and involvement of citizens in the procedures for making decisions about public goods and services.[8] In other words, such governance depends on the interaction that the public administration (irrespective of its organisational level) has with the public through the use of specific participatory and consultative procedures.[9]

Deliberative democracy is based on the collective action of community members and leads to specific decisions. However, it would be simplistic to suggest that it is exclusively based on forms of direct democracy, since the participation of community members is combined with elements of representative democracy. There are numerous mechanisms for participation in the management of public affairs, the classification of which depends on the degree of civic participation.

The first mode of participation involves very little citizen participation, since its boils down to an exchange of information between the local

---

7 A. Chmielarz-Grochal, *Obywatelska inicjatywa ustawodawcza jako instytucja demokracji deliberatywnej i wyraz świadomości konstytucyjnej obywateli*, "Roczniki Administracji i Prawa" 2019, vol. XIX (special edition), p. 35.

8 A. Ziętek, *Publiczne zarządzanie partycypacyjne. O narzędziach włączania obywateli w procesy decyzyjne*, "Studia Politologiczne" 2022, vol. 64, p. 44.

9 K. Peter-Bombik, A. Szczudlińska-Kanoś, *Zarządzanie partycypacyjne we wspólnotach lokalnych*, "Prace Naukowe Uniwersytetu Ekonomicznego we Wrocławiu" 2015, no. 391, p. 86.

authority and community members. The information is transmitted to citizens, who are the addressees. Here, the role of citizens can be passive – when the addressees merely become acquainted with the data (e.g. from published resources, notice boards, public information bulletins), or active – when citizens take action to obtain the information previously made available by the local authority. However, the flow can also go the other way, as when community members provide the local authority with specific information (applications, complaints, petitions). In the latter case, the level of activity is higher and is related to the citizens' willingness to provide specific information.

The second participation mode goes beyond the informational (opinion-forming) dimension highlighted thus far. It includes consultations (also opinion-forming), which differ from systematic and repetitive information distribution by tending to focus on local rather than individual issues, and to include an element of decision-making, such as when decision-makers respond to the expectations, requests or demands raised in the course of consultations.

The third type of participation in local affairs is policy definition and decision-making. These presuppose interaction between the local authorities and community members at both stages (defining and deciding). The basis for consensus emerges from the collective bodies made up of actors defining community goals (town/ local council meetings) and the actors implementing these goals (the local authority).

The fourth mode of participatory action is joint implementation. An important feature that distinguishes this mode from the previous type is corporate assistance (the human substrate) and funding (private assets) in the planning and implementation of investments. The spectrum of entities involved in the implemented activities is broad, including the third sector, NGOs and private business.

4. The growing interest in participatory budgeting is the result of numerous social and political processes. It should be viewed in a broader perspective – as an effect of globalization; and in a narrower perspective – as evidence of citizens' interest in local politics and as a result of widespread disaffection with national politics.

The origins of participatory budgeting are political and systemic, and are linked to the crisis in forms of representative democracy. In the world's first civic budget in Porto Alegre, the involvement of citizens in deciding urban policy was the result of the Labour Party winning the local elections – this electoral victory being the indirect result of years of dictatorship. The Labour Party promised that, once it came to power in the city, it would allow something that had previously been suppressed, namely that members of the local community would be able to participate in decision-making on local issues, including the municipal budget. The popularity of participatory budgeting, however, need not be associated with evident dysfunction in the state and public authority. It is enough, as the Polish experience shows, to have a dominant parliament with representatives who misunderstand their role and the for the local space to be appropriated by centrally led political parties. Political parties – as permanent organisations that bring together citizens and have a programme capable of making decisions with the aim of solving social problems – should not be limited to formulating programmes, as it is also necessary to put them into practice. As actors in free political competition, parties have a duty to present alternative solutions and strategies, and to act as centres for public debate and discussion – think-tanks of sorts – on political, social and economic reforms. Unfortunately, this expectation is not fulfilled, which reinforces citizens' sense that both of the political class and typical forms of representative democracy are woefully inadequate.

The ephemeral nature of politics as well as the dominance of short-term and even one-off goals in politics also contribute to the growth of interest in participatory budgeting. The handling of public affairs is sequential and single-minded, involving little contibution from those who are not politicians. Meanwhile, stimulating, managing or reforming public affairs should be a continuous, multi-threaded and multi-track process, requiring the involvement of a wide range of actors. The participation of politicians, community members and the so-called third sector is essential.

The participatory budget is also an indirect effect of the development of technology, the Internet, new methods for deciding on public matters such as e-voting, the phenomena of NIMBY (Not In My Back Yard), YIMBY (Yes, In My Back Yard), BANANA (build absolutely nothing anywhere near anything), the increasingly popular – including in Poland – "re-call procedure", and the new regulation of the right to petition. The use of mechanisms by which citizens can make their voice heard in public matters is thus becoming increasingly common.

The ongoing globalization of politics and law is important for the genesis of participatory budgeting. Globalization, although not a new phenomenon, is still not clearly defined. This is not surprising, as it is complex and not amenable to a single logic, a process of "intensification of global social reactions that bind together distant places in such a way that local events are shaped by events occurring in other places many miles away and vice versa."[10]

The lack of definitions is made up for by attempts to describe the phenomenon. Given the limited framework of this study, it is impossible to mention all the features of globalization, nevertheless three key points should be noted.

Firstly, globalization is closely linked to the information revolution, the development of information technology, and the changes in information processing, transmission and management that it brings about.[11] Participatory budgeting is based on modern forms of information processing.

Secondly, globalization is first and foremost a financial phenomenon, since it binds together the numerous banking, insurance and other financial institutions of individual countries (including the World Bank and the International Monetary Fund, which are dependent on the United States).[12] Globalization also has a strong economic dimension, based on the emergence of a global market for capital, goods and services. Globalization is also, of course, a political and military phenomenon. Furthermore, it has a cultural dimension, as along with the global flow of goods, services and information, the patterns (values) developed in one civilizational circle are spreading and displacing local elements.[13]

---

10 A. Giddens, *Runaway World. How Globalisation is Reshaping Our Lives*, Routledge, New York, 2000, cited for: R. Zenderowski, *Czy globalizacja unieważni nacjonalizmy i tożsamości narodowe?*, "Studia Bobolanum" 2011, no. 1, p. 140.

11 R. Piotrowski, *Globalizacja i konstytucja*, "Zagadnienia Sądownictwa Konstytucyjnego" 2012, no. 2.

12 W. Szostak, *Globalizacja a suwerenność państwa współczesnego*, [in:] Kornaś J. (ed.), *Nowoczesny Lewiatan. Studia nad współczesnym państwem*, Wydawnictwo WSEiA, Kielce, 2006, pp. 13–14.

13 *Ibidem*, p. 14.

Finally, it is important to note that globalization is a dynamic phenomenon with far-reaching consequences, but one that is not new in the history of statehood. We are currently witnessing the third wave of globalization. Observing the effects of its two earlier phases – the great geographical discoveries and the industrial revolution – it must be assumed that the effects of 21st century globalization will be wide-ranging.

5. A characteristic feature of the definition of participatory budgeting (PB) is that there are numerous problems in its formulation. The development of a definition is fundamentally difficult, especially given the differences in how participatory budgeting operates in different countries. In its most general formulation, however, participatory budgeting entails that non-representatives (non-elected actors) are involved in the allocation of budgetary resources. Three elements should be distinguished – the *differentia specifica* of such a budget. Firstly, it must be an institution belonging to deliberative democracy. In the most general terms, the budget in question must be seen as a public communication process oriented towards the search for appropriate arguments in favour of certain evaluations of and solutions to the projects under discussion. It is thus about a return to debate and dialogue as a central element of democracy, since deliberation is a discussion that seeks consensus.[14] Secondly, the budget must be an institution that legitimises local political objectives and, by extension, local power itself. This legitimisation is multidimensional: on the one hand the budget clarifies the budgetary realities, while on the other it gives voice to the needs of the inhabitants, and through the choice of objectives it strengthens their identification with the local community and develops attitudes of civil society. The third differentiating element is that society can exercise oversight, since participatory budgeting increases transparency in the financing and functioning of the administration. This objective is served by reiterative design – by linking the record of the past and the future, as the budget provides a picture of what the funds have been allocated for, and what purposes were not covered, and also introduces

14 B. Jabłońska, *W stronę demokracji deliberacyjnej? O politycznym komunikowaniu na tematy europejskie w polskiej prasie*, "Przegląd Socjologiczny" 2008, vol. 57, no. 2, p. 123.

an element of verifying the desirability and effectiveness of the funding of specific investments.

In the literature on social participation, one of the most widely described classifications of citizen budgeting models is the division proposed by Sintomer, Herzberg and Röcke.[15] They distinguished between six participatory budgeting models: the Porto Alegre model in the European version (Spain, Italy), the proximity participation model, the consultation model, the local community participation model, and the multi-stakeholder participation model.

The first model, with strong references to Porto Alegre (PA), is based on the involvement of individual community members elected by the community at open meetings. They also elect councils that set spending targets for the coming year. This is followed by meetings at higher levels (district, city) involving local politicians, representatives of associations, and organisations. There is a two-stage approach in this model. First, proposals for specific projects are put forward at the lower level and voted on by an assembly of community members. Then, local government representatives evaluate the projects, and the final version goes to the city council, which incorporates the list into the city budget. Once the budget has been passed, a body (made up of representatives from both levels) is set up to monitor how the proposed investments are implemented. In this model, there is a far-reaching formalism, with the councillors being obliged to take the residents' proposals into account.

The proximity participation model is purely consultative. It is based on "selective listening", which involves councillors incorporating only those projects previously submitted by community members that meet their defined objectives and interests. Consultation with community members takes place through the media, various forums and the Internet. At the local level, strategic goals are set, and decisions are made by consensus. The consultation is carried out by the local government, the councillors

15 Y. Sintomer, C. Herzberg, A. Röcke, *Participatory Budgeting in Europe: Potentials and Challenges*, "International Journal of Urban and Regional Research" 2008, March, vol. 321, p. 169.

are a party to it, and therefore the implementation of the findings made at the consultation stage can be expected.

The next type of participatory budget is also purely consultative (C). The subject of discussion is financial policy and its transparency. The local authority presents information on these aspects and the policies are then evaluated at meetings with community members selected at random. The meetings are open to other members of the community. The evaluation of the financial policy is either focused on specific tasks (a swimming pool, library, etc.) or from the point of view of balancing the budget. During the meeting, participants can ask questions and make their own proposals.

In the two other models, the local community participation (CP) model and the multi-stakeholder participation (MSP) model, funding for specific goals only partly comes from local budgets, as the goals are co-financed by NGOs or private actors, or even through national programmes. The budgets are thus focused on funds for investment, or on cultural, environmental or social purposes. Budgeting decisions are made by a committee consisting of representatives of the local government and co-financiers. The difference between these models lies in private sector co-financing, which is absent in the local community participation model, while in the multi-stakeholder participation model private sponsors have a say in the allocation of funds (although the bulk of the funds must come from the local budget). On the other hand, when it comes to the extent to which local governments are bound by the opinions of community members, in most countries opinions on the draft budget are not binding, thus local governments are free to accept or reject the proposals of community members, while in some countries justification is required for not taking into account the proposals of community members.[16]

6. Participatory budgeting has many advantages. It directly improves residents' quality of life, promotes the equitable distribution of resources, improves satisfaction with public services, increases responsibility for the common good, encourages involvement in public affairs, and even includes people who are typically excluded from public life. In addition, it improves the image of the city and its inhabitants, increases citizens' identification

16 *Ibidem.*

with the city, unites residents around public issues, improves the management of public funds, promotes sustainable neighbourhood development, is a practical form of civic education, and can contribute to the transparency and credibility of local government. Participatory budgeting can also help develop civil society by solving local development problems.[17] However, in order for community awareness to be enhanced, the budget must be a social process, embedded in the local community. It is necessary to mobilise a wide range of actors in this process, and this requires good management of local human resources.[18] Budget developers and the local authority should define the public institutions and their representatives, NGOs, "urban movements" and informal social groups that could be potential participants in budget preparation.[19] Locating the budget in the local community requires extensive civic education, so as to highlight the benefits not of participatory budgeting per se (although these are indisputable), but of cooperation between members of the local community and the authorities. Without the creation of a real social base and genuine public interest, a bottom-up and sustainable participatory budgeting process simply will not emerge.[20]

An equally important reason for a participatory budget is to raise the substantive level of the participatory budgeting process. To this end, it seems necessary to develop a precise methodology for drawing up a participatory budget, to determine the circle of addressees, to consider the impact of the territorial division of the city and the degree of infrastructural

---

17 M. Burchard-Dziubińska, *Budżet obywatelski jako partycypacyjna forma współrządzenia*, "Studia i Prace Wydziału Nauk Ekonomicznych i Zarządzania" 2014, vol. 2, no. 37, p. 199.

18 B. Wampler, *A guide do Participatory budgeting*, October 2000, p. 7, https://www.commdev.org/userfiles/files/1613_file_GPB.pdf

19 The process of socialization is not easy, as has been shown by the example of Porto Alegre – in 1990, only 976 people took part in public assemblies (5% of the city's budget was decided), in 2004, there were 50,000 participants (including unofficial assemblies – 600,000 – activity Neighborhood Groups, Porto Alegre's Union of Neighborhood Associations and Organizations).

20 Report: *Direct and Participatory Democracy at Grassroots Level: Levers for forging EU citizenship and identity?*, p. 93, http://cor.europa.eu/en/documentation/studies/Documents/direct-participatory-democracy.pdf

development on local needs, and to foster organizational and methodological strengthening and coordination of the process of meetings between community members and local authorities, etc. It seems advisable to establish a team to coordinate the creation and implementation of the participatory budget and to include in its tasks the oversight of the budget – with reference to the effects of previous budgets, voices of dissatisfaction, and possible modifications to the procedure in the next project year. Support from legal experts is also necessary, as citizens are generally not familiar with the legal conditions associated with the processes and investments.

The local authority should also consider the purpose of the participatory budget, as its specific form is always conditioned by the social, political and economic situation of the local community. Anna Rytel-Warzocha is right to draw attention to the various functions that this form of citizen participation in governance fulfils. For example, the German experience shows that it is a way to modernise and improve decision-making processes, in Africa these mechanisms are seen primarily as an element of good administration, while in Spain and the United Kingdom participatory budgeting is recognized as a tool for realising the principle of social justice.[21] Each of these functions pursues different objectives. Thus, it is important whether the local community aims to obtain more amenities in the city thanks to the budget, or to try to eliminate infrastructural differences in specific parts of the local area, or whether the objective of the budget is to level the playing field or improve the quality of life.

The role of the municipality can hardly be overestimated when it comes to helping to identify individual projects for funding. The Polish experience shows that it can make sense to formulate the projects to be funded in advance,[22] and that the choice of local community members should be limited.

---

21 A. Rytel-Warzocha, *Partycypacja społeczne w sprawach budżetowych. Model Porto Alegre jako pierwowzór rozwiązań europejskich*, "Przegląd Prawa Konstytucyjnego" 2007, no. 1, p. 96.

22 One of the investments selected for implementation under the Łódź civic budget was training for officials of the Road and Transport Authority in the field of tree protection and planting methods in the metropolitan area. 245 votes were cast for this project. This idea sparked criticism – see *Szkolenia dla urzędników*

7. The legal regulation of participatory budgeting is sparse. Pursuant to Article 5a(3) of the Polish Law on Municipal Self-Government, the civic budget is classed as a special form of social consultation.[23] The legislator uses the concept of "civic budget." Although in sematic terms civic budgeting is a narrower concept than participatory budgeting, as it implies that only citizens can participate, the Polish Constitution provides that all residents can participate, regardless of their citizenship. Given that the civic budget was first used in Porto Alegre,[24] the most accurate term for this institution taken from Portuguese is "participatory budgeting."

ZDiT, czyli… kpina z budżetu obywatelskiego "Express Ilustrowany" 2015, 18 October.

23 Ustawa z dnia 8 marca 1990 r. o samorządzie gminnym [Act of 8 March 1990 on Municipal Self-Government] (Journal of Laws 2022, item 559).

24 The issue of participatory budgeting has become the subject of extensive discussion – see, *inter alia*, L. Avritzer, *Sociedad civil, espacio publico y poder local:un analisis del presupuesto particpativo*, [in:] E. Dagnino (ed.), *Sociedad civil, esfera publica y democratizacion en America Latina*, Fondo de Cultura Econimica, Mexico, 2002; L. Avritzer, *Democracy and the public space in Latin America*, Princeton University Press, Princeton, 2002; L. Avritzer, *Models of democratic deliberation: participatory budgeting in Brazil*, [in:] B. de Sousa Santos (ed.), *Democratizing democracy: beyond the liberal democratic canon*, Verso, New York, 2006; L. Avritzer, *Participatory Institutions in Democratic Brazil*, Johns Hopkins University Press, Baltimore, 2009; G. Baiocchi, *Militants and citizens: the politics of participation in Porto Alegre*, University Press, Stanford, 2005; B. Wampler, *Orçamento Participativo: uma explicação para as amplas variaçoes nos resultados. In A inovação democratica no brasil. Edited by Leonardo Avritzer and Zander Navarro* (in English: *Participatory Budgeting: An explanation of the broad variations in outcomes*), Cortez, São Paulo, 2003; B. Wampler, L. Avritzer, *The Spread of Participatory Budgeting in Brazil: From Radical Democracy to Participatory Good Government*, "Journal Of Latin American Urban Studies" 2005, New York, vol. 7, pp. 37–52; B. Wampler, *Participatory Budgeting in Brazil: contestation, cooperation, and accountability*, Pennsylvania State University Press, Pennsylvania, 2008; E. Aaragones, S. Sanches-Pages, *A theory of participatory democracy based on the real case of Porto Alegre*, "European Economic Review" 2008, vol. 53, no. 1; A. Marquetti, C.E. Schonerwald da Silva, A. Campbell, *Participatory Economic Democracy in Action: Participatory Budgeting in Porto Alegre, 1989–2004,*Originally prepared for and presented at the Eastern Economic Association meetings February 27–March 1, 2009, http://content.csbs.utah.edu/~al/articles/Sub_PB1.pdf

However, the term "civic budget" dominates in Poland – probably due to the "linguistically rather complicated but also politically less attractive character" of the former.[25]

Being slightly more extensive than the original regulations, the regulations devoted to the civic budget were introduced into the Law on Municipal Self-Government by virtue of the Act of 11 January 2018 on amending certain acts to increase the participation of citizens in the process of electing, functioning and controlling certain public authorities.[26] By virtue of this amendment, the institution of the civic budget was also introduced into the Law on County Self-government and the Law on Local Self-government (see Article 2(1)(b) and Article 3(1)(b) of the amending act).

Under Article 5a(3) of the Law on Municipal Self-Government, the legislator classes the civic budget as a special form of social consultation. Monika Augustyniak and Roman Marchaj are right in stating that, from the point of view of the provisions of the Law on Municipal Self-Government, this formulation may be surprising, since, in legal terms, numerous differences can be discerned between the two legal institutions at the very basic level of their functioning. First and foremost, public consultations are of an advisory nature, while – as results from Article 5a(4) of the Municipal Self-Government Act – the civic budget serves the purpose of enabling residents to make decisions on the spending of public funds, and thus has a decisive character.[27] The civic budget as described in the Law on Municipal Self-Government is a form of direct democracy of a decisive nature. Justification for this thesis is found directly in the content of Article 5a(4) of the Law on Municipal Self-Government, which by force of law requires that the tasks selected as part of the civic budget be included in the budget resolution. In addition, the aforementioned provision prohibits the municipal council, in the course of work on the draft budget

25 U.K. Zawadzka-Pąk, *Ochrona dobra wspólnego poprzez budżet partycypacyjny (obywatelski). Studium aksjologiczno-prawne*, Temida 2, Białystok, 2019, p. 12.

26 "Journal of Laws", item 130.

27 M. Augustyniak, R. Marchaj, *Komentarz do art. 5a*, [in:] G. Dolnicki (ed.), *Ustawa o samorządzie gminnym. Komentarz*, Wolters Kluwer, Warszawa, 2021, p. 97.

resolution, from removing or significantly changing the tasks selected by residents.

The subjective scope of the consultation covers only the inhabitants of the municipality, i.e. persons permanently residing in the area in question. As pointed out by the Voivodeship administrative court in Opole: “Since, in principle, the place of residence depends on the intention, i.e. on the will of a particular person, and the nature of the residence is also determined by the factual circumstances indicating the actual intention, therefore persons who meet the above-mentioned prerequisites are residents of the municipality, no other criteria should determine the recognition of a person as a resident of the municipality.”[28] Similarly, the Voivodeship Administrative Court in Rzeszów, in its judgment of 5 February 2019, indicated that when interpreting Article 5a of the Law on Municipal Self-Government, “it must be borne in mind that the institution of the civic budget was introduced into the Law on Municipal Self-Government in order to increase the participation of citizens in the process of electing, functioning and controlling certain public bodies. The civic budget serves the purpose of involving citizens in the process of deciding which public tasks in a specific financial year should be implemented and, consequently, financed from public funds. The decision-makers in this respect therefore cannot include persons who are not residents of the municipality.”[29]

As part of the civic budget, the inhabitants decide annually, by direct voting, on a part of the expenditures of the municipal budget (art. 5a sec. 4, first sentence of the Law on Municipal Self-Government). By law, the tasks selected as part of the civic budget are included in the municipal budget resolution. In the course of work on the draft budget resolution, the municipal council may not remove or substantially change the tasks selected as part of the civic budget (Article 5a, paragraph 4, second and third sentences of the Law on Municipal Self-Government). It should be emphasised that the civic budget may be applied at the level of the entire municipality or to only its part. Pursuant to Article 5a(6) of the Law on

28 The judgment of the Voivodeship administrative court in Opole of 13 June 2006 issued in case no. II SA/Op 213/06, available in CBOSA.

29 The judgment of the Voivodeship administrative court in Rzeszów of 5 February 2019, issued in the case ref. II SA/Rz 1185/18, available in CBOSA.

Municipal Self-Government, funds spent under the civic budget may be divided into pools covering the entire municipality and its parts in the form of auxiliary units or groups of auxiliary units.

However, it should be emphasised that pursuant to Article 5a(5) of Law on Municipal Self-Government, in municipalities which are cities with poviat (county) rights, the establishment of a civic budget is obligatory, with the proviso that the amount of the civic budget is at least 0.5% of the municipality expenditures included in the last submitted budget execution report. It follows from this regulation that in other municipalities the civic budget is optional, and that no minimum level of funds has been defined for them that has to be allocated.[30]

The provision of Article 5a(7) of the Law on Municipal Self-Government constitutes a general competence norm for the municipal council to adopt resolutions on matters defining the principles and procedure for implementing the civic budget. Pursuant to this provision, the municipal council determines, by way of a resolution, the requirements to be met by a civic budget project, in particular: (1) the formal requirements to be met by the submitted projects; (2) the required number of signatures of residents supporting the project, which may not be greater than 0.1% of the residents of the area covered by the civic budget pool in which the project is submitted; (3) the principles for evaluating the submitted projects in terms of their compliance with the law, technical feasibility, compliance with formal requirements, and the procedure for appealing against a decision not to admit a project to voting; and (4) the principles for conducting the voting, determining the results and making them public, taking into account that the principles for conducting the voting must ensure the equality and directness of voting. Any resolution specifying the rules and procedure for its conduct should be classed as an act of local law.

On the basis of the above regulation, following Monika Korolewska and Kamila Marchewka-Bartkowiak, four stages of the civic budget process can be distinguished. The first stage begins on the part of local government units. It involves carrying out the formal procedure of accepting

30 A. Misiejko, *Budżet obywatelski w praktyce samorządów*, Wolters Kluwer, Warszawa, 2020, p. 26.

the amounts and principles of the civic budget (e.g. mayor's ordinance, city council resolution), as well as appointing employees of organisational units or special commissions for formal and content-related evaluation in the office. Some local governments also create special teams for the initial selection of projects, composed of representatives of the local government and residents. During the second stage of the procedure, applications, proposals, and projects for proposed civic investments are submitted. These proposals are reviewed by local government employees and/or by an evaluation team, which selects the best ones, indicating their value or assigning them a predetermined rank. The third stage involves voting on the proposals included in the announced list of proposed investments. Voting is usually conducted electronically (e.g. via the budget website), although it is also possible to cast votes at specially created points or locations (e.g. in libraries). The fourth stage of the civic budget procedure is the announcement of the projects selected for implementation. This stage involves including the winning tasks submitted in the civic budget in the general budget of the local authority, as well as – if necessary – in long-term investment plans.[31]

8. The practice of civic budgets is not free from controversy. Some of them were highlighted by the Supreme Audit Office (SOA) in the summary report of the functioning of the civic budget institution in Poland.[32] Following the audit, the SOA proposed a legislative initiative to amend Art. 5a of the Law on Municipal Self-Government, consisting in: (1) clarifying who can take part in consultations regarding the civic budget, on the one hand to ensure the statutory equality of voting in all municipalities for civic projects and, on the other hand, to define the right to participate in these votes for persons who are fully aware of their choices, or possibly including in the law a mandate for the municipal council to determine in a resolution which residents can participate in the consultations. The above

31 M. Korolewska, K. Marchewka-Bartkowiak, *Budżet obywatelski jako przejaw aktywności społecznej – analiza doświadczeń na przykładzie jednostek samorządu terytorialnego*, „Studia BAS" 2015, no. 4, pp. 130–134.

32 Information on the results of the inspection: "Funkcjonowanie budżetów partycypacyjnych (obywatelskich)", No. 20/2019/P/18/064/LGD https://www.nik.gov.pl/plik/id,21187,vp,23819.pdf, p. 11.

should be done with a guarantee of the right to create civic budgets for a specific part (group) of residents, e.g. youth civic budgets; (2) removal of the restriction related to the possibility of dividing funds spent under the civic budget only into pools covering the entire municipality and its parts in the form of auxiliary units or groups of auxiliary units; and (3) consideration of abandoning the required number of signatures of residents supporting the project (not more than 0.1% of the residents of the area covered by the civic budget pool in which the project is submitted), as specified in Article 5a(7)(2) of the aforementioned law. The Supreme Audit Office pointed out that in the practice of the local self-government units until 2018, in some cities no support of the applications was required from the applicants. The introduction of the requirement to collect signatures of people supporting the project limited the number of applications submitted. This is because some residents with interesting and socially relevant ideas do not want to get involved in drawing up lists of support for their proposals. It should also be borne in mind that the full verification of the quality and value of a project for the local community takes place at the stage of voting on the projects, not at the time of their creation.[33]

However, it is crucial to emphasise that the consultative nature of the budget is insufficient to guarantee real public participation. Without the introduction of a decision-making mechanism, the functions of the budget will be distorted. A participatory budget should be based on the joint decision of community members, on participation in all stages of the budget preparation, on debating the hierarchy of objectives and the substantive importance of the project for different spheres of social life, and on considering the possibilities for its introduction and the consequences that result from its implementation. The budget preparation process is long and arduous, involving real and substantive participation in the governance of the city. This leads to a fetishization of the vote, perhaps to an improvement in ratings, but at the same time to the preparation of the budget "by shortcuts" in a non-deliberate and time-consuming way.[34]

---

33 *Ibidem.*

34 For a critical appraisal of the functioning of participatory budgets in Poland, see B. Martela, *Budżet partycypacyjny w Polsce – wdrożenie i perspektywy*, http://cejsh.icm.edu.pl/cejsh/element/bwmeta1.element.desklight-80e82

The reception of a participatory budget should not be limited to getting certain groups of community members interested in proposing municipal projects worthy of funding. A participatory budget should not be a plebiscite but an instrument of democratic deliberation, and it only makes sense if the procedures are properly introduced, taking into account the basic conditions that ensure the proper functioning of a mechanism leading to real social change, rather than simply calling any procedure a participatory budget. As Markus Miessen has rightly pointed out, the participatory budget may do the opposite of empowering citizens and local communities, serving instead to legitimise the actions of government. This can happen when it is implemented in a way that gives citizens the illusion of a sense of agency over, for example, one per cent of the funds held by a given authority, while at the same time dissuading people from considering the spending of the other 99 per cent of the budget. This effectively eliminates conflicts and potential protests. The civic budget then becomes an additional plebiscite, instead of a real discussion on the shape of the development of the locality.[35]

d42-f701-4c5e-8baa-21e885295160/c/budzet-partycypacyjny-w-polsce-wdroze nie-i-perspektywy.pdf

35 Cited after J. Piekutowski, *Partycypacyjność czy anarchizacja? O „koszmarze partycypacji" słów kilka*, "Kierunki Zmian" 2015, no. 1(5), p. 33

Bibliography

Aaragones, E., Sanches-Pages, S., *A Theory of Participatory Democracy Based on the Real Case of Porto Alegre*, "European Economic Review" 2008, vol. 53, no. 1.

Augustyniak, M., Marchaj, R., *Komentarz do art. 5a*, [in:] G. Dolnicki (ed.), *Ustawa o samorządzie gminnym. Komentarz*, Wolters Kluwer, Warszawa, 2021.

Avritzer, L., *Democracy and the Public Space in Latin America*, Princeton University Press, Princeton, 2002.

Avritzer, L., *Models of Democratic Deliberation: Participatory Budgeting in Brazil*, [in:] B. de Sousa Santos (ed.), *Democratizing Democracy: Beyond the Liberal Democratic Canon*, Verso, New York, 2006.

Avritzer, L., *Participatory Institutions in Democratic Brazil*, Johns Hopkins University Press, Baltimore, 2009.

Avritzer, L., *Sociedad civil, espacio publico y poder local:un analisis del presupuesto particpativo*, [in:] E. Dagnino (ed.), *Sociedad civil, esfera publica y democratizacion en America Latina*, Fondo de Cultura Econimica, Mexico, 2002.

Baiocchi, G., *Militants and Citizens: The Politics of Participation in Porto Alegre*, University Press, Stanford, 2005.

Burchard-Dziubińska, M., *Budżet obywatelski jako partycypacyjna forma współrządzenia*, "Studia i Prace Wydziału Nauk Ekonomicznych i Zarządzania" 2014, vol. 2, no. 37.

Chmielarz-Grochal, A., *Obywatelska inicjatywa ustawodawcza jako instytucja demokracji deliberatywnej i wyraz świadomości konstytucyjnej obywateli*, "Roczniki Administracji i Prawa" 2019, vol. XIX (special edition).

Direct and Participatory Democracy at Grassroots Level: Levers for forging EU citizenship and identity?, http://cor.europa.eu/en/documentation/studies/Documents/direct-participatory-democracy.pdf

"Funkcjonowanie budżetów partycypacyjnych (obywatelskich)", No. 20/2019/P/18/064/LGD, https://www.nik.gov.pl/plik/id,21187,vp,23819.pdf

Giddens, A., *Runaway World. How Globalisation is Reshaping Our Lives*, Routledge, New York, 2000.

Habermas, J., *Faktyczność i obowiązywanie. Teoria dyskursu wobec zagadnień prawa i demokratycznego państwa prawnego* (trans. A. Romaniuk, R. Marszałek), Wydawnictwo Naukowe Scholar, Warszawa, 2005.

Jabłońska, B., *W stronę demokracji deliberacyjnej? O politycznym komunikowaniu na tematy europejskie w polskiej prasie*, "Przegląd Socjologiczny" 2008, vol. 57, no. 2.

Juchacz, P.W., *Deliberacja – demokracja – partycypacja. Szkice z teorii demokracji ateńskiej i współczesnej*, Poznań, 2006.

Korolewska, M., Marchewka-Bartkowiak, K., *Budżet obywatelski jako przejaw aktywności społecznej – analiza doświadczeń na przykładzie jednostek samorządu terytorialnego*, "Studia BAS" 2015, no. 4.

Landau, D., *Abusive Constitutionalism*, "UC Davis Law Review" 2013, no. 1.

Marquetti, A., Schonerwald da Silva, C.E., Campbell, A., *Participatory Economic Democracy in Action: Participatory Budgeting in Porto Alegre, 1989–2004, Originally Prepared for and Presented at the Eastern Economic Association meetings February 27 – March 1, 2009*, http://content.csbs.utah.edu/~al/articles/Sub_PB1.pdf

Martela, B., *Budżet partycypacyjny w Polsce – wdrożenie i perspektywy*, http://cejsh.icm.edu.pl/cejsh/element/bwmeta1.element.desklight-80e82d42-f701-4c5e-8baa-21e885295160/c/budzet-partycypacyjny-w-polsce-wdrozenie-i-perspektywy.pdf

Misiejko, A., *Budżet obywatelski w praktyce samorządów*, Wolters Kluwer, Warszawa, 2020.

Peter-Bombik, K., Szczudlińska-Kanoś, A., *Zarządzanie partycypacyjne we wspólnotach lokalnych*, "Prace Naukowe Uniwersytetu Ekonomicznego we Wrocławiu" 2015, no. 391.

Piekutowski, J., *Partycypacyjność czy anarchizacja? O „koszmarze partycypacji" słów kilka*, "Kierunki Zmian" 2015, no. 1(5).

Piotrowski, R., *Globalizacja i konstytucja*, "Zagadnienia Sądownictwa Konstytucyjnego" 2012, no. 2.

Rytel-Warzocha, A., *Partycypacja społeczne w sprawach budżetowych. Model Porto Alegre jako pierwowzór rozwiązań europejskich*, "Przegląd Prawa Konstytucyjnego" 2007, no. 1.

Sintomer, Y., Herzberg C., Röcke A., *Participatory Budgeting in Europe: Potentials and Challenges*, "International Journal of Urban and Regional Research" 2008, March, vol. 321.

Skąpska, G., *Znieważający konstytucjonalizm i konstytucjonalizm znieważony. Refleksja socjologiczna na temat kryzysu liberalno-demokratycznego konstytucjonalizmu w Europie postkomunistycznej*, "Filozofia Publiczna i Edukacja Demokratyczna" 2018, no. 1.

Szkolenia dla urzędników ZDiT, czyli... kpina z budżetu obywatelskiego, "Express Ilustrowany" 2015, 18 October.

Szostak, W., *Globalizacja a suwerenność państwa współczesnego*, [in:] J. Kornaś (ed.), *Nowoczesny Lewiatan. Studia nad współczesnym państwem*, Wydawnictwo WSEiA, Kielce, 2006.

Wampler, B., *A Guide do Participatory Budgeting*, October 2000, https://www.commdev.org/userfiles/files/1613_file_GPB.pdf

Wampler, B., *Orçamento Participativo: uma explicação para as amplas variaçoes nos resultados. In A inovação democratica no brasil. Edited by Leonardo Avritzer and Zander Navarro* [in English: *Participatory Budgeting: An Eexplanation of the Broad Variations in Outcomes*], Cortez, São Paulo, 2003.

Wampler, B., *Participatory Budgeting in Brazil: Contestation, Cooperation, and Accountability*, Pennsylvania State University Press, Pennsylvania, 2008.

Wampler, B., Avritzer L., *The Spread of Participatory Budgeting in Brazil: From Radical Democracy to Participatory Good Government*, "Journal of Latin American Urban Studies" 2005, New York, vol. 7.

Zawadzka-Pąk, U.K., *Ochrona dobra wspólnego poprzez budżet partycypacyjny (obywatelski). Studium aksjologiczno-prawne*, Temida 2, Białystok, 2019.

Zenderowski, R., *Czy globalizacja unieważni nacjonalizmy i tożsamości narodowe?*, "Studia Bobolanum" 2011, no. 1.

Ziętek, A., *Publiczne zarządzanie partycypacyjne. O narzędziach włączania obywateli w procesy decyzyjne*, " Studia Politologiczne" 2022, vol. 64.

DIA-LOGOS
Schriften zu Philosophie und Sozialwissenschaften
Studies in Philosophy and Social Sciences

Herausgegeben von
Edited by
Piotr W. Juchacz

"*Dia-Logos. Studies in Philosophy and Social Sciences* is a peer-reviewed book series publishing valuable monographs and edited volumes on various aspects of philosophy and social sciences. The series is intended to be an interdisciplinary forum of deliberation according to our firm belief that challenges of the contemporary world require common and multilevel research. The *Dia-Logos* series does not represent a single ideology or school of thought, but it is open to different trends and various styles of reflection, trying to understand better the contemporary world. We invite the submission of manuscripts of monographs and edited volumes from academic philosophers and social scientists."

Bd. / Vol. 1 Piotr W. Juchacz / Roman Kozłowski (Hrsg.): Freiheit und Verantwortung. Moral, Recht und Politik. 2002.

Bd. / Vol. 2 Norbert Leśniewski / Ewa Nowak-Juchacz (Hrsg.): Die Zeit Heideggers. 2002.

Bd. / Vol. 3 Marek Kwiek (ed.): The University, Globalization, Central Europe. 2003.

Bd. / Vol. 4 Ewa Czerwińska-Schupp (Hrsg.): Philosophie an der Schwelle des 21. Jahrhunderts. Geschichte der Philosophie, Philosophische Anthropologie, Ethik, Wissenschaftstheorie, Politische Philosophie. 2003.

Bd. / Vol. 5 Danuta Sobczyńska / Pawel Zeidler / Ewa Zielonacka-Lis (eds.): Chemistry in the Philosophical Melting Pot. 2004.

Bd. / Vol. 6 Marek Kwiek: Intellectuals, Power, and Knowledge. Studies in the Philosophy of Culture and Education. 2004.

Bd. / Vol. 7 Marek Kwiek: The University and the State. A Study into Global Transformations. 2006.

Bd. / Vol. 8 Andrzej Przylebski (Hrsg.): Das Erbe Gadamers. 2006.

Bd. / Vol. 9 Ewa Czerwińska-Schupp (ed.): Values and Norms in the Age of Globalization. 2007.

Bd. / Vol. 10 Tadeusz Buksiński (ed.): Democracy in Western and Post-Communist Countries. Twenty Years after the Fall of Communism. 2009.

Bd. / Vol. 11 Marek Zirk-Sadowski / Mariusz Golecki / Bartosz Wojciechowski (eds.): Multicentrism as an Emerging Paradigm in Legal Theory. 2009.

Bd. / Vol. 12 Bartosz Wojciechowski: Philosophical Approach to the Interculturality of Criminal Law. 2010.

Bd. / Vol. 13 Marek Nowak / Michał Nowosielski (eds.): (Post)transformational Migration. Inequalities, Welfare State, and Horizontal Mobility. 2011.

Bd. / Vol. 14 Tadeusz Buksiński (ed.): Religions in the Public Spheres. 2011.

Bd. / Vol. 15 Bartosz Wojciechowski / Piotr W. Juchacz / Karolina M. Cern (eds.): Legal Rules, Moral Norms and Democratic Principles. 2013.

Bd. / Vol. 16 Ewa Nowak / Dawn E. Schrader / Boris Zizek (eds.): Educating Competencies for Democracy. 2013.

Bd. / Vol. 17 Tadeusz Buksiński (ed.): Identities and Modernizations. 2013.

Bd. / Vol. 18 Karolina M. Cern: The Counterfactual Yardstick. Normativity, Self-Constitutionalisation and the Public Sphere. 2014.

Bd. / Vol. 19 Vito Breda / Lidia Rodak (eds.). Diverse Narratives of Legal Objectivity. An Interdisciplinary Perspective. 2016.

Bd. / Vol. 20 Marek Woszczek: Platonic Wholes and Quantum Ontology. Translated by Katarzyna Kretkowska. 2015.

Bd./Vol. 21 Roman Hauser / Marek Zirk-Sadowski / Bartosz Wojciechowski (eds.): The Common European Constitutional Culture. Its Sources, Limits and Identity. 2016.

Bd./Vol. 22 Aigerim Raimzhanova: Hard, Soft, and Smart Power – Education as a Power Resource. 2017.

Bd./Vol. 23 Roberto Franzini Tibaldeo / Graziano Lingua (eds.): Philosophy and Community Practices. 2018.

Bd./Vol. 24 Marta Soniewicka: After God – The Normative Power of the Will from the Nietzschean Perspective. 2017.

Bd./Vol. 25 Tomasz Jarmużek: On the Sea Battle Tomorrow That May Not Happen. A Logical and Philosophical Analysis of the Master Argument. 2018.

Bd./Vol. 26 Krzysztof Brzechczyn (ed.): New Perspectives in Transnational History of Communism in East Central Europe. 2019.

Bd./Vol. 27 Ewa Nowak: Advancing the Human Self. 2020.

Bd./Vol. 28 Lidia Rodak: Judicial Objectivity. 2020.

Bd./Vol. 29 Tomasz Pietrzykowski: Naturalism and the Frontiers of Legal Science. 2021.

Bd./Vol. 30 Wojciech Piątek (ed.): Supervision over Courts and Judges. 2021.

Bd./Vol. 31 Skirgailė Žalimienė / Bartosz Wojciechowski (eds.): Constitutional Consciousness. In Search of a Remedy for the Crisis of Discourse and Democracy Deficit in the European Union. 2023.

www.peterlang.com

www.ingramcontent.com/pod-product-compliance
Ingram Content Group UK Ltd.
Pitfield, Milton Keynes, MK11 3LW, UK
UKHW041447071026
15587UKWH00010B/531

9 783631 895566